PUNCH A HOLE IN THE WIND

RACING POST

PUNCH A HOLE IN THE WIND

The Stories Behind 50 of the Greatest Flat Racehorses Since the Dawn of Film

Oli Hein

Foreword by Michael Bell

*In memory of my father Pierre: outstanding surgeon,
tireless parent, loving grandfather, athlete, agent provocateur
and the ultimate horseracing purist.*

Photographic acknowledgements

All images copyright of Getty except the following:
pages 45, 53, 73, 153 copyright of Alamy
pages 184, 192 copyright of the Racing Post

First published by Pitch Publishing on behalf of the Racing Post, 2022

Pitch Publishing
Pitch Publishing,
9 Donnington Park,
85 Birdham Road,
Chichester,
West Sussex, PO20 7AJ

www.pitchpublishing.co.uk
info@pitchpublishing.co.uk
www.racingpost.com/shop

© 2022, Oli Hein

Every effort has been made to trace the copyright. Any oversight will be rectified in future editions at the earliest opportunity by the publisher.

All rights reserved. No part of this book may be reproduced, sold or utilised in any form or transmitted in any form or by any means, electronic or mechanical, including photocopying, recording or by any information storage and retrieval system, without prior permission in writing from the Publisher.

A CIP catalogue record is available for this book
from the British Library.

ISBN 9781839500992

Typesetting and origination by Pitch Publishing
Printed and bound by TJ Books Limited

CONTENTS

Foreword			7
Introduction			9
Name	Where they were trained	Year they were foaled	Page
Man O' War	USA	1917	13
Epinard	FRANCE	1920	17
Mumtaz Mahal	UK	1921	21
Phar Lap	AUSTRALIA	1926	25
Windsor Lad	UK	1931	29
Brantome	FRANCE	1931	33
Bahram	UK	1932	37
Nearco	ITALY	1935	41
Pharis	FRANCE	1936	45
Sun Chariot	UK	1939	49
Bernborough	AUSTRALIA	1939	53
Count Fleet	USA	1940	57
Tudor Minstrel	UK	1944	61
Citation	USA	1945	65
Tantieme	FRANCE	1947	69
Tom Fool	USA	1949	73
Native Dancer	USA	1951	77
Ribot	ITALY	1952	81
Swaps	USA	1952	85
Tulloch	AUSTRALIA	1953	89
Kelso	USA	1957	93
Sea-Bird	FRANCE	1962	113
Dr Fager	USA	1964	117
Vaguely Noble	UK/FRANCE	1965	121
Nijinsky	IRELAND	1967	125
Brigadier Gerard	UK	1968	129
Mill Reef	UK	1968	133

PUNCH A HOLE IN THE WIND

Name	Where they were trained	Year they were foaled	Page
Secretariat	USA	1970	137
Allez France	FRANCE	1970	141
Ruffian	USA	1972	145
Seattle Slew	USA	1974	149
Alleged	IRELAND	1974	153
Affirmed	USA	1975	157
Kingston Town	AUSTRALIA	1976	161
Spectacular Bid	USA	1976	166
Shergar	UK	1978	170
Dancing Brave	UK	1983	175
Miesque	FRANCE	1984	180
Dayjur	UK	1987	184
Cigar	USA	1990	188
Dubai Millennium	DUBAI	1996	192
Montjeu	FRANCE	1996	196
Silent Witness	HONG KONG	1999	200
Deep Impact	JAPAN	2002	205
Zenyatta	USA	2004	210
Sea The Stars	IRELAND	2006	214
Black Caviar	AUSTRALIA	2006	218
Frankel	UK	2008	222
Winx	AUSTRALIA	2011	227
American Pharoah	USA	2012	231

Epilogue   235

FOREWORD

It is sometimes hard to overstate the sheer variety in ability and attitude within the breed that we call the thoroughbred. Like humans, their size, temperament and natural gifts can range from the sublime to the ridiculous. I shall confess that several of the latter, over the years, have passed through the gates of my stables at Fitzroy House in Newmarket. Unsurprisingly, interacting with the shamelessly optimistic owners of said horses needs a proper dollop of diplomacy and endless good cheer which, in the scheme of things, is hardly a bad way to pass the day.

But when, just occasionally, you are fortunate to come across something special that comes to the yard, a colt or filly that reveals such a profound ability as to make your heart flutter that tiny bit more, then it is your own turn, as a trainer, to be the hopeless dreamer. As the mysterious forces of genetics, luck and circumstance align to create a four-legged wonder, these are the moments that we treasure most. I am fortunate enough to have trained, amongst others, a winner of both the Epsom Derby and Epsom Oaks. Both the colt (Motivator) and filly (Sariska) in question were wonderful and my memories of their successes and the ensuing joy are likely as vivid as those of their owners.

But this book is about some of those very few racehorses who take it to the next level still.

I first met Oli at my stables, where he happily described himself as one of those very owners who, in a relentless triumph of hope over experience and evidence, frivolously believed that the horse of which he was part-owner would defy all logic and land him a Group 1. But I quickly realised that this lopsided love for his own horse stood in stark contrast to his clear, level-headed assessment of those greats of years gone by in which he did not have a personal stake.

We bonded also over shared experiences from our families' professional lives in years gone by, and I was pleasantly surprised when he unearthed for me a letter that my grandfather, a wartime security chief, wrote to his staff when the end of the war was declared. Clearly Oli knew where to dig to find interesting things.

You may well have read other books that capture the lives of some of the great horses who have graced the world's tracks over the years. What makes this one different?

I would say three things. First, its sheer international outlook. Racing is an intense and all-consuming sport, so it is only natural that both fans and professionals within it don't necessarily have the time or energy to explore the racing horizons from further afield with a dispassionate eye. It is refreshing, therefore, to see greats from Europe, Australia, North America and elsewhere all sitting side by side here, and not being directly – and unnecessarily – compared.

Second, the research. Oli has demonstrably gone over his sources again and again to try to reconcile conflicting evidence, correct misunderstandings and dig out some more obscure nuggets that may not be familiar to even the most seasoned racing reader. These 50 chapters are each long enough to properly immerse you in the ups and downs of the champions it describes.

Third is the passion and entertaining humour that weaves its way into the pages that follow. Writing with equal verve, whether about an unbeaten Australian heroine of this century or a French champion of the 1920s who came to a tragic end, it is evident here that the horse is king (or queen), and not the flag. Nevertheless, underpinning this are some fascinating insights into some of the well-known and also more obscure racing characters who have helped, in their own way, to shape the racing scene over the decades.

The seed was sown for my passion in horseracing watching the majestic, multiple Cheltenham Gold Cup winning Arkle when he was at his pomp in the mid-60s. I was five or six, sitting by the grainy, black-and-white television watching his exploits being called home by Peter O'Sullevan. He was a majestic horse with great presence and any books about Arkle got devoured immediately. Later in life, I bought a hunter chaser who managed to lug me successfully around Cheltenham a couple of times, and one of the reasons that encouraged me to buy this horse – Ten Cherries – was that he was a very close relation of Arkle as their dams were closely related. So my fondness for Arkle will live long and it is one of my great regrets that I never saw him in the flesh; tragically he lost his life too soon, in 1970.

Clearly this book is not designed to 'change your mind' about your own heroes. Indeed, hopefully it will enrich your knowledge and love of them as it has mine, and introduce you to new ones. It will provoke conversations – and what's wrong with that? Perhaps it will leave you (as it did me) desperate to revisit many of these races via the magic of video.

Above all, though, it will transport you, repeatedly, to another time and another place and make you realise once more why you love this sport and the wonderful creature that rightfully takes centre stage within it.

Michael Bell

INTRODUCTION

Let's not sugar-coat it: this book is conceptually flawed from the very outset. A list of 50 of the greatest thoroughbreds over so many generations, running over a huge range of distances in four corners of the globe – how is anyone supposed to measure all that?

Fundamentally, they *aren't* supposed to. True, we are an unrelentingly judgmental species, constantly daring to compare and contrast, even if those being compared are young apples and old oranges. So let's be abundantly clear: this is purely *my* chronological list of 50 of the greatest flat racing thoroughbreds of the last century or so; it's not a definitive countdown of the top 50, as that simply can't be done, no matter who says so. What each of these horses *does* have is a unique story to tell.

But let's rejoice in that fact, rather than shake our fist in frustration. This book is a celebration, not a competition. Since the thoroughbred was first developed over three centuries ago in Great Britain – three Arab stallions being brought over and bred with local mares to produce a stronger, faster but more capricious animal – these magnificent creatures have given the race-going public limitless joy, and filled our memories with wonder and respect. Every horse that has ever raced has given its connections, and many others besides, an unbridled feeling of elation, even in brave defeat. They were each, in their own way, 'great'.

Therefore, no two lists will ever look the same; indeed, some may differ violently, but that should just be the trigger for an engaging (albeit unwinnable) debate. Putting this tome together has been both immensely enjoyable and deeply upsetting. Enjoyable, because it has given me an easy excuse to abuse YouTube and watch so many heroes of the past show me yet again that they were just that little bit more special than the others, often for reasons one can't put one's finger on; but upsetting because I only have space here to explore 50 horses, which means hundreds – literally *hundreds* – had to be discounted. It felt like a betrayal, even though all have been eulogised in passages elsewhere and will, we hope, never be forgotten.

I was clear when I started this endeavour that I simply had to lay down some really tough criteria at the outset, more for reasons of sanity than anything else. Some of these will seem straightforward enough; others will come across as borderline sacrilegious. But believe me that, without them, this task would have been absurdly unrealistic.

So, for the sake of clarity:

1) These are only Flat racing horses. I adore jump racing too, but it felt one step too far amalgamating the two into what could have been a rather

incongruous mash-up of five-furlong sprinters and four-and-a-half-mile Aintree Grand National winners. It is hard to overstate, too, how global an enterprise Flat racing has become in the last two generations, in a way that jump racing has not. For lovers of Arkle, Red Rum, Flyingbolt, Desert Orchid and others, please accept my apologies now.

2) Linked to the global theme was a desire to rectify what I have come across time and again during my lifelong love of racing, which is the predictably parochial approach that so many take when working out who they think are the best. Ask the question to anyone knowledgeable in Europe, and they will instinctively refer to *Timeform* ratings or similar, and probably list a succession of uniquely British, French and Irish horses. Similarly, go to the US experts, and their top 20 will likely leave you feeling that horseracing is a uniquely North American pastime. Imagine how this, in turn, will wind up the Australians, Japanese and others, each of whom has had the world's top-rated racehorse in recent years. You only have to read the comments in any number of online videos – please resist that urge, I implore you – to see how quickly this descends into grubby flag-waving. So this is my attempt to put the jingoism that always clouds judgment firmly in its corner, and really explore the merits of horses in many parts of the world, and not just the two usual cornerstones of Europe and the US.

3) In turn, I wanted to depersonalise this as much possible, as such intrusions – heartfelt though they are – tend to upset the integrity of any such compilation. Despite being a lifelong racegoer, sad to say that I have seen very few of these legends running in the flesh, nor bet successfully on any of them, nor owned any of them, but maybe that's an advantage; my aim is to be as passionate about them all when writing about them, whilst being as dispassionate as possible in my rationale for including them.

4) And now I'm going to be really provocative. My final self-imposed criterion will risk leaving some to shake their heads in despair. I decided, with such a wealth of greats to choose from, that I wanted to be able to *see* the horses in action alongside writing about them, and I wanted the reader to be able to do likewise. Consequently, I am only looking at horses that have been captured on film for posterity, with a video camera that doesn't lie in a way that a 19th-century reporter could (and often did).

'What about Eclipse?' you may scream; or Triple Crown winner Gladiateur, the 'Avenger of Waterloo'?; Or Carbine, one of Australia's greatest ever? Or even that magnificent Hungarian mare Kincsem, unbeaten in 54 races across Europe? Or

INTRODUCTION

West Australian, or St Simon, or Ormonde? Wonderful horses, all, along with so many others. But the undeniable truth is that we live in an interactive age, and I wanted this book to be as interactive as a book can be; I want the reader to be inspired by stories they already thought they knew as well as races they probably didn't, so that they can then satisfy that lust online and watch them immediately after reading about them. And, heartbreakingly, we will simply never be able to do that with all the great horses of the Victorian era or before. Take heart in the fact that their stories are captured in loving words elsewhere.

That said, any book with a historical element to it has a hurdle to overcome. As one sage once reflected, 'There is a propensity in each of us to exalt the past and to deprecate the present, particularly as we reach our more senior years.' I can assure you that I am both conscious of that and, when looking at the even spread of these 50 champions across the decades that span the existence of racing on film, believe that it is a trap that I have avoided.

My earliest racing memories are of the Champs de Mars, the six-and-a-half furlong oval in the Mauritian capital Port Louis, with the spectacular backdrop of the Moka Range mountains only heightening the atmosphere. My grandfather and uncle were both chief stewards there, proud of Mauritius having the oldest Jockey Club in the Southern Hemisphere, even if it still has just the one tiny racecourse, and even though a Mauritian horse is unlikely to make this list anytime soon. But I hope that this detached, remote upbringing absolves me, at least partially, from accusations of geographical favouritism. My travels since have taken me to watch racing throughout the UK and France in particular, as well as Australia, South Africa, the US and even Turkmenistan, where the thoroughbred makes way for the staggeringly beautiful Akhal-Teke, its unique metallic sheen sparkling in the spartan desert surroundings.

Superficially, these places have little in common. Yet peel back the veneer of difference and the key similarity shines through: we all love to watch the harmonious magic of a well-trained horse and a skilled jockey working in glorious tandem, striving to go that little bit quicker than the others.

You are unlikely to have this book in your hands if you don't love racing in the first place. I therefore urge you to bear all of these criteria in mind whilst reading the chapters that follow. And if any of it spurs you to make your own list, or triggers stimulating conversation with other race lovers, or even prompts a spontaneous trip to a racecourse to remind yourself of the beauty of a thoroughbred racehorse in action, then so much the better.

PUNCH A HOLE IN THE WIND

A NOTE ON DISTANCES

Different countries measure distance in different ways. This applies equally to their measuring distances for horse races.

The most common global unit of measurement is now the metric system of kilometres, metres, centimetres, etc., as practised in Australia, France and elsewhere. In the USA and the UK, the imperial system of miles and yards is usually preferred. However, this is a book about horses, and we are fortunate that thoroughbreds have a distance that is pretty much unique to their sport: the furlong. Equal to 200m or 220 yards, I have chosen to use the furlong as the standard measurement in this book, firstly because it is still one of the most universally recognised measurements amongst horse lovers, but also to celebrate the uniqueness of it within this sport.

That being said, should you be more familiar with another system, the chart below spells out the various equivalents:

Race distance	Metric	Imperial	Example
1 furlong	200m	1/8 mile	
2 furlongs	400m	¼ mile	
4 furlongs	800m	½ mile	
5 furlongs	1000m	5/8 mile	Nunthorpe Stakes, Hong Kong Sprint
6 furlongs	1200m	¾ mile	Breeders' Cup Sprint, Golden Slipper Stakes
8 furlongs	1600m	1 mile	2000 Guineas, Prix Jacques Le Marois
10 furlongs	2000m	1 ¼ miles	Kentucky Derby, Breeders' Cup Classic
12 furlongs	2400m	1 ½ miles	Prix de l'Arc de Triomphe, Epsom Derby
16 furlongs	3200m	2 miles	Melbourne Cup, Tenno Sho

MAN O'WAR

'The mostest hoss that ever was.' Man O'War's reputation – and his myth – have only grown with time. Seen here in a morning workout at Belmont, July 1920.

We should be more than a little grateful to the nameless camera operator who filmed Man O'War racing in 1920 – considered, in fact, to be the first recording of a full horse race in North America. It means he can be included in this book without breaking the strict, self-imposed criteria. Just as well, as omitting him would have rendered its whole integrity obsolete. He was the earliest great to be foaled of any horse described here and, to many, he remains the near-mythical benchmark of equine perfection.

By Fair Play out of Mahubah, a daughter of English Triple Crown-winner Rock Sand, Man O'War was sold as a yearling at the Saratoga Sales for $5,000 to Pennsylvania textile magnate Samuel Riddle, and trained by Louis Feustel. Initially, it was touch-and-go as to whether he would ever race: he was wilful to the extreme and refused to be broken in; he was too smart by half. Eventually he acceded but – the trainer would later say – the horse never forgave them.

His 21 races were spread quite evenly across his two and three-year-old seasons. He demonstrated a colossal stride that would only later be rivalled in North America by Secretariat and Native Dancer. He looked different too. Standing over 16.2 hands and an almost golden chestnut, his withers properly stuck out, his long back dipped more than average and he possessed an almost supercilious look in his eye. His first six races, run over five and six furlongs, and starting with a six-length victory at Belmont Park, were all won in a canter. His fan club grew quickly as word spread of a horse that was running like no other before. He was sent to the six-furlong Sanford Memorial Stakes at Saratoga for what was planned to be another procession. But whilst Saratoga was at the time the US's premier racetrack, it also had a well-earned nickname: 'The Graveyard of Champions'.

We can easily forget that this was the era before starting stalls; there was nothing but a thin tape, and jockeys needed to position themselves well for the off. With Johnny Loftus aboard, as he would be throughout Big Red's first season, Man O' War was facing fully backwards when the tape went up, losing many lengths. His immense stride caught him up with the pack, only to get boxed in by the tiring horses in front of him. Still he found a way through, but the finish line came too quickly. Half a length in front of him was a well-regarded colt whom he had already beaten easily in a previous race at Saratoga, and to whom he was conceding 15 pounds. The colt's name – and you couldn't make it up – was Upset.

Journalists and public alike – who had watched the hapless start and breathtaking finish – were unequivocal that only bad luck (and perhaps poor jockeyship) accounted for the defeat, thus his reputation, ironically, only grew in defeat. For the record, they met three times more over their careers, and Upset never again got near him – then again, neither did any other thoroughbred. Man O' War finished the year as two-year-old champion, a colossal 16 pounds clear of his nearest peer in the rankings.

There would be no blemishes, unfortunate or otherwise, in Man O' War's second season. That said, there was a glaring omission: he was not entered in the Kentucky Derby. The reasons were twofold and utterly spurious: Riddle believed that a three-year-old shouldn't race 'as far as 10 furlongs' so early in the season; second, the Preakness Stakes in that year was run only a few days later, and it was only his preferred target because of Pimlico's proximity to Riddle's farm where Man O' War had wintered. We shirk at the narrow-mindedness of it now, but it is worth recalling that the US Triple Crown as we now know it did not become recognised as such until the 1930s. Regardless, having never raced beyond six furlongs, and ridden by new jockey Clarence Kummer, he still won the nine-furlong Classic in record time.

Just 11 days later he was back in Belmont Park, first winning the eight-furlong Withers Stakes in a US record of 1min 35.8secs before, in June, destroying a class field in the Belmont Stakes (then 11 furlongs) by 20 lengths in a time of 2min 14secs – a world record on dirt that would stand, incredibly, until 1991.

MAN O'WAR

Several more victories followed, sometimes with starting odds of 100-1 on – the stingiest anyone could remember in track history. Further superlatives were on show at the Lawrence Realization Stakes at Saratoga, where every horse but one – Hoodwink, owned by Riddle's niece – had run scared despite the $15,000 prize. Reports state clearly that Kummer did little more than sit quietly for 13 furlongs. Man O'War still reduced the world record by nearly two seconds to 2min 40.8secs, and officially won by 100 lengths – the stewards sensibly rounding it down to a memorable figure as photos showed that Man O'War had won by *over two furlongs*.

Only once was he properly tested. Facing only one opponent, the top-class John P Grier, in the Dwyer Stakes at Aqueduct, Big Red was still expected to win, despite carrying 18 pounds more. Man O'War led for most of it until the home stretch, when John P Grier ranged up beside him. Clarence Kummer drew the whip on his mount, allowing the distance to grow, only for Eddie Ambrose on his opponent to do likewise and draw back level. This happened once more before finally John P Grier could take no more and wilted in the final furlong. The *New York Times* loved every minute of it: 'The contestants had set such a dazzling pace from the very start that they seemed to fairly fly through space rather than to touch ground.' The world record for nine furlongs had predictably been broken too.

After a few more facile successes, and with an enormous following fan club, Man O'War's career finished with a match race for the ten-furlong Kenilworth Park Gold Cup in Ontario against Sir Barton, who had won the Triple Crown the previous year (even if it had not been called that at the time). Here, finally, Big Red is captured at glorious full tilt on film, albeit at the accelerated frame speed of what was still primitive technology. We see him lead from the start, high head carriage reminiscent of Sea-Bird many years later, and we see just how far before the end Kummer starts pulling him up whilst still winning in absurdly easy fashion by seven lengths.

With Man O'War thereafter facing crippling handicap weights as a four-year-old, Riddle instead chose to retire his hero but, quirky to the last, restricted his stallion to a mere 25 mares a year, many of which were either his own or those of friends. Living to the ripe old age of 30, Man O'War still sired 64 stakes winners – War Admiral pre-eminent amongst them – but one feels it could have been so much more. His devoted stallion hand Will Harburt didn't care, calling him 'The mostest hoss that ever was'.

Certain racing and breeding experts – trying to take a more objective view – have called Man O'War the 'sacred cow' of US racing. The challenge is fair. In the same way that some consider it borderline illegal for a Brit to criticise a Shakespeare play, Man O'War's reputation within certain US racing circles sometimes feels similar: to question his achievements is simply not the done thing. To many, he has long passed through the wormhole of history and can now only be viewed through the prism of myth.

Two tempering factors are perhaps worth reflecting upon: one of quality and the other of quantity. First, the quality of US bloodstock improved – gradually but undeniably – between the start and the end of the 20th century, which doesn't undermine Man O'War's incredible individual achievements but might put into question the overall strength in depth of his challengers. Second, in the lean years of World War One, there were a mere 1,680 thoroughbreds foaled in the US that year, the second lowest of the century (after 1919) and far fewer than in later years, perhaps reducing the chances of a genuine competitor for Man O'War to prove himself against – which, again, he surely would have.

Yet at a time when heroes as timeless as Ty Cobb, Babe Ruth and Jack Dempsey loomed so large in the US sporting public's eye, it is telling that the most popular of all of them was a headstrong horse whose trainer had once said of him that 'he was hell to break, a headache to handle, and a catapult to ride'. Perhaps. But he was also an imperious legend.

That so many should have turned up for his funeral was unsurprising for, as was said in the eulogy that day, 'he touched the imagination of men and they saw different things in him. But one thing they will all remember was that he brought exaltation into their hearts.'

FACTFILE

Description: **Chestnut Colt**
Size: **16.2 hands**
Dates: **1917-47**
Racing seasons: **1919-20**
Where were they trained?: **USA**
Trainer: **Louis Feustel**
Owner: **Samuel Riddle**
Jockey: **Johnny Loftus, Clarence Kummer and Andy Schuttinger**

Sire: **Fair Play**
Dam: **Mahubah**
Damsire: **Rock Sand**
Record: **21: 20-1-0**
Most impressive victory: **Belmont Stakes, 1920**
Nickname: **Big Red**

EPINARD

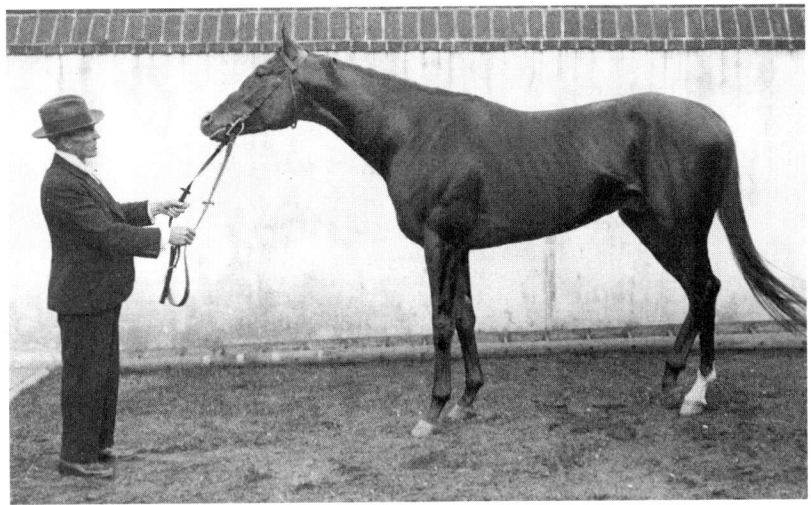

Having already conquered Europe, the wonderful Epinard arrives in the USA in 1924.

One of the only two films in existence that definitely shows Epinard racing is of him coming second. Further, his greatest-ever performance was when he again finished second. Then again, you can take almost anything out of context and twist it. In fact, there is nothing incongruous about Epinard's place amongst these exalted thoroughbreds. He won plenty too, in deeply impressive fashion, and was enough of a European star to have the US beckoning him to challenge their best as long ago as the 1920s, thus blazing a trail that many decades later would morph into the Breeders' Cup.

Owned and bred by Chanel co-founder Pierre Wertheimer, Epinard (French for spinach) was an underwhelming yearling, but he was sent into training with French-based American Eugene Leigh. At the start of his two-year-old season, they weren't sure what to make of him; by the end of it, he was Champion European two-year-old against an outstanding crop of peers. It started in Deauville in the Prix Yacowlef, primarily against a two-year-old whom leading trainer Willie Pratt swore was his best, and Epinard gave him a five-length panning. Soaking it all up at the glamorous seaside resort that day was a certain Ernest Hemingway, who proudly recalled later, 'Epinard won in a breeze, and I was able to support myself for six or eight months with my earnings.' One can only imagine how.

Epinard, soon after, effortlessly annexed the Grand Criterium, Criterium de Maisons-Laffitte and the Prix de la Foret (against older horses), with his sole loss being in the Prix Morny where, as was not uncommon in those days, he was left at the start facing the wrong way.

By age three, Epinard was an imposing, muscular and handsome chestnut, but had not been entered in the Classics on either side of the Channel, partly because his speed suggested he would never stay for a Derby distance anyway. Nevertheless, he crushed all-comers in France in his first four races that year over distances from six to nine furlongs, including the Prix d'Ispahan and the Prix du Gros-Chene, usually ridden by another Euro-based American, Everett Haynes. Ambitions then grew to send him to topple England's best. The most prestigious sprint handicap at the time was the six-furlong Stewards' Cup at Goodwood. His reputation being what it was, he was allotted 8st 6lb – far bigger than a three-year-old had ever carried to victory in that race. It made no difference and he cantered in by two lengths. It was clear that the Brits were in awe of him as much as the French.

He then returned to England in the autumn to take on the nine-furlong Cambridgeshire Handicap, another of the very top prizes at the time. This time he would be burdened with 9st 2lb – considered impossible. Stabled at Newmarket in the week leading up to the race, he undertook a mile-long gallop, witnessed by jockey and subsequent journalist Jack Leach, who was on a parallel gallop starting fully a furlong ahead: 'We jumped off and came a good gallop. As we [reached the end], Epinard was with us. In fact, he pulled up in the bunch as if he had been with us all the way. I have never been so astonished in my life!'

Epinard, in fact, didn't win the Cambridgeshire, although he should have. That being said, he still blew the audience away. Drawn high, Haynes had been told to bring him straight to the stand rails, which Epinard did almost violently. He then let him go and Epinard was fully six lengths clear, and with his swerving had gone so much further than his competitors. He was caught at the death by Verdict, carrying nearly two stone less, and who would go on to win the Coronation Cup the next year. Even in defeat, the audience knew what they had witnessed, with the word 'astonishing' mentioned liberally. 'The performance, by common consent, stamped Epinard as the best three-year-old in the world up to a mile and a little over,' wrote the no-nonsense *Bloodstock Breeders' Review*.

The US Racing scene agreed and wanted to see more. To that end, a series of international races were set up between the European champion and the cream from across the pond. As usual, it was the European horse who had to travel. It wasn't so easy in those days, but after some negotiating Epinard and his team set sail in July 1924 from Cherbourg on the *Berengaria*, whose owners

EPINARD

had adapted part of the ship to accommodate their special cargo. Indeed, Epinard was big news at the time and there were daily cables sent from the ship to the press to keep the public up to date. If the *New York Times* was anything to go by, the Americans were mostly amused that Epinard was being accompanied by 40 barrels of Evian spring water to quench his thirst on the journey. Bearing in mind the horse was originally born near Bordeaux, they speculated, mischievously, why was he not being given wine?

Thus, as a four-year-old, after a long sea crossing, Epinard took in four races, all on dirt that he clearly loathed, and with increasingly sore hooves, which were abnormally prone to getting thrush infections. He ran against sprinters over five furlongs, then milers, and finally against middle-distance horses over ten furlongs. Despite being given lumps more weight to carry, he came a close second in all of them, with the Americans realising that, despite these defeats, he would patently have won on turf if not in agony. Even so, the starts of his races were by all accounts a sight to behold, as they had been throughout his career. In the days before starting gates, many swore that they had never seen a horse reach full tilt so quickly from a standing start. 'Once launched, he went like an arrow,' one admiring US hack wrote. Another more melodramatic journalist in *The Free Lance* reflected after the last of these gallant defeats: 'Whether it be beast or man, the French die gloriously.'

In fact, Epinard's feet were so painful on the day of a match race with Sir Gallahad III that he had to be literally dragged to the racetrack. He still only lost by a neck. In the fourth race, the Laurel Stakes, his tender hoof finally cracked after five furlongs and he pulled himself up in searing pain. The US had seen enough and made him Champion American older horse. Subsequently retired, and a hero on both sides of the ocean, each wanted a piece of Epinard, so he was shuttled repeatedly between studs in the US and France, which wouldn't have done his condition much good – his immediate output was unspectacular, although it is pleasing to note that many, many generations down the line, his distant, direct ancestor Goldikova would carry those same famous Wertheimer colours to victory in three successive Breeders' Cup Miles. His closest companion was an old Airedale terrier named Peter, who had travelled to the US and back with him, and whom he would tenderly carry around by the neck.

Years later, doubt swirled around Epinard's death. Initially it was thought that the Germans had commandeered him post-invasion in 1941 and had worked him to death as a carthorse near Chartres – a harrowing enough tale, and one announced by French radio in 1942, but it was then thought that eyewitnesses may have been mistaken. So racing historian John Hervey dug deeper …

PUNCH A HOLE IN THE WIND

Dunkirk, Spring 1940. A never-ending grey beach, smothered in a colossal, retreating British land force, pincered on the coastline with limited protection from an equally under-pressure French army and with a huge Nazi war machine bearing down remorselessly. On the shore, in amongst hundreds of thousands of desperate soldiers, were countless horses, and one of them – more likely than not – was Epinard. Stolen from his stud, and doubtless still in pain from his sensitive hooves that never really recovered, the gentle, 20-year-old stallion would likely have been filled with fear and confusion. With a flotilla of fishing boats soon to appear from England, a miracle would eventually arrive for the soldiers, but sadly there was no miracle for Epinard. We cannot know whether in his last moments – before likely becoming a meal to starving soldiers – he still remembered those glorious performances of 17 years before, but moved as we are by this haunting image, we can only hope that his end was quick, respectful and merciful. It was the very least that this pioneering champion deserved.

FACTFILE

Description: Chestnut Colt
Size: 16.2 hands
Dates: 1920-40
Racing seasons: 1922-24
Where were they trained?: France
Trainer: Eugene Leigh
Owner: Pierre Wertheimer
Jockey: Everett Haynes

Sire: Badajoz
Dam: Epine Blanche
Damsire: Rock Sand
Record: 20: 12-6-0
Most impressive victory: Stewards' Cup 1923
Nickname: The Great Gentleman

MUMTAZ MAHAL

Mumtaz Mahal - 'The Flying Filly' - with George Hulme up, in the parade ring before the Champagne Stakes at Doncaster, September 1923.

Horseracing, like pretty much every other popular sport, is imbued with cliché. Sometimes it is self-aware; other times it is eye-rollingly lazy. To that end, it is not uncommon to hear the latest sprint filly who wins a race well being referred to as 'the flying filly'. But on this there are two points worth making. First, there was an original flying filly who was first given that moniker, and her name was Mumtaz Mahal. Second, it is highly unlikely that any of the more recent horses were anywhere near as quick as her. She was very likely the fastest filly to ever run in Europe.

For this she had her sire The Tetrarch to thank. There is enough evidence to suggest with conviction that The Tetrarch was the fastest two-year-old ever seen, the strangest-looking thoroughbred in history and also the most mysterious. His initially chestnut coat was scatter-gunned with bizarre black blotches, and then it randomly changed colour to a grey coat with white blotches. This gave him the initial nickname the 'Rocking Horse', which rapidly changed to the 'Spotted Wonder' when he won all his races with consummate ease, breaking track records along the way. Even as a juvenile, he had the fully developed body of a four-year-old; and his jockey, the usually down-to-earth ten-time UK champion Steve Donoghue, swore that it couldn't have been his first time on earth as he essentially trained himself and knew exactly what to do before being taught. 'Freak' was never a more apt term.

Mumtaz Mahal, although slightly more compact, inherited a toned-down version of her sire's odd coat. She was descried as 'nicely proportioned with a regal head and a deep, dark, intelligent eye'. She also obtained class from her tough dam, Lady Josephine. It was The Hon. George Lambton who chose and bought her on behalf of the Aga Khan. Lambton had politely turned down being the latter's trainer as he was retained by Lord Derby, but helped him in other ways – including picking up the most expensive lot at that year's Doncaster sales for a hefty 9,100gns – the most anyone had parted with in the UK for a filly since the wonderful Sceptre over 20 years earlier.

She was sent to train with Dick Dawson in Oxfordshire. At two, before she had run or even been tested, Dawson wanted to see exactly what he had on his hands so did a trial between her and stable companion Friar's Daughter, who had already won that season, and would in due course be the dam of Triple Crown-winner Bahram. Despite carrying a 28-pound heavier jockey, the Aga Khan's filly humiliated the other, and Dawson, in his own words, 'was so astonished and excited that I nearly fell off my hack'. Word quickly spread that there was something special at the yard, so when she appeared in May over five furlongs at Newmarket, there were expectations. She justified them under regular rider George Hulme by absolutely cantering up in 57.8 seconds, smashing the course record, and a time still unrivalled for a two-year-old at the track.

She then went the following month to Royal Ascot and the Queen Mary Stakes, also five furlongs, where she bolted clear to win by fully ten lengths, displaying a beautiful, rangy action. The *Daily Mirror* newspaper wrote an article called 'Flying Filly Wins Again', going on to say, '[She] literally lost her rivals in the Queen Mary Stakes … After standing as quiet as a sheep at the gate, she went off with the same wonderful burst of speed she had shown when making her record-breaking debut at Newmarket, and before a furlong had been covered she must have been at least half a dozen lengths clear.' The nickname immediately stuck and The Aga Khan had a superstar on his hands.

Three more pulverising victories came in relatively quick succession: the National Breeders' Produce Stakes at Sandown, The Molecomb Stakes at Goodwood (where she started at 40-1 on, and walloped her opponent by ten lengths), and the Champagne Stakes at Doncaster, where she was upped to six furlongs. Film footage of this day shows her bucking and kicking exuberantly in the parade ring before trotting up in the race itself in front of an adoring public. She was a deeply impressive athlete.

Her only blip was on her final outing at Kempton, again over six furlongs. Dawson wanted to withdraw her as she hated very heavy going but no one could get through to the Aga Khan (who was in Switzerland) for his blessing, so she had to run. In the event, with the mud dulling her speed and her zest, she was caught at the line by the colt Arcade, to whom she was giving seven pounds.

The big question as she entered her Classic year was: with such phenomenal speed, could she stay? She returned from the winter bigger and stronger and was thrown in at the deep end in the 1,000 Guineas over a mile, for no other reason than this is 'what was expected' of a champion filly. When five furlongs in she was, predictably, six lengths clear, but in the final furlong her stamina completely gave out, although her class and genuine nature meant that she still came second, this time to Plack.

As though unconvinced of the seemingly obvious evidence, connections tried once more over a mile at the Coronation Stakes at Royal Ascot where again she simply couldn't stay. She was an outrageously good sprinter, pure and simple. The penny having finally dropped, her final two outings were back over five and six furlongs respectively at the King George Stakes at Goodwood and the Nunthorpe Stakes at York. And, of course, she once again destroyed the opposition, by six lengths in the latter. Mumty, as the hugely popular filly was now affectionately known, had proved that when it came to pure speed, no colt or filly could touch her – not then, and likely never since.

Her racing career over, Mumtaz Mahal proceeded to become a legend for a second time. Living first at her owner's Sheshoon Stud near The Curragh, and then in England, some have accurately asserted that she is '… considered part of the fabric of the modern Thoroughbred'. Via her grandsons Nasrullah, Abernant, Royal Charger and Mahmoud, amongst many others, her genes seep into every successful line you can think of. She was, naturally, the spider at the centre of the web of the Aga Khan's inter-war dominance of British racing.

And as a consequence, if you are a fan of grey horses, then more than any horse you have Mumtaz Mahal to thank. In the early 20th century there were fewer and fewer around, as the UK was going through 'grey scepticism' at the time. Mumty's watershed popularity changed all that, as Native Dancer would in the US 30 years later. Her immense success as a broodmare, carrying those special units of grey inheritance, ensured that these scarcer but no less beautiful thoroughbreds would carry on successfully – and popularly – to this day.

Completing her post-racing European odyssey, she had her final few foals when resident at the Aga Khan's Haras Marly-la-Ville stud farm just north of Paris, her legacy was more than secured. The Flying Filly, now a stately mare, passed away in 1945 on her own terms, and oblivious to the final throes of war around her. But as one breeding specialist put it: 'Great broodmares never really die. Neither do they simply fade away like old soldiers. Instead they live, virtually, forever. And it is difficult to find a pedigree anywhere in the world today in which Mumtaz Mahal's influence is not felt.'

One could almost forget, in fact, that before her breed-defining input, this feisty, spotted grey filly displayed an unearthly speed on the racetracks of England never seen since. Almost, but not quite.

FACTFILE

Description: Grey Filly
Size: 15.2 hands
Dates: 1921-45
Racing seasons: 1923-24
Where were they trained?: UK
Trainer: Dick Dawson
Owner: His Highness Aga Khan III
Jockey: George Hulme, George Archibald

Sire: The Tetrarch
Dam: Lady Josephine
Damsire: Sundridge
Record: 10: 7-2-0
Most impressive victory: Queen Mary Stakes 1923
Nickname: The Flying Filly, Mumty

PHAR LAP

Happy times: Phar Lap with his devoted 'strapper' and best friend, Tommy Woodcock.

I make no apologies for the fact that I watched the 1983 movie of *Phar Lap* over 30 times when I was a child, thanks to a knock-off VHS tape that my uncle – under strict instructions – picked up for me in Bangkok. Even if I hadn't been obsessed with him, Phar Lap would have to make this list for any number of reasons. He still tussles with Carbine in lists of Australia's greatest-ever, but as the latter can't make the strict criteria of this book, we are free to indulge this magnificent thoroughbred – and his heartbreakingly short life – that little bit more.

One of the few geldings in this list, the red chestnut's story started on 4 October 1926, in Alick Roberts's Seadown Stud near Timaru on New Zealand's South Island. In contrast to the freakish ability he would ultimately show, he possessed a rather underwhelming pedigree, by Night Raid (never won), out of Entreaty (unplaced on her only start). Nevertheless, Sydney trainer Harry Telford thought there was something further back in his breeding that warranted an unsighted punt, so he persuaded businessman David Davis to buy the colt at auction, based on those distant bloodlines alone, for 160gns. But the horse's skinny frame and warty face horrified everyone when he arrived in Australia. Davis – a Russian-born but Australian-based American citizen who had made his wealth from importing fine china and silver – was furious, and only agreed to proceed with the purchase if Telford trained the horse for free in exchange for two-thirds of his winnings.

His rather pedestrian performances on the training grounds early on earned him the nickname 'Lightning' among those watching the gallops. Amongst them, a Sinhalese speaking medical student at the University of Sydney by the name of Aubrey Ping suggested 'farlap' – his own language's word for 'lightning' – as a name for the horse. And so 'Phar Lap' – as Telford thought a champion needed two words and seven letters in its name – was christened, later to be supplemented by many other nicknames, including the ubiquitous 'Big Red', 'Red Terror' and 'Bobby'. The latter was given by his devoted lad Tommy Woodcock who, after Phar Lap's first few unedifying performances, suggested settling him towards the rear and giving him a target to aim for.

The tactic worked, and how. At three, and now filling a magnificent 17-hand frame, he won the Rosehill Guineas, AJC Derby and Craven Plate in great style, and proved near-unbeatable. Aged four, and with the Melbourne Cup approaching, his increasing untouchability meant bookmakers stood to lose a fortune if he won. Unknown gun-toting criminals made an attempt on his life just three days before the Cup, but fortunately missed both him and Woodcock. Incredibly, Phar Lap won the Melbourne Stakes that very afternoon, and just three days later – after nearly missing the race altogether due to a truck breaking down on the way to Flemington – he was duly crowned in 'The Race that Stops the Nation' at odds of 11-8 on. Under his now-regular rider, the imperturbable Jim Pike, he carried a huge 9st 12lbs to a three-length victory. No Melbourne Cup runner has ever started at shorter odds since. Phar Lap stayed at Flemington and, to demonstrate his unbelievable powers of recovery, just two days later won the Linlithgow Stakes, and 48 hours after *that* the CB Fisher Plate.

Indeed, 1930 and 1931 saw him cement his reputation as a true great, winning 14 straight races over the two seasons, over a wide range of distances. He nixed two Cox Plates, two Melbourne Stakes, the Futurity Stakes and many more, usually with a devastating burst of speed when coming from behind. Nothing could stop him … except crippling weight. The only time in his final 35 races that he ever finished out of the first two was when the Victoria racing authorities lumped him with an utterly unheard of 10st 10lb for the 1931 Melbourne Cup, where even coming a close eighth was deeply impressive against a winner carrying over three stone less.

With nothing else to prove in the Antipodes, and the big handicaps in Australia prohibitive because of the weight allocations, Davis chose – against Telford's wishes – to send him to race in the US, initially in the Agua Caliente Handicap, on the Mexican-US border, and at the time the richest race in North America. As an invite-only event over ten furlongs, Phar Lap faced the best that the continent had to offer.

The odds were stacked against him. He had endured a long sea crossing on the *Ulimaroa*, including a lengthy stay over in New Zealand, and then getting stressed any time his best friend Woodcock was out of sight. He was also running on dirt for the first time, had cracked a hoof, and was carrying top weight of 9st 3lbs. Ridden by lighter jockey Billy Elliot, and with Woodcock acting as the trainer in Telford's absence, Phar Lap was dropped straight to the rear of the field – a tactic virtually unheard of in US racing at the time. But between the five and four-furlong poles, the afterburners kicked in, and Phar Lap astonishingly overtook the rest of the field to suddenly be three lengths clear. As jockey Johnny Longden, riding the high-class colt Bahamas, recalled: 'I was leading the field to the three-eighths pole. About that point the big New Zealander [sic] went by the rest of us like we were tied to the fence …' He held that lead until the end, smashing the track record and with US champion Reveille Boy no match.

He was unofficial world champion, and being lauded as one of the best ever. As writer William R. Nack recounted, 'After Secretariat's triumph in the Triple Crown, [I] asked the elderly Francis Dunne, then a steward in New York, whether Man O'War or Secretariat was the greatest horse he had ever seen. 'Neither,' said Francis. 'I saw Phar Lap.'

Yet 18 days later, he was no more. We will never know for sure what happened at the private ranch near Menlo Pack in California on the night of 4 to 5 April 1932. Woodcock was woken by his beloved charge grunting in agony, clearly in horrific pain and sweating profusely. The vet tried to treat him for colic but with no great success. Woodcock did all he could to keep his beloved horse moving in the stable, but eventually he collapsed. With blood and other fluid coming out of his nostril, he haemorrhaged to death in a distraught Woodcock's arms.

The autopsy revealed an inflamed stomach and intestine, possibly suggesting massive arsenic poisoning, which chimed with a 2006 study by an Australian research group. Illegal bookmaking groups were very active at the time and might have felt threatened by Phar Lap's invincibility, although there is no compelling evidence. Further, a necropsy in 2000 believed that it had identified bacterial gastroenteritis as the culprit. So which was it? All we do know is that Telford used to administer mysterious 'tonics' to his horses, and some believed many years later that they had evidence to suggest that Woodcock – himself a hero in Australia – had admitted to giving his horse an accidental overdose. Perhaps it was more simple than that. Subsequent investigation at Menlo ranch showed that some trees had recently been sprayed with an arsenic–based insecticide, which could easily have drifted onto the juicy grass in Phar Lap's paddock.

Either way, the adoring Australian public were in disbelief that their global hero was dead, and aged only five (by Southern hemisphere dating). Even the Australian Prime Minister Joseph Lyons called it 'a great tragedy'. But unlike so many equine champions, his memory didn't rapidly descend into obscurity, but only grew. Streets were named after him throughout the country, songs were written about him, and a decent movie was made – refreshingly free of schmaltz, and with Woodcock's direct input. His gigantic heart – three times the average size – remains the most requested exhibit at the National Museum in Canberra; his stuffed hide takes pride of place at the Melbourne Museum; and his skeleton has returned to his land of birth, seen by millions at the Te Papa National Museum in Wellington. An incredible legacy – but a completely fitting one.

Like his fellow 'Big Red' Man O'War, Phar Lap the horse has been gradually usurped by Phar Lap the legend. But let us not lose sight of the reality underpinning this: he could only have drifted into myth by repeatedly displaying awesome power, ability and an unparalleled will to win in the first place. It ultimately isn't hard to see how he ensnared Australia's hearts during hard economic times. Among the multitude of poems devoted to the horse who carried a nation's soul upon his back, Peter Porter's spare words capture it best: 'It was his simple excellence to be the best.'

And maybe he was.

FACTFILE

Description: Chestnut Gelding
Size: 17.1 hands
Dates: 1926-32
Racing seasons: 1928-32
Where were they trained?: Australia
Trainer: Harry Telford
Owner: David Davis
Jockey: Jim Pike, Billy Elliot, Jack Baker, James L. Munro, Bobbie Lewis

Sire: Night Raid
Dam: Entreaty
Damsire: Winkie
Record: 51: 37-3-2
Most impressive victory: Agua Caliente Handicap 1932
Nickname: Big Red, The Red Terror, Bobby

WINDSOR LAD

Windsor Lad was bought in his Epsom Derby-winning year by bookmaker Martin Benson, who rapidly nicknamed him 'Lazy Bones'.

It had happened before and would happen many times again: A horse is branded 'a great', 'The best since X', 'Horse of the Century'… and then they lose fair and square. The excuses come tumbling out, yet as often as not a simple fact is overlooked: they were beaten by an unheralded, but truly exceptional, horse. This is how Windsor Lad first made his name – by accident. But by the end of his career, he was the one casting the shadow of greatness not just over his own generation, but others too.

By champion sire Blandford out of Epsom Oaks runner-up Resplendent, genetics were certainly on Windsor Lad's side. This was certainly noticed by trainer Marcus Marsh at the 1932 Newmarket yearling sales, scouting on behalf of one of his owners, the splendid and ambitious horse-lover Maharan Vijaysindhji, Maharajah of Rajpipla. Ruler of the 4,000 sq km Rajpipla district near Bombay, many of the racing fraternity visited his huge estates and 'Pip' – as he was lovingly referred to – became a stalwart of the British racing scene.

Indeed, it seemed at one stage that Pip was attending every single race meeting held in Britain, such was his obsession both with the horses and with the high-society folk he would likely befriend there. It was his lifelong dream to win the Epsom Derby, and he believed Windsor Lad, picked up for 1,300gns, would be the one who would finally present it to him. He was so named because Pip summered every year in the town of Windsor, deliberately keeping himself within spitting distance of British royalty, on the off-chance that they might invite him into the castle for tea and biscuits.

As a two-year-old, Windsor Lad seemed good, if not sensational, winning both his races well whilst displaying some immaturity. But over the winter he grew into a strong specimen, proving as much by annexing two recognised Derby Trails in the Chester Vase and the Newmarket Stakes. But he crept in under the radar, as the only horse on anyone's lips for the previous 12 months had been a certain Colombo. He had won all seven of his juvenile races, easily topped the end of year English Free Handicap, and cemented this with workmanlike victories in the Craven Stakes and 2,000 Guineas. The press, keen to create a hero during hard economic times, had decided to latch onto him as the 'Horse of the Century', meaning that he started the Epsom Derby as a strong favourite, despite never having been tested over further than a mile.

Pip and his team were not sucked into the madness, as they knew that their charge stayed well. As it turned out, the 1934 Epsom Derby delivered a controversy on a grand scale, in front of fully half-a-million race-goers, and vast swathes of the Royal Family, and it all revolved around the styles and characters of several top jockeys. French-based Australian Rae Johnstone was on Colombo. Well-fancied Easton had the inimitable Gordon Richards on board. Medieval Knight had Derby legend Steve Donoghue on top. Windsor Lad, meanwhile, was always partnered by Charlie Smirke.

Smirke was as mercurial as they came, and proud of his Cockney roots. He had recently returned from a five-year ban for 'stopping' a 'sure thing' – a horse of ultimate inconsequence called Welcome Gift – from even starting a race at Gatwick races. In fact, the poorly named horse refused to start at any of his subsequent races, backing up Smirke's claims that he had done everything he could. The lofty, class-conscious authorities couldn't possibly be seen to apologise to a jockey from the East End of London, so kept his ban in place and offered no compensation. His unplanned break saw him working as a beach hand in Brighton for pennies, leaving him essentially homeless and often sleeping on the beach. He felt that he had much to prove.

Coming down Tattenham Hill, the front-running Medieval Knight quickly slowed into Colombo. Johnstone found himself trapped but didn't call Donoghue for room. Windsor Lad and Easton got themselves into place far earlier, with Colombo joining the party late, with all three in a line with a furlong to go. But then the unthinkable happened: Colombo slowed, and

WINDSOR LAD

Windsor Lad pulled easily away to win from Easton, equalling the race record set just the year before by the pocket-rocket Hyperion. Johnstone received a savage press, including from the cocksure Donoghue, all conveniently ignoring the obvious fact – echoed by Johnstone – that Colombo simply didn't stay.

Some punters were happy though, quoting a prophecy from Romany fortune teller Gypsy Lee fully 50 years before, who had stated confidently, if rather nebulously, that a horse with a 'W' in its name would win the 1934 Derby. As cheers of 'Good old Pip!' echoed around the Downs, the King invited the hugely popular Maharajah to the Royal Box, toasting the first Indian-owned winner of the great race. Pip hosted a party the following night at the Savoy Hotel in London and, true to his Indian roots, organised for an elephant to rise up from the floor, the mighty beast fully garlanded in Pip's purple-and-cream colours. It was not something that happened in London with alarming regularity, but then Pip wasn't your regular owner.

In the Eclipse Stakes at Sandown a few weeks later, it was Smirke who came crashing down to earth. He rode a shocker, finding himself trapped against the rail, rallying too late to come third to the patently inferior four-year-old King Salmon, whom he was three lengths clear of 50m past the post. Pip, crashing back down to earth, was convinced that Smirke was up to his old tricks, and sacked him whilst also being unable to resist a £50,000 offer from bookmaker Martin Benson to buy the horse. Benson watched him train, immediately nicknamed him Lazy Bones, and decided to give Smirke another go. In his two subsequent races at three, he trotted up in the Great Yorkshire Stakes, before demolishing the St Leger field, once again in a record time.

By this stage both public and experts were realising that he was something special. And perhaps conscious of the failed shooting attempt on Phar Lap in the build up to the 1930 Melbourne Cup, Windsor Lad now travelled with a pair of bodyguards – referred to less dramatically in the press as 'detectives'. Either way, the only people not over the moon with Leger success were the bookmakers, as Windsor Lad had won at 9-4 on and looked to be getting better with each race, so the precautions were perhaps understandable. The Americans, meanwhile, were also impressed and, after the trailblazing of Epinard in the 1920s, tried to organise races between their champion Cavalcade, leading French horse Admiral Drake and Windsor Lad, but the logistics proved impossible.

It was the norm at the time for champion three-year-olds to try to win the 20-furlong marathon of the Ascot Gold Cup at four. Benson, however, likely balked at the chance for his valuable colt to face up against France's own 'horse of the century' at the time, Brantome, whose story is told elsewhere. Instead, he took in the Coronation Cup back at Epsom, beating Easton very easily over the latter's preferred trip, and then won the Rous Memorial at Royal Ascot over an inadequate seven-and-a-half furlongs. He then tried his hand at the Eclipse for the second time. It proved to be his final race and his bravest. In the home straight, with the race this time at his mercy, Windsor Lad suddenly fell lame, and ran the entire straight with essentially three functioning legs. He dug deeper than ever before, and incredibly beat top three-year-old Theft by three-quarters of a length, leaving adults weeping on the track in face of such courage.

Sadly Windsor Lad never really had a chance to prove himself at stud, as sinus problems proved too debilitating and he was eventually euthanised in 1943. Pip didn't forget him, though. At the height of World War Two, he donated two Spitfires to the RAF, naming one 'Rajpipla' and the other 'Windsor Lad'. The Press were ecstatic, running the headline 'Windsor Lad will fly'. But for those who had seen his immense, understated abilities at Epsom, Ascot and Sandown, they believed that he already had.

FACTFILE

Description: Bay Colt
Size: 16 Hands
Dates: 1931-43
Racing seasons: 1933-35
Where were they trained?: UK
Trainer: Marcus Marsh
Owner: The Maharajah of Rajpipla, Martin Benson

Jockey: Charlie Smirke
Sire: Blandford
Dam: Resplendent
Damsire: By George!
Record: 13: 10-0-1
Most impressive victory: St Leger Stakes 1934
Nickname: Lazy Bones

BRANTOME

Brantome and Charles Bouillon return to the winner's enclosure after a facile victory in the Poules d'Essai des Poulains (French 2,000 Guineas), Longchamp, May 1934.

Sometimes it can be the most random thing that ultimately makes the difference between being regarded as an all-time great or being largely overlooked. Brantome was unquestionably one of the best, yet if it hadn't been for a moment of madness on a busy street in Chantilly one morning, his reputation would undoubtedly be even further up there with the very best than it already is.

He certainly had a breeding head-start, being by multiple British champion sire Blandford out of Prix Jacques Le Marois winner Vitamine. Owned and bred by Edouard de Rothschild at his sublime Haras de Meautry stud outside Deauville, he was decidedly on the small side, with some sources claiming him to be 15.1 hands – photographs suggest this to be a slight exaggeration. They also show, however, a noticeably straight set of hind legs. Trained by Lucien Robert at Chantilly, and ridden by Charles Bouillon, his two-year-old season was spectacular. After a comfortable five-furlong lung opener in the Prix Martinvast in June 1933, he went straight to the six-furlong Prix Robert Papin, cruising to a two-length victory and then annexing the Prix Morny at Deauville in August. Hot favourite for the mile-long Grand Criterium at Longchamp, he crushed the best of his peers yet again, thus completing the rare French

'Juvenile Triple Crown'. The obvious ease of his victories ensured that he led the end-of-year Free Handicap ratings by a street, being allocated one pound shy of 10st (139lb, 63kg). For a juvenile, this was pretty much unprecedented, yet, as things would pan out, completely justified.

And this itself was telling as in the UK, Colombo was taking all before him, with the Brits wasting no time in calling *him* 'Horse of the Century' (See Windsor Lad entry). But in 1934 there was no doubt who the champion really was. A warm-up demolition by six lengths in the Prix de Sevres tuned Brantome up for a tilt, 11 days later, in the Poules d'Essai des Poulains (French 2,000 Guineas), where he again displayed a killer turn of foot to destroy the best of the rest, Admiral Drake, by an easy three lengths. A fortnight later it was time to take in the top French Derby trial, the ten-and-a-half-furlong Prix Lupin where, once Bouillon gave him his head, he strolled home by an easy two-and-a-half lengths.

By now his reputation was sky high on both sides of the Channel. His diminutive size had initially caused the English press to dismiss him as a 'polo pony', and indeed he didn't walk like a world-class athlete. He was certainly of delicate build, but he used this to his advantage from the very start, for his running style was sublime. His effortless, liquid stride and perfect balance transcended his size, making it seem as though he simply wasn't trying, despite polishing off one Group 1 after another. But then bad luck struck as Robert's entire string was overwhelmed by a severe bout of coughing. It compromised the champion's entire summer, as both the Prix du Jockey Club (French Derby) and Grand Prix de Paris went begging, with Brantome sick in his stable. The former race went to Duplex, the latter to Admiral Drake; Brantome had pulverised both in the past.

This pause was extra frustrating for connections as the US racing community was working hard to bring the top European horses over to challenge their best, with Epsom Derby winner Windsor Lad and Admiral Drake on the list in Brantome's absence. Ultimately it came to nothing, but Brantome had the beating of the latter and at aged three was almost certainly ahead of the former too. His connections took no chances with him, however, waiting until September's Prix Royal Oak (French St Leger) where, despite having to run wide around a wall of horses, he still unleashed his legendary acceleration and snuck in by a neck from Astronomer, in what was described by journalists as a finish for the ages.

The Prix de l'Arc de Triomphe loomed, and the line-up for 1934 was one of the strongest yet assembled: Duplex, Admiral Drake and Astronomer were all there, as well as easy Ascot Gold Cup winner Felicitation and Assuerus, victor of the Prix du President de la Republique (which became the Grand Prix de Saint-Cloud). Even so, there was a respect for Rothschild's colt that ensured he would start at near even-money favourite.

Heavy ground threatened to blunt Brantome's speed, but despite sweating heavily in the preliminaries, he completed his season in sensational style. When the time was right, Bouillon pressed the invisible button and Brantome rushed past the rest of the field, idled a bit, and then accelerated again, winning from Assuerus by nearly three lengths, with *Le Petit Parisien* stating unequivocally in their write up that 'his acceleration would never be forgotten by those who saw it'. In an extra strong year, Brantome was unbeaten and devastating; now it was the turn of the Parisian *turfistes* to proclaim their own '*Cheval du siecle*'. The crowds adored him, with horse and owner 'receiving the greatest popular demonstration ever heard on a French racecourse'. Fans also flocked to the cinema soon after to watch the short film *Brantome: Invincible Horse*, in the days when the movie-theatres were able to celebrate a different kind of superhero.

His four-year-old season was completely focussed on winning the two-and-a-half mile Ascot Gold Cup, still the pinnacle at the time for older European horses, and the race where he would finally meet British champion Windsor Lad. Easy victory in the Prix Edgar Gillas at Le Tremblay was followed by a mesmerising course record in the 'French Gold Cup', le Prix Du Cadran, by a staggering 15 lengths. What could go wrong?

Two things, in fact. First, Windsor Lad was withdrawn from the Gold Cup in what looked awfully like his owner Martin Benson running scared. Second, Brantome had become increasingly highly strung, and on his way to Chantilly racecourse for his final warm-up race, the Prix de Dangu, he escaped his groom and charged down the main road at full tilt. How he didn't get run over will never be known, but for an hour he galloped and smashed his way up and down the avenue. He lost three shoes, got himself a huge gash on his leg and was eventually caught, shattered and terrified. Given a tetanus shot, he missed the next four days' training, and likely displayed a reaction to his jab when running strangely after being taken back out to the training grounds.

99 out of 100 owners – certainly in more recent times – would have withdrawn their horse from the imminent Gold Cup, but the incredibly sporting Rothschild chose to go ahead – 'I knew that such a wide interest was taken in him and the Gold Cup that I wanted to keep faith with the English public' – and the inevitable happened. The clearly ailing Brantome lost his first race, trailing in fifth behind the rather ordinary Tiberius. The French public literally

couldn't believe it, with many calling their friends in England to double-check the result.

Despite winning the Prix du Prince d'Orange in September, he still bore the scars of his escapade, and the following month he came fourth when trying to retain his Arc crown. Indeed, the calamity-prone colt may have injured himself yet again in the course of the race, and, in the days before larger railings lined the track, hit a stake in the ground that marked the course. Whether hurt or not, he was gracefully retired, with many realising that, but for his moment of madness, he would likely never have been beaten and remain the yardstick for so many future generations.

In 1940 it was no great surprise that the Nazi invaders deliberately sought him out – along with a few choice others (see Pharis) – to be exported to Germany to sire future German champions. Fortunately, he was repatriated in 1946 to stand at his birthplace, and although not a great stallion in his own right, his son Vieux Manoir ensured that his line would ultimately produce Arc winners All Along, Exbury and Ivanjica, as well as the ill-fated Epsom Derby-winner Shergar.

Bloodstock Breeders' Review, not known for their hyperbole, said of him: 'As success followed success, the praises in his honour became louder and louder, and he was generally pronounced a "crack" and the horse of the century.'
Not bad for a 'Polo Pony'.

FACTFILE

Description: Bay Colt
Size: 15.1 hands
Dates: 1931-52
Racing seasons: 1933-35
Where were they trained?: France
Trainer: Lucien Robert
Owner: Baron Edouard De Rothschild

Jockey: Charles Bouillon
Sire: Blandford
Dam: Vitamine
Damsire: Clarissimus
Record: 14: 12-0-0
Most impressive victory: Prix du Cadran 1935
Nickname: Le Petit Roi

BAHRAM

The Aga Khan leads his Epsom Derby-winning hero Barham to the winner's enclosure as his son Prince Aly Khan converses with jockey Freddie Fox. Ever-present tipster 'Prince Monolulu' lurks in the background.

To go through a racing career unbeaten is rare. To win a Triple Crown – in whichever country – is also an occasional treat. To have the pair of these claims together is something only very few horses can claim, but Bahram was one. And at a time when his owner, the Aga Khan, had become one of the most prolific and successful owner-breeders in British racing history, there was no real doubt who his best ever was.

But just how good was he? The bottom line was no one really knew, as Bahram was an enigma, even to his closest connections. There was no faulting his looks. By champion sire Blandford out of top broodmare Friar's Daughter (who featured in Mumtaz Mahal's story), his imposing frame was matched with perfect conformation, perhaps second only to Nearco. He was named after the Aga Khan's cousin, Princess Bahram, who had drowned when the SS *Sussex* was torpedoed during World War One, and was trained by veteran Frank Butters at Newmarket.

Bahram's first eight years were intertwined with that of his owner-breeder. Sir Sultan Mahomed Shah – known to the world, and especially to the Nizari Ismaeli Muslims to whom he was their spiritual leader, as The Aga Khan – was at the start of that period a popular fellow in UK Racing circles. Born in Karachi but educated at Eton and Cambridge, his ways were very much those of the British aristocrat. He outdid his school friends by coming from a family even more fabulously wealthy than theirs. With a background like this, it was hardly surprising that he took an interest in the sport of kings.

Yet it was an interest driven purely by commercial concerns. His success was immense and of profound – and initially positive – influence on UK racing. As leading owner seven times, and with five prestigious studs in Ireland alone to satisfy his breeding interests, his wealth bought popularity across society. Yet the exterior investment in blue-blooded thoroughbreds hid an inner stinginess that raised an eyebrow or two in social circles. When it came to tipping, for example, he threw money around like a man with no arms.

Bahram was foaled at one of his breeder's Irish studs, possessing a handsome head with a unique ice-cream cone white marking. At two, he wasn't initially thought to be the best in the yard. Partly this was because of the easy success of stable companion Theft in the Windsor Castle Stakes at Royal Ascot. It was also because Bahram was so outrageously lazy. To say that this sleep-obsessed colt did the bare minimum was an understatement. Yet when he made his debut under regular-rider Freddie Fox at Sandown in the National Breeders' Produce Stakes, facing off against Theft, he came home the victor by a neck at 20-1 – clearly there had been little stable confidence at the time with this big and leggy colt.

Yet he soon backed it up with victories in the Rous Memorial at Goodwood and the prestigious Gimcrack Stakes at York, each time showing both little urge to make an effort, but being deeply impressive when compelled to. He completed his season with two wins on home turf at Newmarket, including the Group 1 Middle Park Stakes, where he almost casually notched up a six-furlong course record of 1min 11.2secs. It was no surprise that he headed the Free Handicap at the end of the year.

Triple Crown plans brewed that winter, as Bahram blossomed into a strong and imposing colt, but after missing his warm-up race for the 2,000 Guineas there were question marks about his sharpness and ability to run the full mile. Neither posed any problem, and he ambled away to win the first Classic 'comfortably' by a length-and-a-half from old rival Theft. He was sent off a month later as a hot favourite for the Epsom Derby, where the usual half-a-million-strong crowd descended. Those seeing him for the first time, including seasoned racing experts, believed that they had never seen a horse move more smoothly to post, but his stamina was untested. Confidence was high, though: the owner's son Aly Khan admitted afterwards that he placed the largest bet of his life that very morning.

BAHRAM

He needn't have fretted. Despite Freddie Fox finding himself boxed in at the rails halfway through, fellow jockey Harry Wragg on whipping boy Theft obligingly gave him the space he needed, and Bahram sauntered away for a victory so seemingly without trying that only Sea-Bird's 30 years later would ever be mentioned in the same breath. To prove that speed hadn't deserted him, he reverted back to a mile later in the same month at Royal Ascot's St James Palace Stakes, again trotting up to win at the prohibitive odds of 1-8.

The first spanner in the works came at the height of summer when a coughing epidemic made one of its periodic visits to Newmarket, and Butters' yard was hit. Although Bahram escaped it, his training was disrupted, but he still made it to Doncaster in September to complete the rare Triple Crown in the one-mile-six-furlong St Leger. Fox, however, did not, having been involved in a horror fall the day before, and cheeky cockney Charlie Smirke was handed the plum ride. Putting in only as much effort as he needed to, Bahram still coasted to perhaps his easiest victory yet, finishing five lengths clear of Solar Ray, with the ever-confident Smirke stating afterwards that his horse 'would have won carrying 12 stone and two riders'. Perhaps he could have.

And thus this legend of the turf was retired, undefeated over five furlongs, 14 furlongs, and everywhere in between. Yet still he had his detractors. Some claimed, spuriously, that 'he never beat a good horse'. Others claimed that he was kept apart from the other good horses because they were mostly all owned by … the Aga Khan. But this simply doesn't stand up to scrutiny; there was nothing to suggest that Bahram's peers were any inferior to usual, and in truth no one really ever tested him. Conversely, it is true that he never faced older horses, and a 1935 clash between him and either Brantome or Windsor Lad would have been mouth-watering.

Part of this apathy was because of his attitude. Chilled beyond belief, his unique and signature pose was to lean against the stable wall, cross his front legs in an anthropomorphic way and survey everything around him. You sense that, if he had been human, he would likely have been drawn to surfing. In turn, he flummoxed those around him. Butters confided, 'I never really knew how good he was.'

What could be disputed was the wisdom of what happened to him thereafter. All-powerful the Aga Khan may have been but – unlike the purer path chosen by his grandson in later years – to him racehorses were commodities, not purveyors of sporting dreams and culture. He enjoyed his victories, but he certainly enjoyed the winners' cheques even more. He retired all his champions at three rather than let them develop further at four; he then swore to the public that he would never sell Bahram, only to go back on his word in 1940 and sell *all* of his Derby winners to the highest bidder – inevitably the US. In Bahram's case, a syndicate which included Walter P. Chrysler, S. W. Labrot, James Cox Brady and the highly influential Alfred G. Vanderbilt bought him for £40,000 pounds ($160,000 at the time) and he went to ply his trade in Maryland and then Virginia.

It has been persuasively argued by breeding experts that this exporting of many of the great bloodlines away from the UK acted as one of the greatest catalysts for the westward shift in power over the ensuing decades. The year he left, Bahram was second leading sire in the UK, and just 18 months after he departed, his son Big Game, owned by King George VI, won the 2,000 Guineas, showing the British public again what might have been. Formerly huge fans, they now found it very hard to forgive the Aga Khan, who moved that very year, with the war at its zenith, to neutral Switzerland.

Bahram was part of this sad exodus and, after siring a few stakes winners, was sold on aged 13 to Argentina where, again, his offspring didn't set the racetracks on fire. By the strange vagaries of lineage, his descendants were only found for many years in Germany. Only with the unexpected success of their stallion Monsun have his distant descendants once again been seen succeeding on top tracks. His death at 24 passed by without much fanfare. Yet for those 16 months where he so effortlessly swatted away everything in his lazy path on the racecourse, there were many who swore that they'd never seen better.

FACTFILE

Description: Bay Colt
Size: 16.2 Hands
Dates: 1932-56
Racing seasons: 1934-35
Where were they trained?: UK
Trainer: Frank Butters
Owner: HH Aga Khan

Jockey: Freddie Fox, Charlie Smirke
Sire: Blandford
Dam: Friar's Daughter
Damsire: Friar Marcus
Record: 9:9-0-0
Most impressive victory: St Leger 1935

NEARCO

Nearco - 'the perfect thoroughbred' - after winning the Gran Premio del Re (Italian Derby) by a distance, May 1938.

Ask ten breeders what they think the ideal thoroughbred racehorse should look like, and you will likely get quite a bit of general overlap, followed by ten divergent views on more detailed aspects. So far, so predictable. But here's the thing: what so many of them will find themselves agreeing on is that Italian champion racehorse Nearco had pretty much the most perfect conformation of any racehorse in history. Fortunately for us, his sheer brilliance on the racecourse was matched by his potency in the breeding shed. Indeed, nearly a century on, Nearco is as ubiquitous as any thoroughbred sire has ever been.

One man is to thank for all this: Federico Tesio. Snobbish, fussy and self-centred he may have been, but it is possible that there may have been no greater breeder in the 20th century. He possessed an indefinable magic touch that made him something of an international breeding star. His mantra was: 'A good horse walks with his legs, gallops with his lungs, resists with his heart, but wins only with his spirit and character'. As one historian remarked, 'If you carefully research performance pedigrees right around the world you will find the hand of Tesio in so many great horses – no matter what the sport – and no matter what the breed.'

Together with his wife, the former Marchesa Lydia Serramezzana Flori, they set up a stud at Dormello, but uniquely Tesio was a trainer too, so his training stables were in Milan. From his paddocks near Rome – and three generations in the planning – in 1934 he sent one of his mares, the absolutely tiny Italian Guineas winner Nogara, to Pharos – his second choice behind Pharos's brother Fairway. The resultant foal wasn't huge either at first, but he steadily grew into 16 hands of perfection: his intelligent head, his withers, his shoulders, his croup, his fetlocks, his back, his balance, his symmetry … you just couldn't fault him.

And sure enough, as Tesio tested him in training, he developed into the mightiest runner his country had hitherto produced. At two, he won all seven races with frightening ease, from five to eight furlongs, including the Gran Criterium and Premio Chiusura. It would be premature to assume that competition in Italian racing was in some way inferior at the time; there had been plenty of Italian winners abroad before. Yet incredibly, despite this endless success, at the end of Nearco's two-year-old season, Tesio tried to sell him, because he thought he was *too* fast. Rare it is that a horse can show such precocious speed at two yet see out the longer-distance Classic races and beyond at three and older, and those were the races that Tesio coveted. For once, Tesio's incredible horse instincts let him down, and it was to Tesio's – and likely our – eternal good luck that he couldn't find a buyer, and so this special animal stayed where he was.

To that end, at three, Nearco came into his own. First, he cantered to the Premio Parioli (Italian 2,000 Guineas) at Capannelle by six lengths. In the Gran Premio Del Re (Italian Derby), he won officially by a distance – video evidence suggests it was nearer 20 lengths, but either way he was crushing all the opposition with contempt, and always with a stunning turn of foot.

He then went to Milan and trotted up in the Gran Premio d'Italia (12 furlongs) before stepping up to 15 furlongs for the Gran Premio Di Milano. It was far longer than he ideally wanted, but it made no difference. Unbeaten and utterly untested in 13 races, Nearco had nothing left to prove at home, so needed to be tested against the best that Europe had to offer. But this was 1938 and Europe was not a happy place.

The biggest all-age race at the time, attracting the best that the continent had to offer, was the Grand Prix de Paris at Longchamp, again run over 15 furlongs. With the stench of imminent war so pungent in the air, Tesio had to seek permission from Mussolini himself to send his horse to enemy territory. Tesio only sought to achieve pure horseracing supremacy, but of course for Il Duce it represented so much more. Seldom has there been a more 'political' race in history.

NEARCO

The line-up was outstanding, including the winners of both the Prix Du Jockey Club (French Derby), Cillas, and the Epsom Derby, Bois Roussel. The stands were rammed, with the local supporters cheering their home challengers – and even the British horses – as much as they jeered the Italian imposter. He was hissed by tens of thousands, as it was said that his near-black colour represented the black heart of fascism itself. How the usually fractious Nearco managed to remain composed in the face of all this we'll never know.

But jeers don't down class, and even over a distance that was well beyond his comfort zone, Nearco won far more easily than the length-and-a-half margin suggests. As they entered the winner's enclosure, and as payback to the reception that his horse had been given, jockey Pietro Gubellini unleashed a fascist salute. It is frankly a miracle that World War Two didn't start there and then. Regardless, Nearco had conquered Europe in a way Il Duce would not. The more dispassionate elements of the racing press acknowledged that the unbeaten colt was truly one of the greats.

After what he had witnessed in Paris, Tesio realised that Nearco couldn't stay in Italy as he would likely be in the firing line of war sooner rather than later. He therefore retired him and sold him for a record £60,000 to English bookmaker Martin Benson – who, after Windsor Lad, was making a habit of buying champions – and Nearco went to stand at Beech House Stud in Newmarket. But Nearco wasn't a normal sire. He was recognised as being the most valuable animal in the country, so when war did indeed arrive, he was built a special bomb shelter, and learned to walk into it when the air raid sirens went off.

But the investment was worth it, as we now look back and realise that Nearco's sire line, via three of his sons in particular – Nearctic, Nasrullah and Royal Charger – permeates almost every single pedigree on both sides of the Atlantic. There has never been a sire over the last century whose ancestors dominate like Nearco's – not just in quality but in quantity. As France Galop noted, every single winner from 1985 to 2010 of Europe's touchstone middle-distance race, the Prix de l'Arc de Triomphe, can be traced back to him. Domination doesn't come much more complete than that. And it wasn't just quality, but strength in numbers that proved to be Nearco's other secret weapon. In all, more than 100 of his sons have themselves stood at stud around the world, which is a record only surpassed since the late 19th century by the legendary St Simon.

Potent he may have been, but Nearco was also incredibly temperamental as a stallion, and the first ten grooms who tried to look after him utterly failed. Only the 11th, Ernie Lee, was able to finally get Nearco to accept him – the horse loathed being touched, but trusted Ernie, who adored him, for all his character issues. As an aged Nearco developed cancer of the hip and an ailing digestive tract, the devoted Lee had to hand-feed him a special mash of grain and hay for several months, until eventually he had to be euthanised. Lee walked away there and then from the world of racing, never to return. He would never look after another horse as brilliant and beautiful as Nearco.

And, some might argue, nor would anyone else.

FACTFILE

Description: Brown colt
Size: 16.05 Hands
Dates: 1935-57
Racing seasons: 1937-38
Where were they trained?: Italy
Trainer: Federico Tesio
Owner: Federico Tesio
Jockey: Pietro Gubellini, Ilario Grassini

Sire: Pharos
Dam: Nogara
Damsire: Havresac II
Record: 14: 14-0-0
Most impressive victory: Grand Prix de Paris 1938

PHARIS

'As black as a crow': Charlie Elliot aboad the astonishing and enigmatic Pharis, June 1939.

It is a truth universally acknowledged that European horses, on average, run fewer races than their US and Australian counterparts. Even so, having only three races in a career seems absurd, and to have such a barely exposed horse in this book might seem, on the face of it, ludicrous. But it's not as simple as that. Dig deeper, and you realise that Pharis absolutely deserves his place here for several reasons, and the first of those is the towering figure of Marcel Boussac. Textiles magnate Boussac was small, dapper, wealthy and immensely astute. His revolutionary approach to breeding utterly dominated first the French and then the European racing scene for decades, but went far wider. His canny ability to push the limits of inbreeding to maintain brilliance without compromising health was soon practised elsewhere. He changed the design of what a standard stud farm should look like, with his trailblazing Haras de Fresnay-le-Buffard stud in Normandy as a template; the Americans soon copied him.

He was leading owner in France 19 times, leading breeder 17 times, won a staggering 36 French Classics and six Prix de l'Arc de Triomphes. Soon enough, his famous orange-and-grey silks also became the Jolly Roger to the British racing scene, as he launched successful raids and plundered all the top races there too. After winning the Epsom Derby in 1950 with Galcador, he was overheard to say casually in the winner's enclosure, 'I have six better than him back in France' – and in all honesty he wasn't joking. In fact, he didn't joke at all, and you'll be hard pushed to find a photo of him smiling. In short, this was a pioneer who was peerless in his knowledge of horses, so when he said later in life that Pharis was unquestionably the best racehorse he had ever seen, let alone bred, you did well to listen.

By Pharos (like Nearco) and out of Boussac's moderate mare Carissima, very few thoroughbreds are genuinely black, but the stunning Pharis was one of them – 'as black as a crow,' the Parisian Turfistes wrote. He grew to have an imposing presence with quite a long back and powerful hindquarters, but being quite scopey, he took a while to grow into his frame so did not run at two. Placed into training with one of Boussac's retained trainers, the Paris-based Englishman Albert Swann, Pharis finally saw the racecourse in May 1939 in the 12-furlong Prix Noailles at Longchamp, where, under Charlie Elliot, he cruised to a three-length victory. He looked very promising.

Just three weeks later he was thrown in at the deep end of the Prix Du Jockey Club (French Derby). Respected French racing journalist Michel Bouchet would see an amazing 80 French Derbies in person, and he was unequivocal that Pharis's victory was the best that he had ever seen: 'Blocked in at the back of the field, the jockey pulled the horse wide and, showing an incredible turn of foot, passed the whole field to win comfortably by two-and-a-half lengths from Galerian.' The crowd was genuinely thrilled to see a burgeoning superstar.

A mere fortnight after that, and the biggest European prize of all at the time, the Grand Prix de Paris, beckoned. Longchamp was properly attended in those days. A record 59,797 spectators turned up, amongst them the new French President Albert Lebrun and the 'exiled' Duke and Duchess of Windsor. Perhaps they were all there for the socialising, but they also had the good fortune to witness greatness.

Just a year earlier Nearco's victory had almost caused an international incident, and more drama would follow this year, fortunately this time within the confines of the race. As the 19 horses in the high-quality international field rounded the final turn of the 15-furlong race, the more tired ones blocked Pharis, who was still near the back, and he stumbled, pretty much falling to his knees; he just recovered his stride. Elliot then found a gap on the inside, and despite the slow ground and the long race, Pharis unleashed a quite breathtaking turn of foot to storm past the others horses.

Watching it now is proper jaw-dropping stuff. Despite being in the pack and nearly at a standstill with two furlongs to go, photographic and video evidence shows that his winning margin was fully six lengths and not the arbitrary two-and-a-half lengths that the judges asserted. The testimonials flooded in. 'Like the winged horse of the Arab Legend,' wrote one admiring English journalist. French Daily *Le Figaro*, meanwhile, thought nothing of publishing a spontaneously written verse by leading poet Leon-Paul Fargue, also in the audience and 'dumbfounded and inspired' by what he had seen. Elsewhere in the same edition, their racing correspondent wrote, 'At last, now, when older generations tell us tales of Gladiateur and the like we will contend that we saw the greatest horse of them all – his name was Pharis.' He further waxed lyrical that what he had seen was '… an education. The winner was no longer just the best, by far, of his generation. He was changing the goalposts.'

Jockey Elliot, a winner of 14 Classics in the UK and France, declared that there was simply no competition amongst which was the best horse that he had ridden. More prosaically, Charles Bouillon, who had ridden the runner-up and had himself ridden champion Brantome just a few years earlier, was almost baffled afterwards: 'When I heard a horse coming up behind me, I immediately looked round, but he had already gone past'. In a championship race, Pharis had put up a champion's performance, displaying a turn of foot that to this day has seldom been replicated, especially in a 15-furlong race.

There was frantic excitement as he was then sent over to England for the St Leger in September where he was due to square up to the English hero Blue Peter. This equally handsome horse – an intelligent white-blazed chestnut – had taken all before him in that fateful English summer, including the first two legs of the Triple Crown as well as the Eclipse Stakes against his elders. Indeed, the two horses were cousins of a kind, as Blue Peter's grandsire Fairway was a full brother to Pharis's father Pharos. The press on both sides of the Channel went into giddy overdrive, dubbing it the 'Duel on Town Moor' and whipping up something of a frenzy. Both sides exuded confidence, with more favouring Pharis because he potentially had more improvement in him, having only graced the racetrack in anger three times.

But if Nearco's year had smelled war on the horizon, Pharis's year saw it put off no longer. Just as Pharis was being settled into the yard of Steve Donoghue – former champion jockey and now trying it as a trainer – Germany invaded Poland. Within two days, the UK declared war. It being only 72 hours before the St Leger, there was no option but to cancel the final Classic. Most fully understood, but not everyone. Possibly apocryphal – yet how we desperately hope that it isn't – the UK ambassador to France was allegedly heard to say, 'It is inconceivable that in a country of sport-lovers like ours, war should have been declared before the St Leger, which was to be the race of the century and for which I especially planned my holidays.'

But there was to be no duel. Pharis's other target, the Arc, was likewise abandoned soon after. Meanwhile, Boussac had no choice but to hurry his supreme black racer back onto the ship to Normandy and retire him: three races, three increasingly stunning victories, a sky-high reputation and frustration as to what might have been.

Pharis's story doesn't end there. In his first year at stud, the Nazi invaders found him and sent him to Germany to pair up with various German mares. Fortunately, he was returned unharmed in 1945, but Boussac understandably refused to recognise any of his sire's supposed offspring, most notably the filly Asterblüte, who captured the German Derby, 1,000 Guineas and Oaks in 1946. (Interestingly, fast-forward five generations in her family and you would find future Arc winner and broodmare *extraordinaire* Urban Sea.) Perhaps Pharis's German sojourn was a blessing; Boussac's dual Arc-winning mare Corrida was not taken from his Normandy stud in 1940, but later disappeared soon after D-Day, almost certainly ending up as meat for hungry soldiers.

Pharis's immediate success on his return, with his first 13 foals producing ten winners including a Prix du Jockey Club and Arc winner, showed yet again that likely his best breeding years were stolen in the same way as his racing years had been. But some experts, like Michel Bouchet, felt that they had seen enough in his final race: 'In the last 200 metres he would have beaten Sea-Bird, no matter what.' And if the grainy evidence is anything to go by, it's not a crazy assertion.

FACTFILE

Description: Black Colt
Size: 16.2 hands
Dates: 1936–57
Racing seasons: 1939
Where were they trained?: France
Trainer: Albert Swann
Owner: Marcel Boussac

Jockey: Charlie Elliot
Sire: Pharos
Dam: Carissima
Damsire: Clarissimus
Record: 3:3-0-0
Most impressive victory: Grand Prix de Paris 1939
Nickname: Le Cheval du Siecle

SUN CHARIOT

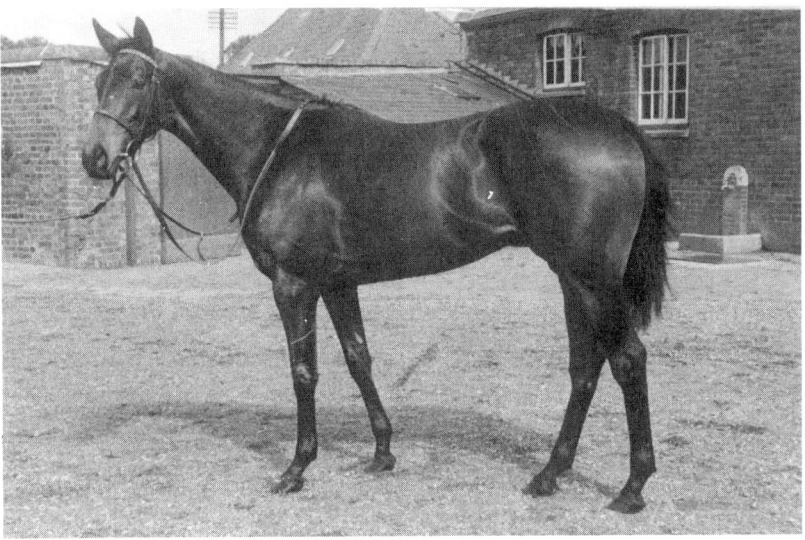

The not-particularly-straightforward Sun Chariot just prior to her sensational performance in the Oaks, run that year at Newmarket, June 1942.

War is miserable and World War Two was as awful as any. Putting on horse races was hardly a priority for the governments of the world, yet somehow they found a way. Options, however, were necessarily limited. In England, as on the continent, those racecourses that hadn't been damaged by bombs were requisitioned by the armed forces as excellent substitute airfields. There were a few exceptions, and one of them was the largest racecourse in the world, Newmarket, and this was where all of the country's Triple Crown races needed to be held until normality once again returned. Several horses made their mark there, but none more so than Sun Chariot. When discussing her at the time, all experts were in agreement about two things. First, she was utterly mad. Second, she was quite, quite brilliant.

But there was an extra angle to her that thrust her into the limelight: she was owned by King George VI. In fact, it was strictly speaking the National Stud that owned her and loaned her out to the King, but to the adoring public this was a mere technicality; she was a royal horse and should be treated as such. To the shy, stuttering King, doing his level best during those dark, consequential days to instil warmth, solace and hope in the face of limitless horrors, she became a beacon, if not of hope then of distraction.

When she reached two, the monarch sent her to the Beckhampton stables of one of his trainers, Fred Darling. Darling's success and brilliance as a trainer was unparalleled in English racing. He annexed championships and records as a matter of course, and could prepare a horse for a specific race like no other, although it was also noted that he had no real affection for any of them. By all accounts, he was a genius when dealing with the equine form. What he couldn't do, however, was people. To call him 'cold' was to be generous to ice. He deliberately shunned any form of human friendship but didn't stop there: he actively discouraged all those connected to his yard (lads, jockeys, grooms) to have any form of social interaction either.

Enter Sun Chariot, with all her naughty and unpredictable behaviours, in stark contrast to her charming and lazy father Hyperion, the tiny Epsom Derby-winner-turned-supersire. She initially refused to be trained, and Darling was on the cusp of returning her to the stud in disgust. It was largely thanks to a groom called Warren that she didn't, as he seemed to find a way to get her to comply. He proceeded to ride her in her work at home, and finally it dawned on them that when she put her mind to it, she was something special. She was also growing into a real beauty, not that Darling would have cared.

It came as little surprise, therefore, when she won her first race at Newbury quite easily. Ridden in that first year by Harry Wragg, because stable jockey and champion Gordon Richards was injured all year, she won easily. Richards, though, had heard all about the unhinged filly, and managed to put a bet on her from hospital. Perhaps in an attempt to please the regal owner, Darling next entered her in the Queen Mary Stakes, which usually formed part of Royal Ascot. Even over an inadequate five furlongs she trotted up, and that was when plans and dreams reached the next level.

One of the top end-of-year races in England for two-year-olds remains the Middle Park Stakes, now open only to colts but then open to fillies too. It was very rare for trainers to even bother entering fillies into it, yet Sun Chariot not only ran but she won going away by three lengths from Ujiji. Behind them was Watling Street, who would win the following year's Epsom Derby. No filly had won the race since 1921. The British public unquestionably now had a heroine to rally around.

What they remained largely unaware of, however, was her temperament, which if anything became even more of a time bomb the following year. By now, Richards was fit again to ride and was desperate to finally get a chance to see what she could do. Their partnership started ignominiously. With the target being the 1,000 Guineas, Darling chose a six-furlong warm-up race at his local track of Salisbury, often seen as a tough but fair racecourse to get horses back into the groove of racing. Yet there was nothing fair about Sun Chariot's behaviour that

SUN CHARIOT

day, even with the godly skills of Richards aboard. He tried to be boss, and she was having none of it. She steadfastly refused to take hold of the bit and deliberately tried to shake him off. It was her first defeat, and also her last.

There was much apprehension, therefore, when she lined up for the first Classic of the season, yet perhaps the only thing more infuriating than a horse who always behaves like a punk is one that only does so on certain, unpredictable occasions. Aside from swishing her tail violently, she decided to try, and charged past the field to win effortlessly by four lengths. The King, for good measure, also won the 2,000 Guineas with Big Game, also trained by Darling.

The most shameful moment of her life, though, followed in the run up to her next assignment, the Epsom Oaks. With the two royal horses favourites for the upcoming Classics, the King and his consort – the future Queen Mother – decided to descend upon Darling's stables and watch their thoroughbreds in action on the training grounds. Big Game was fine; Sun Chariot absolutely disgraced herself. In a stultifyingly petulant mood, even by her exacting standards, the head lad on her back decided to give her a smack. Sun Chariot bolted off the course and ran headlong into a neighbouring ploughed field. Once there, and for reasons known only to her lunatic self, she sat herself on her knees and, according to all those present, 'proceeded to roar like a bull'. Oh to have been a fly on the King's lapel to witness his reaction to this Pythonesque behaviour. Darling was apparently mortified, although it's hard to see how anyone could tell.

Her second most dreadful moment happened in the Oaks itself. The saving grace this time was that it was coupled with one of the most astonishing performances in a Classic race in European history. At the start, like a toddler after too much sugar, she was all over the place, and ruined three attempted starts. At the fourth try, the starter had rightly had enough and just let them go. Sun Chariot immediately flew off to the left and then stopped. Richards recounted later that the field had gone fully a furlong (straight), by the time he had gone 50 yards, to the left – and Richards was never one to exaggerate. Yet only then did she decide to play ball and, incredibly, over the next mile, she caught them up, making up an untold number of lengths. Mere mortal horses would have collapsed at this effort, yet somehow Sun Chariot hit the front a furlong from home and held on to win by a length. Richards, with saucer-eyed wonder, unsurprisingly called it, 'One of the most amazing performances I have ever known'. A beaming King George led his filly into the enclosure, perhaps still unsure of the incredible performance she had just put in, and briefly the country forgot its woes.

PUNCH A HOLE IN THE WIND

Yet there were still grumblings in some elements of the public that wartime racing felt frivolous, never more so than when 50,000 people had attended the previous year's Derby at Newmarket. Whilst this offered an insight into these clearly austere times, it perhaps also illuminated the occasional British habit of deliberately not wanting to enjoy oneself, or not letting others do so. Others felt that rallying round the King's horse was the best cure. To that end, it was now inevitable that Sun Chariot would try for the Fillies Triple Crown by running in the St Leger. It was to be her last race and, in her own version of appeasement, she behaved, meaning that victory was an easy formality. In scintillating style, she came from last to first, and won by three lengths from Watling Street, who had beaten Big Game to victory in the Epsom Derby. This Leger performance made plenty of folk believe that this one-off filly would likely have won the Derby itself given a chance.

With little else to prove, the King decided to retire her, and she bred seven winners, including two by Big Game. Richards it was who recalled in his memoirs, 'She was a machine and a character! I've a few grey hairs and she gave them to me.' Equally, he asserted that, 'she was probably the greatest racehorse I've ever come across'. And coming from a 26-time champion jockey, it's a statement that's hard to ignore. But then again, ignoring Sun Chariot was the last thing you wanted to do.

FACTFILE

Description: Bay Filly
Size: 16 Hands
Dates: 1939-63
Racing seasons: 1941-42
Where were they trained?: UK
Trainer: Fred Darling
Owner: King George VI, The National Stud

Jockey: Gordon Richards, Harry Wragg
Sire: Hyperion
Dam: Clarence
Damsire: Diligence
Record: 9: 8-0-1
Most impressive victory: Epsom Oaks, 1942

BERNBOROUGH

Bernborough and work rider Billie Nielsen warm up for a morning gallop, where he would doubtless unleash his monumental stride.

There are two kinds of 'war hero'. The first is the actual soldier who fights bravely for their country, laying their life on the line if necessary. The other kind is the 'diversion' – someone or something that the civil population needs to rally around during dark times to offer them hope and inspiration of a different kind. During World War Two in Australia there were countless folk who fitted the first category, but as for the second, many Australians chose their escapism via horseracing, and the overwhelming hero for them was Bernborough. Yet he wasn't just a conveniently good horse who popped up at the right time. His massive size was forever matched by his massive ability.

His origins were inauspicious. Foaled in Dalby, Queensland, and by imported UK stallion Ernborough out of elderly mare Bern Maid, his most notable feature was a mane that fell to the left rather than the right – a rarity in thoroughbreds. When bought as part of a wider dispersal lot by Jack and Frank Bach, he was described as the 'lousiest thing' they'd ever seen, and soon leased to Albert Hadwen. Trained by Bobby Mitchell, at two the lousy thing was now a 17.1 hand monster, with a huge girth and ground-guzzling stride; it was no surprise that he would eventually remind so many of Australia's previous great, Phar Lap. He balanced his massive frame well, and ran in a unique way, with his back legs splayed much further apart than other horses.

Yet despite winning nine of his first 14 races in his first two seasons, he was restricted to the bush track of Toowoomba, 80 miles west of Brisbane. This was because Frank Bach had been found guilty by the Queensland authorities years before of running a 'ringer' – i.e. swapping one horse for a lookalike in a race – and had banned him from running any horse outside of Toowoomba. Bach no longer 'owned' the horse but the Queensland Turf Club wanted to send a message, and the loser was the increasingly brilliant Bernborough. Twice he was sent to race in Sydney and Brisbane hoping for leniency, but each time was barred at the last minute. To further distance him from disrepute, he was sent as a five-year-old to be trained by Harry Plant in Sydney and sold outright for 2600gns to restaurateur Azzalin Romano, whose eponymous restaurant was the place for Hollywood and actual royalty to be seen when harbour-side. This move was sufficient to allow the Toowoomba Tornado, now with a proper countrywide reputation, to run against all-comers. From now on he would be running in his fifth set of colours. But these ones – orange, purple and black – would be the ones that he would forever be associated with.

Plant had to manage his huge charge cleverly. He was to be burdened with crushing weights, and as a horse that always tried his hardest, that meant risking his legs; he had already had several cases of corns in his tender hooves. His first race in Sydney was an average fourth, and the locals began to consider that the horse from the bush was over-rated. This was spectacularly misguided, for what followed has entered Australian racing lore. Bernborough would notch up victory in each of his next 15 races, across the big racing centres of Sydney, Melbourne and Brisbane, from all distances between six to 11 furlongs, each time with colossal weights on his back and in the top-ranked races, including the Newmarket Handicap, the Chipping Norton Stakes, the VATC Futurity Stakes and the Rawson. He had become invincible and his growing legion of fans loved it as a distraction from the on-going horrors of war.

During this amazing streak, his lightweight jockey, Athol Mulley, quickly realised that Bernborough was most comfortable following a set routine. At the start, he would be kept right back and relax, often 20 lengths behind the leaders, before going through the gears in the home straight and unleashing a pulverising turn of foot. It worked a charm every time, and more than once his final four furlongs in a mile race was timed at 46 seconds – an otherworldly time in a turf race considering he was carrying over 10 stone (140 lb) at the time. His secret weapon, aside from his courage, could well have been his stride. At full tilt, it was regularly measured at 8.6m (28ft), thought to be the longest of any accurately measured thoroughbred.

Old Aussie fans had their favourite of his races: the Newmarket Handicap. 28 runners, no starting gates, a sodden track, visibility not great. As the peloton of horses entered the straight, radio commentator Jim Carroll was more honest than many in a similar situation: 'I just cannot find the favourite.' Eventually he found him, achingly far behind, with 15 horses in front of him and two furlongs to run. But as one eye witness recalled, 'And then, through a great heap of horses – as though he wanted to make as dramatic an enterprise as possible – exploded the massive form of Bernborough, mane flying and head extended.' Impossibly, he got up by a head. Of course he did.

The pinnacle amongst this immense streak was the 1946 Doomben Cup, over just shy of 11 furlongs. Bernborough had been assigned an unbelievable 10st 11lbs (151 lbs) – a weight that not even Carbine or Phar Lap had ever been asked to carry. Plant, who genuinely cared for the big horse's welfare, was coerced into running by the ebullient Romano. The story that Plant, whilst saddling Bernborough, was heard to say 'You wouldn't run if I owned you, old fella,' was not apocryphal.

In front of a huge, partisan crowd and against a vast field of 27, Mulley played his usual game, dropping 'Bernie' 15 lengths shy of the leaders. Halfway through he pushed the go button, only for his big mount to run straight into the retreating filly Tea Cake, and almost fall. The situation almost repeated itself a furlong later. With time running out and the rails jammed, Mulley had no option but to swing his mighty horse around a wall of six horses to the extreme outside and do it the hard way. Incredibly, despite these challenges and the weight of a train on his back, Bernborough won by a length in a track record. Performances like this were once-on-a-lifetime treasures, and all this by a seven-year-old.

Yet all good things have to end, and in Bernborough's case it was nearly the very end. After running poorly in the Caulfield Cup, Mulley was replaced by Bill Briscoe, who chose to ride differently in the November 1946 LKS MacKinnon Stakes. Up against one of the great Australian fillies Flight (whom he had beaten several times before), and challenging for the lead under another monstrous weight, Briscoe heard what he swore was a gunshot, but was in fact Bernborough's right foreleg sesamoid bone snapping. All were in shock, and the camera proceeded to ignore Flight's win and focussed on the distressed Bernborough instead. Often a horse will be euthanised in such awful circumstances, but this smart colt quickly learned to minimise the pain by walking only on his three good legs, and lying down whenever he could. He would never run again but he had saved himself for a career at stud.

Australia heaved a sigh of relief and then reflected on what this giant bay had achieved. *The Daily Telegraph* didn't hold back, putting together a 33-page tribute. He had an appeal that spanned all ages. Visitors to the stable had always been allowed to put their toddlers safely on his back as he was a truly gentle soul. It is only fitting that a statue was eventually raised in his honour, in his initial hunting ground of Toowoomba. Fittingly, it is the largest bronze horse sculpture in the Southern Hemisphere.

Bought by admiring movie mogul Louis B. Mayer for the highest price ever paid at the time for an imported stallion, he was given a tearful adieu before boarding for California, and eventually Kentucky. He was a fair success as a stallion, siring winners across all of Latin America, as well the US and the UK, where he was even Grandsire to Grand National winner Jay Trump. He died in 1960 of a heart attack in his paddock, his head cradled in his heartbroken handler's arms. But in Australia, he will always be more than special, as a horse that could seemingly do the impossible and who in turn helped the country forget the turmoil of war. As journalist Joe McCarthy wrote in awe, 'He could carry the grandstand and win.' And with it, one senses, he carried the heart of a nation.

FACTFILE

Description: Bay Colt
Size: 17.1 hands
Dates: 1939–60
Racing seasons: 1941–47
Where were they trained?: Australia
Trainer: Gordon Neale, Bobby Mitchell, Dinny Callinan, Francis Roberts, Harry Plant
Owner: Frank and John R. Bach, A.E.Hadwin, Azzalin O. Romano
Jockey: George Mulley, Billy Briscoe
Sire: Ernborough
Dam: Bern Maid
Damsire: Bernard
Record: 37: 26-2-1
Most impressive victory: The Doomben Cup, 1946
Nickname: Bernie, The Toowoomba Tornado

COUNT FLEET

Count Fleet, with Johnny Longden aboard, already has his rivals in trouble rounding the final turn in the Preakness Stakes, which he would win by eight lengths, May 1943.

It sounds obvious, but it's worth listening to jockeys: ultimately it is they who sit on a thoroughbred, take it through its paces, and pick up either nuanced concerns from the way a horse is running or, more happily, good vibes if their mount is offering something out of the ordinary. To that end, we should be grateful that John Hertz, founder of the eponymous car rental empire and owner of a self-bred yearling called Count Fleet, listened to jockey Johnny Longden when the former was on the verge of selling him. Longden – known to his weighing-room colleagues as The Pumper – felt it worth sticking up for the horse, who he sensed had more to give. Hertz relented, and we hope later in life offered Longden a bonus, as Count Fleet would soon become one of the greats of 20th-century North American racing.

Hertz's misgivings were understandable: Count Fleet, who both started and finished his life at Hertz's Stoner Creek Stud in Kentucky, was no oil painting. Breeding commentator Abram Hewitt described him as 'narrow, light-waisted, and flat-muscled with less than ideal action'. His head was charitably referred to as 'plain', and experts deemed him 'too leggy'. But no one could fault his energy. Following Longden's prescient advice, the son of unfashionable Kentucky Derby winner Reigh Count and aptly named dam Quickly was sent into training with former World War One balloon pilot Don Cameron.

After two green and slightly erratic runs as runner-up, he got his act together by sprinting to an easy victory at Aqueduct, just shy of the course record despite displaying his tendency to run very wide around the bends. He followed up with a slew of victories and the odd second place over several east-coast tracks, including Belmont and Empire City, over five and six furlongs, sometimes against his great two-year-old rival Occupation. They traded wins, with some thinking Occupation the better. But at one morning gallop, a few days before their third match-up in the big-pursed Belmont Futurity, Longden couldn't control the boisterous colt who, in front of many stopwatch-holding onlookers, proceeded to run six furlongs in 1min 8.2secs. It was one of the fastest training runs by any horse of any age, and suddenly the racing world realised that they had a rocket on their hands.

Soon enough, only the superb horseman Longden was allowed to ride the colt at home or on track. In one incident at training in Belmont, The Count was going for it, and as Longden spotted two horses coming towards him from the other direction, tried to veer his colt away to safety – as though this equine lunatic was going to listen. He refused to slow or change direction, forcing Longden – incredibly – to thread himself between the two closely paired incomers, at a combined speed of nearly 80 miles an hour. Ever his favourite horse's apologist, Longden would point out, 'He was not a mean horse … Just one full of the devil.'

Unsurprisingly, in the Futurity itself, he let his exuberance get the better of him, cut his front hooves with his back legs, came third, and then carried on uncontrollably galloping for an extra six furlongs past the winning post. But this time there were extenuating circumstances, as Count Fleet liked the ladies. In the field was top filly Askmenow who, it transpired later, was in season. She was just trying to run her race, but to the excitable Count Fleet she was all cooing and wiggles. As an exasperated Longden recounted after, 'He kept alongside Askmenow, nose and nose, and nothing interested him except to remain in her companionship. If she spurted, the Count would spurt with her; if she slowed stride, so did he. I tried everything that was possible to end his fascination and pull away from her—but nothing helped.' He would never lose again.

With connections realising two things – that he needed further, and that he was slightly mad – a week later he ran over a mile at Belmont's Champagne Stakes. Not only did he crush his rivals by six lengths, but his time of 1min 34.8secs was a world record for a juvenile over the distance. After another six-length victory in an allowance race, he once again took on Occupation over eight and a half furlongs, this time with no injury. Evenly matched down the

COUNT FLEET

backstretch, the Count's class then told as he peeled six lengths ahead in another course record. He rounded off his season with an amazing 30-length victory in the Walden Stakes at Pimlico and the US now emphatically knew who their two-year-old champ was, his figure of 132 being the highest ever assigned to a two-year-old at the Experimental Free Handicap.

It being 1942, and the world still in the depths of war, he spent an atypical winter in Arkansas, before he returned for his Classic season. Still only weighing barely 1,000lb (454 kg), he kicked off with a facile allowance race over an extended mile in New York, before plundering the Wood Memorial by an easy three-and-a-half lengths. The Kentucky Derby – and history – beckoned.

Yet it might so easily not have been. Transport restrictions were in place and unnecessary travel much reduced; thus, out-of-state visitors were limited. Further, no one was permitted to arrive by car. The 1943 Run for the Roses was therefore dubbed the 'Streetcar Derby' but the 60,000-strong crowd still sent Count Fleet off as odds-on favourite. He didn't disappoint. Gradually pouring it on, Longden only gave him one little shake and he took off again, ambling home by three lengths. The Preakness a week later was even easier, with the Count cruising to an eight-length victory over just three opponents. Before the Belmont Stakes, his boundless energy was so high that Cameron ran him in the Withers Stakes over a muddy mile – a five-length victory in a quick time, despite again demonstrating his odd preference to round the turn incredibly wide.

So to the Belmont, where now only two rivals had the courage to oppose him. Laws forbad his starting price to get any lower than 20-1 on. He led throughout, and with Longden essentially motionless, he pulled further and further ahead, finishing 25 lengths clear of his nearest pursuer in a new stakes record. Indeed, everyone in the crowd agreed the judge's estimate had been conservative to the point of stinginess, and that the true figure was – like Secretariat three decades later – over 30 lengths. Exhibiting true wartime spirit, his silks were auctioned off in the unsaddling enclosure straight after, raising US$50,000 in war bonds. Was his the strongest-ever Triple Crown in terms of competition? Probably not but, notwithstanding Citation, Secretariat and others, it was undoubtedly the most ridiculously easy in terms of execution.

It also, sadly, marked his racing end. What the crowd hadn't realised was that this remarkable victory was in fact even more incredible than it first seemed. His eternal vitality had got the better of him and again he had injured his left fore ankle early on in running. In Longden's biography he states, 'He fractured a bone in his left front leg. I felt him bobble in the long stretch and knew he had hurt himself … I started to pull him up but he'd have none of it. He just grabbed the bit in that bull-headed way of his and took off again.' Months of treatment ensued but it just couldn't heal. Tragically, Hertz had to take the decision to retire his wonder colt at the height of his powers, with the Horse of the Year title already a shoe-in.

Count Fleet proved to be a successful stallion, twice topping the US rankings. His 1951 insurance policy, at $550,000 the heftiest for a stallion at the time, only reinforced the incredibly high regard in which he was still held. Even so, his effervescence slowly morphed into rambunctiousness, whilst bizarrely he also developed a fear of the dark, insisting on being taken to his barn before twilight, rain or shine. Fully 33 years, eight months and seven days after his foaling, the old Count's front legs gave up. He was already the longest-lived Kentucky Derby winner in history, but still valiantly spent two days trying to stand. It was not to be, and his patient and loving handlers sent the ebullient colt on his final journey.

FACTFILE

Description: Dark Bay/Brown Colt
Size: 16 hands
Dates: 1940–73
Racing seasons: 1942–43
Where were they trained?: USA
Trainer: Don Cameron
Owner: Fannie and John Hertz
Jockey: Johnny Longden

Sire: Reigh Count
Dam: Quickly
Damsire: Haste
Record: 21: 16-4-1
Most impressive victory: Belmont Stakes 1943
Nickname: The Count of Stoner Creek

TUDOR MINSTREL

Coming in after the 2,000 Guineas at Newmarket, May 1947, and Gordon Richards still can't quite believe his colt's performance.

Many horses – even the great ones – have their quirks, and some of them are explored in these pages. Tudor Minstrel's was an extreme version of one that is not as uncommon as you might think: he couldn't run left-handed. It's just as well, of course, that he wasn't trained in the US, as then he and his brilliance would have been as lost to history as a cough in a hurricane. Fortunately, he had enough straight and right-handed tracks in the UK to show the racing world that, on the right course at the right distance, there was essentially no beating him.

Tudor Minstrel's dam Sansonnet had been passed down into ownership to John Arthur Dewar, whose Uncle Thomas was a huge whisky magnate. Hence Dewar Jr ended up with the young colt, whom he sent into training with one of England's most successful trainers, Fred Darling. 'Successful', of course, doesn't mean 'nice'. As noted under Sun Chariot's entry, words used to describe this inter-war training colossus were notable in their polarity. 'Genius', 'greatest' and 'record-breaking' were all used and true, as were 'ruthless', 'friendless' and 'weird'. Utterly lacking in emotional intelligence he may have been, but Darling was also respected, and he saw that Tudor Minstrel was maturing early as a two-year-old, and plotted an ambitious path for him. Tudor Minstrel's sire was Owen Tudor, winner of the 1941 Epsom Derby, whilst his dam's sire Sansovino won the same race in 1924. To that end, all assumed that he would have been imbued with enough stamina to eventually do likewise. Hold that thought.

The brown colt's first two forays onto the course were in Bath and Salisbury where, ridden as he always would be by seemingly eternal champion UK jockey Gordon Richards, he trotted away from the opposition, showing that he had bags of potential. He was then, in June, thrown in at the deep end of Royal Ascot's Coventry Stakes where, unfazed, he again put four lengths between himself and the best of his peers. He confirmed this form the following month in the equally prestigious National Breeders' Produce Stakes at Sandown, winning by the same distance. Interestingly, despite having such an exciting colt and it only being July, Darling decided that that would be that for the season, which still had months to go. He would still easily top the end of season Free Handicap ratings.

At three, although powerful and muscular, Tudor Minstrel hadn't grown enormously in height, and he maintained the ever-so-slightly short-legged build reminiscent of his champion grandfather Hyperion. He negated this, however, with exceptional balance and bulging hindquarters. With the 2,000 Guineas at Newmarket as his first main target, he returned to Bath for his seven-furlong warm-up race, which he won with consummate ease, priming him perfectly for the first colt's Classic of the season.

And so the stage was set for what many commentators present – as well as many who weren't – swore to their dying day was the most dominant display in a European Classic race in the whole of the 20th century. Tudor Minstrel took off at the start, and piled it on, and on, and on over Newmarket's straight mile. It was by no means an inferior year of colts, yet the son of Owen Tudor, displaying astonishing speed, balance and energy, crushed his opponents physically by half way, and most likely mentally too by the end. Long before he reached the post, Richards had stopped pushing and was seen by all to be patting his colt and even playfully tweaking his ears – unheard of in most races, let alone a Classic. The official margin of victory was eight lengths, but photographic evidence shows it to be a bare minimum of 11 and likely more. Reliable eye-witness reports backed this up, all agreeing that if Richards had bothered to make any effort in the last two furlongs, the winning distance could easily have been 20 lengths.

And so the drooling reports and accounts started flooding in, starting with Richards: 'Tudor Minstrel galloped us all stone cold. I have had the easiest ride of my life.' 'We have all seen races which were a foregone conclusion some way from home,' wrote Quintin Gilbey later, 'but it was inconceivable that the Two Thousand Guineas should have been over and done with before the horses had travelled half a mile.' 'The most astonishing Classic victory I have ever seen,' scribbled *Daily Graphic* columnist Gimcrack straightforwardly for the following morning's edition.

Meanwhile, Phil Bull, who had recently founded horseracing data provider *Timeform* and whose mercurial write-ups were matched only by his stringent adherence to what the data was telling him, was equally unequivocal: 'So far as I know I have never yet described any horse as a world-beater, but, with this reservation about distance, I think I am prepared so to describe Tudor Minstrel … The memory of Tudor Minstrel's strolling home the length of a street in front of everything else will remain with me for the rest of my life.' There were elements of the day that were to be eerily emulated 64 years later by Frankel. Not only did the latter also put on an incredible 2,000 Guineas display, but it was set against the backdrop of a trainer enduring extreme ill health. Then it would be the great Henry Cecil; here it was Darling, who also had to miss some of his great horse's performances in person, and who would sell his stables at the end of the season as a consequence.

Even so, amongst this near-hagiographic response to what had been a mind-blowing display, the true clue was hidden in the canny Bull's write-up. He thought the colt was simply too fast to be as effective over the mile and a half of Epsom's Derby – indeed, he thought he might even be better suited to seven furlongs than a mile. Nevertheless, by early June the mesmerised public were having none of it, and backed him down to be the shortest-priced favourite for the Derby in 40 years, not least as his pedigree suggested stamina wouldn't be a problem. What the public didn't know was what had happened two weeks earlier.

Ever the perfectionist, Darling had built a left-handed track within his training grounds at Beckhampton, specifically for potential Derby horses to practise on. Although he had twice won at Bath, Tudor Minstrel now decided that he simply wasn't going to run left-handed, and kept forcing himself to go right. Richards jumped off in shock, telling Darling: 'This fellow's action is all *right*. He can't get onto the other leg. If he does, he's all at sea!' Thinking it might pass, they kept their revelations to themselves.

The miserable and cold day of the Epsom Derby itself (the first iteration of the old race ever held on a Saturday) was a fair reflection of Tudor Minstrel's – and Gordon Richards's – experience that day. The angry colt fought from the very start, mouth wide open, head almost at right-angles, and shooting off to the right whenever the master jockey let him try to settle. Seeing a nightmare unfold, he had no choice but to push him to the front and hope his stamina held out. It didn't, with the colt's energy having already been spent. Tasting defeat for the first time, he finished a forlorn fourth, the race being won emphatically by French outsider Pearl Diver.

PUNCH A HOLE IN THE WIND

The recriminations began almost immediately from the disbelieving public. Richards explained what he had been through, and stated clearly that 'my colt just could not stay'. But the newspapers the following day were still in a state of unforgiving shock. Consider this slice of hyperbole from the *News of the World*: 'At eight minutes past three yesterday afternoon a song died in the heart of Britain. On the muddied field of Epsom lay buried many million hopes – the hope that at long last our tarnished Turf prestige would shine again and that we should be back on the racing map.' Worthy of note in these melodramatic words were both the astonishing levels of expectation which that 2,000 Guineas victory had brought on, as well as the navel-gazing attitude of the British racing scene at the time, which had until recently considered itself all-dominant. Richards, meanwhile, started receiving letters, phone calls and more from angry, unforgiving punters looking for a scapegoat for this whole unfortunate debacle.

Darling wisely decided to revert Tudor Minstrel later in the month both to a mile and a right-handed course, namely Ascot for the Royal meeting's St James Palace Stakes. Unsurprisingly, the colt absolutely trotted up, showing that he was as good as there had ever been over the distance. But in the Eclipse Stakes over ten furlongs in July on a soft Sandown track, the stamina again gave way, and he was outstayed by Migoli, who would win the following year's Arc de Triomphe. The public was now finally understanding that the colt was just too fast for middle distances. He finished off his season, and his career, back at Ascot's mile in the Group 1 Knight's Royal Stakes – which would mutate later into the Queen Elizabeth II Stakes – and again won from Vagabond, some claiming it was a cosy victory, others that he was pushed at the end.

Regardless, as Tudor Minstrel was becoming more headstrong, it was decided to retire him to stud. He would achieve a rating over a mile that only the mighty Brigadier Gerard would match in the 20th century. And it came as a surprise to few that, although he sired a Kentucky Derby winner in Tomy Lee, almost all his other offspring were notable purely for one thing: speed.

FACTFILE

Description: **Brown Colt**
Size: **15.3 hands**
Dates: **1944-71**
Racing seasons: **1946-47**
Where were they trained?: **UK**
Trainer: **Fred Darling**
Owner: **John Arthur Dewar**

Jockey: **Gordon Richards**
Sire: **Owen Tudor**
Dam: **Sansonnet**
Damsire: **Sansovino**
Record: **10:8-1-0**
Most impressive victory: **2,000 Guineas 1947**

CITATION

The imperious Citation (Eddie Arcaro) poses after effortlessly completing the US Triple Crown, June 1948.

That Citation is not instinctively mentioned by every US racing fan in the same breath as Secretariat and Man O'War is simply wrong. And it is due to one thing only: greed. Citation was a spellbinding colt, but one who bucks a certain trend: whilst so many great horses discussed here seemed to get better at age four, Citation should have been retired at three. But brilliance has a price, and in Citation's case that price was exactly $1 million.

With Bull Lea as a sire and Hydroplane (a daughter of Hyperion) as a dam, Citation had the blue blood to match the blue grass of Kentucky, where he was foaled at the all-conquering Calumet Farm. He quickly matured at two, so trainer Ben Jones sent him out nine times in 1947, each time under Al Snider. He won eight, only once coming second to his stable companion, Bewitch, in the Washington Park Futurity. He was still named champion two-year-old.

It was in February 1948, however, that Jones finally appreciated that he had an absolute world-beater on his hands. Citation was about to embark on an unparalleled three-year-old season. He had grown a little over the winter to 16 hands, but was so well put together (despite a long, flat croup) that his athleticism came to the fore. Before even starting his prep races for the Triple Crown, Jones entered him in two all-age handicaps – highly unconventional so early in a three-year-old's season, when they are still growing. Citation easily beat top-rated older horse Armed and now people really took notice. The charismatic, posing colt quite liked the attention.

Next, though, there was tragedy. A few days after riding Citation to victory in the Flamingo Stakes, Snider took a short fishing trip off the Florida Keys with two friends. Out of nowhere, a nasty squall appeared. Eight days later their upside-down skiff was found, but of the three men nothing was ever seen again.

Distraught, Jones quickly secured the services of Eddie Arcaro, 'The Master', and the most naturally gifted and stylish jockey of his generation – albeit possessor of an equally world-class temper. The partnership started poorly, with Citation being defeated by unfancied Saggy over six furlongs at the now defunct Havre de Grace track in Maryland. Excuses abounded, and there was talk of it being as shocking as Man O'War/Upset 29 years earlier, but ultimately it was a blip, and a mere five days later the two horses met again with the placings comprehensively reversed.

Meanwhile, the Triple Crown itself beckoned next, and Citation took each leg more easily than the last. It wasn't set up to be a cakewalk, however. Up against him was a horse with – at the time – an equally lofty reputation. Stablemate Coaltown, also a son of Bull Lea, had hacked up in the Blue Grass Stakes, was unbeaten in five races, and was going to make a race of it. Despite the unpleasantly muddy ground, Coaltown bolted six lengths clear in the back stretch, but Arcaro bided his time, reeled him in and won going away by three-and-a-half lengths. It was the third of a record eight Kentucky Derbies that Calumet would take in their pomp. In a heart-warming gesture, Arcaro gave half his winning money to Al Snider's widow.

The Preakness he won by nearly twice as far. And before the Belmont Stakes, Jones squeezed the Jersey Derby in for good measure, Citation romping home by 11 lengths in a track record. The Belmont itself was a procession, Jones's amazing colt surging clear by eight lengths in the home stretch. However, it could so easily not have been. In the build-up, Arcaro confidently stated that, 'The only way I could lose this race is if I fall off the horse.' One can only imagine his heart pounding, therefore, as, leaving stall one, Citation stumbled, nearly heaving Arcaro out of the saddle right at the start. It was also the first Triple Crown race to be shown live on national TV, albeit in front of a limited

CITATION

TV audience. Overall, his Triple Crown was unquestionably every bit as easy and convincing as Secretariat's many years later.

In all, Citation ran no fewer than 20 times that year, losing only that early season race. This included a 15-race winning streak, against top company. Being voted US Horse of the Year was a given. He was utterly versatile in the truest sense: he could charge from behind, or he could lead from the off; he could act on dirt and on grass; he won over seven furlongs and two miles. But equally it speaks volumes to Citation's immense durability and resilience that he kept it up, his smooth, fluid stride and relentless will to win ensuring that he became the biggest sporting draw of the age, in person and in print. The handicapper rated him an unprecedented 15 pounds above his nearest peer. But then the greed took over.

Trying to get as much prize money out of Citation as possible, Jones was still running him in December, and although he won the Tanforan Handicap, he returned lame – not surprising, as the poorly laid track had barely any dirt covering the concrete beneath. A year of endless pounding on hard surfaces meant that Citation had developed an osselet – a stress-induced trauma causing arthritis in his front left fetlock joint. He was sent to recuperate and bar-fired.

The most graceful of retirements should then have ensued; this wonderful horse had nothing left to prove. Except Calumet Farm – spurred by Jones – were desperate for their champion horse to be the first to ever win $1 million. It was obsessional. Citation had to sit out the whole of the 1949 season, where ironically the emerging horse of the year would be none other than stablemate Coaltown, who won 12 of his 13 races and only made Citation's connections and fans think of what might have been.

After what felt like an age but was in fact 13 months later, as a five-year-old back in training, Citation was sent to race after race to try to get to that mythical mark. After winning a small race first time out, he was beaten, again and again, with the injury clearly having taken so much out of him. His nemesis was Noor, an ex-English turf colt brought over to the California dirt, and who thrived in the sun. Again, good as Noor was, there was an overall feeling that pre-injury Citation would have eaten him for breakfast. As 1950 drew to a close, and with Calumet's owner Warren Wright close to his deathbed, he made Jones promise that he would keep Citation in training for as long as it took him to pass that $1 million mark. With Citation clearly not happy, it seemed to some that the on-going infatuation was blinding connections to the central issue of horse welfare.

Finally, now as a six-year-old, and with Wright having passed away, Citation was sent to California, and strung together three victories, including the

Hollywood Gold Cup, ironically beating Bewitch. The mythical barrier was reached, although inflation would soon render the achievement moot. To all who had stood back in wonder at the great colt's early career, it felt like something of a pyrrhic victory. Only then was Citation – by now frankly falling apart – given his long overdue retirement. At stud, he started off well, siring a Preakness winner, from which it went steeply downhill.

His last hurrah came not in the breeding shed, though, but via the whirrings of an extremely primitive computer in 1968, programmed to set up a 'Race of the Century' involving all the big US champion thoroughbreds to that point. Citation found himself winning by a neck from Man O'War, with Native Dancer, Kelso, Count Fleet, Tom Fool and others behind. Make of that what you will. Certainly in ESPN's listing of their greatest 100 North American athletes of the 20th century, Citation was one of only three equines in there – Man O'War and Secretariat, predictably, being the other two.

Arcaro, whose rides over his long, hugely successful career read like a who's who of champions, was unequivocal that Citation was the best that he had ever ridden. But as with so many champions in this book, Citation's greatness should be measured on what he did at his best, and not on the dubious decisions of those who took care of him. And at his best, he really was something truly special.

FACTFILE

Description: **Bay Colt**
Size: **16 Hands**
Dates: **1945-70**
Racing seasons: **1947-51**
Where were they trained?: **USA**
Trainer: **Ben Jones**
Owner: **Calumet Farm**
Jockey: **Al Snider, Eddie Arcaro, Steve Brooks**

Sire: **Bull Lea**
Dam: **Hydroplane**
Damsire: **Hyperion**
Record: **45: 32-10-2**
Most impressive victory: **Belmont Stakes 1948**
Nickname: **The Big Cy**

TANTIEME

Proud owner Francois Dupre brings in his champion Tantieme, with the suprememly confident Jacques Doyasbere aboard, after his second Prix de L'Arc de Triomphe victory, October 1951.

Jockeys will always tell you how the indefinable quality that is known as confidence is so critical when giving their mount its best possible placing. The question is: just how confident do you want a jockey to be? Many jockeys have fallen foul of taking it too far – some subsequently owning up, others possessing more slopey shoulders. But consider the actions of top French rider Jacques Doyasbere in the run-up to Europe's premier race, the Prix de l'Arc de Triomphe, in 1951. Days before the race, he booked a table for 12 at Paris's top restaurant Maxim's *to celebrate his forthcoming victory*. As chutzpah goes, it takes some beating. Fortunately, he was one of the very best. More importantly, so was his mount, Tantieme.

Tantieme was by Deux Pour Cent out of the Indus mare Terka. Bred by hotelier and art collector Francois Dupre, he was trained by former cavalry officer Francois Mathet, a true gentleman – albeit an enigmatic one – at a time when not all in the business could be called one. His star colt was one of the very few European horses who proved to be a champion as a juvenile and then again for his two subsequent seasons. A star he may have been, but you'd be hard pressed to call Tantieme handsome. All the pictures and videos of him show a colt who, despite a decent girth, appears scrawny to the point of gaunt, with ribs poking out everywhere, and long legs. You could charitably muster that he had a pleasant head. Not that any of this slowed him down.

PUNCH A HOLE IN THE WIND

All the clues were there in his juvenile season. In early July he first took on the Prix des Villarmains at Saint-Cloud over a super-short and inadequate four-and-a-half furlongs. He still won comfortably. He next had his only defeat of the year, when he was pitched straight into the six-furlong Group 1 Prix Robert Papin at Maisons-Lafitte. His lacklustre sixth place was readily forgiven when he was found the next day to be lying and sweating in his barn – he'd clearly been ill and had indeed coughed on the day of the race. It was a stronger colt that returned in September to win the Prix de Villiers and then in October the Group 1 Grand Criterium, where he impressively made up a fistful of lengths in the Longchamp straight to take it near the line. As though keen to get ahead of himself, Mathet then tried him in one of the few races where juveniles are able to run against their elders, the Group 1 seven-furlong Prix de la Foret. It didn't make a difference to Tantieme and he won easily. Indeed he would always finish in the money from now on.

Ridden by Roger Poincelet, he started his three-year-old season in 1950 where he left off, showing 'lightning acceleration' in effortlessly taking the Poules d'Essai des Poulains (French 2,000 Guineas) – where he trounced Galcador, who would go on to win the Epsom Derby – before easily winning the top French Derby trial, the Prix Lupin.

It was then that controversy struck, in a finish that still causes arguments in French cafes to this day. Vying for favouritism in the Prix du Jockey Club (French Derby) with the Prix Greffulhe winner, Marcel Boussac's Scratch, the two colts went at it hammer and tongs in the final furlong, drawing well away from the others. As the post arrived, Tantieme appeared to have just got the better. The crowd certainly thought so, as did Poincelet. But Chantilly at the time was the only Parisian course with no photo-finish camera. A photo taken 50m *before* the finish line suggested that Tantieme would have won, but another one taken 50m *after* was not so clear-cut. The only opinion that mattered was that of the judge, Le Comte de Kergorlay. Almost always in such circumstances, it was his instinct to favour the horse further away in such tight finishes, and thus he awarded the race to Scratch.

Mayhem ensued, of course. Punters were livid, the normally unflappable Mathet quietly refused to accept the result to his dying day and swore revenge, whilst Poincelet let out his steam on Scratch's Aussie jockey Rae Johnstone, socking him a right hook on the weighing-out scales and earning himself a 25,000 franc fine for his troubles. Tantieme next travelled to England in July to contest the Queen Elizabeth Stakes – to mutate soon after into the

TANTIEME

Festival of Britain Stakes and then the King George and Queen Elizabeth Stakes – where he beat the previous year's Arc winner Coronation by a head.

After a summer break, the 1950 Arc was next. Tantieme – always a bit fractious – sweated so liberally on what was a sticky October day in Paris that spectators could see it dropping off him. However, now with Jacques Doyasbere on his back, he easily overcame both Scratch and Coronation. Tellingly, in a top all-age race, the first six places were all filled by the three-year-old generation, strongly suggesting that it was a vintage crop, with Tantieme at its head.

Staying on in training as a four-year-old, Tantieme followed the tried-and-tested route of the Prix Ganay at Longchamp followed by the Coronation Cup at Epsom. He won both, although was clearly below his best in the latter as he hated travelling and never displayed his best form abroad, despite usually winning. Indeed, he increasingly hated being anywhere except his own stable. Therefore, when he went over to run in the Festival of Britain Stakes, Mathet planned for him to fly in that morning. It went disastrously. He had to get up so early that he hadn't slept. Once on the plane, a storm blew all morning, the turbulence giving poor Tantieme air sickness, and meaning that he only arrived at Ascot with minutes to spare. He then had a bad passage during the race. That he still finished third was testament to his undoubted class.

It is worth pointing out here that not every horse who travelled from France to England at the time had the best of reputations. With French horses, spearheaded by Marcel Boussac's formidable team, annexing so many top English races, there were strong counter rumours among the notoriously exceptionalist British racing scene that the French thoroughbreds must have been pumped full of performance-enhancing drugs. It was an accusation not entirely without substance. In that very year's St Leger, the French colt Talma sweated like a marathon runner in the pre-parade ring, got bizarrely sexually excited, and then won the race by officially ten lengths – and unofficially 20 lengths – running like a bat out of hell. He was then scooted straight back to the airport with his eyes almost popping out of his head. It looked more than a little strange. Rightly, no one ever suggested this regarding runners from the incorruptible Mathet's stable.

Back in France, the aim was for a second Arc, a feat only achieved three times previously, and now with a huge sum going to the winner. The sense of expectation was palpable: unofficial attendance figures were put above 100,000 and the not-inconsiderable sum of 400 million francs was laid at the Pari-Mutuel, a record at the time. The champion duly delivered under a supremely confident Doyasbere ride, his victory even easier than the year before, and by beating Nuccio by two lengths – a horse who would win the following year's edition – Tantieme became the last French-bred horse to achieve the feat of winning two Arcs in the 20th century, showing once more that he was a horse for the ages. Owner Dupre was jubilant: 'I never had any doubt. I knew what Tantieme could do.' He also had, in Mathet, a master conditioner who had kept this fractious colt at his peak throughout a long season. He retired straight after to Haras d'Ouilly, the Normandy stud where he had been born, becoming French champion sire twice, with his sons Reliance, Tanerko and Match all being top horses in their own right.

The 1950s was a seminal decade for the Arc. With Longchamp teaming up with the Loterie National in 1949, a highly regarded middle-distance race was suddenly transformed, with an injection of 25 million francs, into the richest middle-distance, weight-for-age race in Europe, and very possibly the world. From that stage onwards, it went from strength to strength to cement its position as the most prestigious too. What it needed in those days was for a true champion to act as its flag bearer, and Tantieme rose magnificently to the occasion, with another dual winner to follow soon after, as we shall find out. With his only three defeats coming because of illness, a judge's poor eye-sight and a terrible journey, Tantieme could just as easily have retired unbeaten.

And we have to assume that Jacko Doyasbere made the most of his dinner at Maxim's. Perhaps he had pre-ordered the champagne too.

FACTFILE

Description: Bay Colt
Size: 16.1 Hands
Dates: 1947-66
Racing seasons: 1949-51
Where were they trained?: France
Trainer: Francois Mathet
Owner: Francois Dupre

Jockey: Roger Poincelet, Jacques Doyasbere
Sire: Deux Pour Cent
Dam: Terka
Damsire: Indus
Record: 15: 12-1-1
Most impressive victory: Prix de l'Arc de Triomphe 1951

TOM FOOL

Even at stud, Tom Fool never lost his muscular frame.

Tom Fool. Such a frivolous name. It inspires images of unreliable timewasters and cheeky ragamuffins. To that end, Tom Fool was as poorly named a colt as one could contemplate. For he was the purest of professionals on the track, oozing ability from every one of his bulging muscles, and putting in a season that still acts as the older horse benchmark in the US. He was also synonymous with the 1950s racing scene in New York – both the city and the state. Only two of his 30 races were beyond its borders, but by the end it was for the simple reason that almost no other horse in the country would dare take him on.

Bred at Manchester Farm, Kentucky, by Duval Headley, The son of Menow was picked up as a yearling by siblings John Whitney and Joan Payson (one of the founders of the New York Mets baseball team) for their Greentree Stables. Although some raised eyebrows at the seemingly hefty $20,000 paid for him, that sum seemed like the bargain of the decade by the end of the colt's career. As his trainer John M. Gaver brought him along, he increasingly liked what he saw. The willing colt developed a unique and highly effective running style that the 1954 *American Racing Manual* saw fit to describe: 'When he is in action, he thrusts both forelegs forward and both hind legs behind him, for all the world like a horse clearing a hedge.' As was so often the way with leaky stable staff, word got out that there was a good 'un around, so that when he overcame a case of cracked heels and took in his first juvenile race, a five-and-a-half furlong maiden at Saratoga in

August 1951, he was quickly bet down to 2-1 favourite. He duly obliged, pulling four effortless lengths clear of his rivals.

He was ridden that day, and in every single other race of his career, by Ted Atkinson. Atkinson was a Canadian-born jockey who adored his horses. He had three nicknames: in the weighing room he was 'The Professor', being the only one of his colleagues who enjoyed reading classical literature; to the trainers he was 'The Gentleman' because of his courteous and honest demeanour; and to the less discerning members of the public, he was 'The Slasher' because of his unorthodox technique of using the whip on a horse's rump rather than its flanks. In fact, he used this method as it was both more humane and didn't risk a horse running off a straight line. No guesses which of the three names he didn't appreciate. Tom Fool would remain the apple of Atkinson's eye throughout his career and beyond: 'None of the others I ever rode, on their best days, could measure up with him.'

Two more quick victories ensued at the Sanford Stakes and the Grand Union Hotel Stakes, the latter seeing him easily despatch Cousin, hitherto the season's leading two-year-old. Cousin got his revenge in the Hopeful Stakes, but it was very likely that Tom Fool was suffering from an adverse reaction to a recent tetanus shot, making it all the more remarkable that he still came second. Soon recovered, he polished off both the Futurity and then the East View Stakes at Jamaica Park, the latter on a sloppy track that he clearly resented, easily securing the title of champion two-year-old. Connections spent the winter dreaming of Triple Crown glory, in turn watching their star colt grow to over 16.1 hands.

Yet it was not to be. Indeed, Tom Fool not only didn't win the Triple Crown, he never even made it to the starting gate in any of the three races. It was one of the great 'What ifs?' of US racing. The season had started promisingly. Victory at an allowance race at Jamaica Park boded well, but then in the Wood Memorial he was overtaken late to lose by a neck to Master Fiddle, a colt he would normally defeat with ease. The reason became clear the next day. Tom Fool was feverish and listless in his stable, and coughing violently. Again, it made his performance all the more stunning. But it could not have been more ill-timed, and his ten-week recovery back to something resembling fitness heartbreakingly ruled out the Classics.

The rest of Tom Fool's three-year-old season was a mixed bag by his very high standards. A second and fourth place on his two return racetrack visits strongly suggested that he wasn't yet fully over his debilitating sickness, and connections wondered just how much it had taken out of him. But after a third place in the Midsummer Derby at Saratoga, he signalled that he was in better shape, and barely looked back. He won three and came second in the other two of his five

TOM FOOL

remaining starts, and was now beating the older horses regularly, including a seven-length romp in the Jerome Handicap at Belmont. Tom Fool was still not to be messed with, but he had yet to show his ultimate abilities.

Wintering in Aitken, South Carolina, Tom Fool developed yet further. Always a strong colt, he was now absolutely bulging with muscle ('He even had muscles in his eyebrows,' Atkinson remarked). Further, his mental fortitude, already shown off in many of his races, had also morphed into something altogether more merciless. Perhaps there was something in South Carolina waters. Equine artist Richard Stone Reeves admired him as, '... an archetype of the American handicap horse: docile, a finely chiselled head, broad chest and long straight legs.'

A season of the top handicaps beckoned, but rather than shirk potentially huge weight burdens, many owners saw it as a badge of honour for their horse to be so highly regarded, and the Whitneys were no different. Tom Fool took no prisoners in his four-year-old season, and no amount of crippling weight on his back, or variation in distance, was going to stop him. It started with a five-and-a-half-furlong warm-up victory before he went to Belmont for the Joe H. Palmer Handicap. Even the journalists who had been covering his career for the previous two seasons were overwhelmed by what they saw that day. George F. T. Ryall writing for *The BloodHorse*, wrote: 'I can't remember when I've seen a horse so well turned out as the Greentree Stable's Tom Fool was for the Joe H. Palmer Handicap at Belmont Park. Also, I've seen few smarter performances this season, for although he carried 130 pounds and gave big weight to everything, he simply toyed with what might loosely be called his opposition.'

Connections then aimed him for New York's holy trinity of Handicaps – the Metropolitan, Suburban and Brooklyn. Only won once before by Whisk Broom in 1913, it was a huge ask. Just four days after the Joe H. Palmer, and with the muddy track conditions that he loathed, came the Metropolitan. Tom Fool, with almost pathological determination, still found a way to win by half a length in a rapid time, from Royal Vale. Gerald Strine of the *Washington Post* would later recall, 'Not all male runners look the part of champions, you know. Some are almost effeminate. Others are plain. Tom Fool had the look of a killer. Anybody who would have bet against that look simply didn't like money.'

The two rivals met just a week later at the Suburban at the same track, with Tom Fool again top-weighted at 128lb. He made up three lengths on Royal Vale in the stretch to win by a nose in the second-fastest time ever for the race. Atkinson, ever full of praise, said, 'Not that he's ever run a bad race, but today's was his best.' He was now so strong that before the Brooklyn, Gaver gave him an extra outing in the seven-furlong Carter Handicap, where he carried an immense

135lb to a facile two-length victory. Incredibly, he was asked to carry 136lb–26lb more than the next horse – in the Brooklyn over ten furlongs at Aqueduct, yet poured on in the home stretch, with Atkinson slowing him down well before the line. He had achieved the seemingly impossible.

With a reputation that now dwarfed that of any other rival, it wasn't just other trainers who were running scared, but the bookmakers too. For his final four runs of the season, therefore, no betting was allowed. Whilst this was distressing for many racegoers – after all, as the greats sports writer Hugh McIlvanney once opined, 'Horseracing without betting is like jazz without sex' – it was also an opportunity to focus on a new legend in his pomp. One person, however, didn't watch him – at least not in person. Breeder Duval Headley followed the colt's rise to superstardom with interest, but noted that the only two times that he had seen him run in the flesh, he had finished second. He therefore took this as an omen, and would only ever watch him on television.

Tom Fool predictably destroyed anyone who dared challenge him in those races. He won the Wilson Stakes by eight lengths, the Whitney Handicap by three-and-a-half lengths. Efforts were made to pitch him against that year's star three-year-old, Native Dancer, in the Sysonby Mile, but the latter got injured and it never materialised. 'A smart move on the "Gray Ghost's" part,' asserted Strine, 'because he would have been defeated. No animal on four legs was going to beat Tom Fool that day, not even a cheetah.' He finished with an eight-length crushing in the Pimlico Special in a track record. Ten runs, ten breath-taking victories. The Horse of the Year title was his and, in due course, so was the National Turf Writers Association's title of 'US Horse of the Decade'.

Tom Fool became an important sire, his progeny including 1960s star Buckpasser and Kentucky Derby winner Tim Tam. But even at stud, Atkinson never forgot his old friend, and vice versa. Even many years after his glories on the track, the stallion would recognise Atkinson's call and rush over to see him. Tom Fool was still smart. Somehow, the great ones almost always are.

FACTFILE

Description: Bay Colt
Size: 16.15 Hands
Dates: 1949-76
Racing seasons: 1951-53
Where were they trained?: USA
Trainer: John M. Gaver Sr
Owner: Greentree Stables

Jockey: Ted Atkinson
Sire: Menow
Dam: Gaga
Damsire: Bull Dog
Record: 30: 21-7-1
Most impressive victory: Pimlico Special 1953
Nickname: Tom

NATIVE DANCER

The charmless but brilliant Native Dancer (Eric Guerin up) out for a training gallop at Santa Anita, January 1953.

Native Dancer was utterly odious. He was on record as lifting sleeping grooms by his teeth until they screamed, pulling riders off other horses during exercise by tugging hard at their legs, roaring in anger if anyone entered his field, and launching a collie dog over a 6ft fence because he didn't like the look of it. His apologists called him 'playful'. But you don't have to be nice to be great – and Native Dancer was certainly great, with a far wider impact on racing than his 22 starts alone would suggest.

Owned and bred by Alfred Vanderbilt Jr and trained by Bill Winfrey, his unrepentant schadenfreude was first taken out on his mother, Geisha. Standard horse gestation is 11 months, but Native Dancer refused to budge for an extra month, coming out predictably huge and causing understandable pain to his poor dam. Native Dancer would ultimately be built like an absolute tank: 16.3 hands of rippling, stocky muscle, completed by a striking, dappled grey coat.

PUNCH A HOLE IN THE WIND

Mature early on at two, he raced nine times that season, and was unbeaten throughout. Ranging between five and eight-and-a-half furlongs, he mixed the styles up, sometimes pushing on early from the front, sometimes coming with a blitz from behind. After his first easy victory, he would start odds-on in every race thereafter, mainly that year in Saratoga and Belmont. Winning margins weren't usually spectacular, but there was an air of inevitability about each one, and in the Belmont Futurity over six-and-a-half furlongs he stamped that authority by tying the world record for that distance at 1min 14.4secs – despite still being a juvenile. In the parade ring beforehand, Winfrey had offered regular jockey Guerin his regular advice: 'Just ride him with confidence' – as if Guerin had any other option when riding this surly grey missile. But such were his performances that he was made horse of the year for 1952 – an honour never hitherto achieved by a juvenile.

Expectations were therefore huge for his three-year-old season. But, crucially, so were TV audiences. The advent of TVs in most homes across America and Europe meant more races could be watched live, and the sport built up its sizeable fan base yet further. In the US, Native Dancer was almost solely responsible for that, becoming a cult favourite from early on, partly due to his immense ability and partly because of his striking colouring, which still stood out on black-and-white TV sets.

It is worth stressing just how much so many owners, trainers and punters still had issues with grey horses, even in the 1950s. Racing author Joe Hirsch reflected, 'Greys just were different. It was a sense of racism, I suppose.' And indeed, 70 years before, they very nearly died out of the thoroughbred lines altogether, rescued by French stallion Le Sancy, who is present in the pedigree of every single grey runner you see today. But unequivocally Native Dancer was the Grey – or Gray – that finally dispelled the anti-grey prejudice in the US once and for all.

The Gray Ghost – as he was now lovingly referred to – carried on where he left off, with facile victories in the Gotham Stakes and Wood Memorial. But then the bubble burst in The Big One. Considered a shoe-in for the Kentucky Derby, Native Dancer suffered his one and only defeat. No one, however, blamed the horse. Jockey Eric Guerin did not have his finest hour, dropping Native Dancer too far back off a slow pace, getting badly bumped wide out on the back stretch, and then almost stopping at the top of the home stretch behind a wall of horses on the rail. As one journalist so memorably put it, 'he took the colt just about every place on the track except the ladies' room.' A typical storming run in the last furlong came too late, with Dark Star, under a much cannier ride, prevailing by a rapidly diminishing neck.

NATIVE DANCER

His huge following were crestfallen, but swift consolation followed in the Withers Stakes, before he took the other two legs of the Triple Crown in workmanlike fashion. By now, the uppity Native Dancer was running only as it pleased him, and it was clear to spectators that he *knew* he could win but only he would choose *how*. Later he decided to up his game and in the summer ran at his peak, knocking off the Dwyer Stakes at Aqueduct before coming back to a mile for the Arlington Classic where, clearly in the mood, he gave each of his rivals six pounds in weight and trounced them by nine lengths.

There was then drama in the American Derby at Washington Park. With Guerin suspended, Eddie Arcaro took the ride and, arriving at post, thought the Gray Ghost might be lame and considered withdrawing. Deciding to proceed, he settled his mount near the back and when he got no immediate response at the home turn, Arcaro gave him a crack of the whip. Native Dancer took off even more aggressively than usual and won, going away by two lengths. Some thought it courage, but more likely it was fear: much later in his life at stud, stories continued of how, when riders went to see him carrying a whip prominently, Native Dancer would just about behave; when there was no visible whip, he would unhesitatingly try to harm them.

Arcaro's instinct may have been right. He was next prepared for a whole new challenge: a face-to-face in the Sysonby Stakes with the magnificent Tom Fool. But his lameness kept returning and it was decided to put him away for the rest of the season to aid his recovery. Tom Fool found it rather easy to take that race – and indeed all his others that year – to earn the Horse of the Year award for 1953. It had been something of a toss up either way, with most racegoers just happy to have two such greats on their courses at the same time.

With top four-year-olds in the US at the time only facing the prospect of hideous weights in the big handicaps, there were international ambitions for him to go to either the King George VI and Queen Elizabeth Stakes at Ascot or the Prix de l'Arc de Triomphe at Longchamp. Meanwhile, his loyal fans adored him even more, and he made the cover of *Time* magazine on 31 May that year.

First, however, he settled back in with a conditions race before a dramatic win in the Metropolitan Handicap. Giving up to 24 pounds to his eight rivals, and still seven lengths adrift with two furlongs to go, he decided to start trying, unleashed his monumental stride and charged to the lead with a neck to spare. But after another nine-length handicap win in Saratoga, he again displayed lameness in training, and connections realised that the international dream had to be shelved and he was gracefully retired after a truly outstanding racing career. That he was made horse of the year for 1954, despite having run only three races – a record low – felt more like a reflection of his overall career than that year alone.

But his legacy went much deeper. First, as US TV's first racing superstar, he galvanised an interest in watching live racing that continues fervently to this day. We can only assume that the new fans watching on TV were oblivious to the fact that, in the flesh, their hero displayed all the charm of an ingrowing toenail. And second, his success at stud was so profound as to be all-conquering. There are now very few US horses who don't in some way trace their lineage back to him, usually via his grandsons Northern Dancer and Mr Prospector; in the 2018 Kentucky Derby and 2015 Belmont Stakes, for example, every single runner was his descendant.

Native Dancer, by now a huge pure white bull of a stallion, fell ill on 14 November 1967 and during necessary surgery that evening a tumour and 10ft (3m) of intestine were removed to ease his discomfort, but The Gray gave up the ghost 36 hours later.

Not many of Native Dancer's offspring share his grey coat, but it seems that many have inherited traits of his grumpy character. Very few, however, are quite as brilliant as he was.

FACTFILE

Description: Grey Colt
Size: 16.3 Hands
Dates: 1950-67
Racing seasons: 1952-54
Where were they trained?: USA
Trainer: Bill Winfrey
Owner: Alfred G. Vanderbilt
Jockey: Eric Geurin, Eddie Arcaro
Sire: Polynesian
Dam: Geisha
Damsire: Discovery
Record: 22:21-1-0
Most impressive victory: Arlington Classic 1953
Nickname: The Gray Ghost

RIBOT

Enrico Camici puts the imperious Ribot through his paces in a training gallop, 1956.

Within most horseracing nations, there are never-ending debates about who was the best horse to have been trained and run within that country. In Italy, they have no such conundrum.

It was a sad irony that the greatest horse bred by that glorious owner-breeder Federico Tesio – the mastermind behind Nearco – would only start running just a month after the 85-year-old Tesio's death. Ribot was foaled at the UK's National Stud – then in West Sussex. His sire Tenerani had been a post-war champion in Italy and England, winning both the Goodwood Cup and Queen Elizabeth Stakes, so stamina was unlikely to ever be an issue. Sent into training with Ugo Penco, and always ridden by top veteran Enrico Camici, he was named after slightly obscure 19th-century French realist painter Theodule Ribot.

Yet it all started unassumingly, with Ribot being a tiny yearling, nicknamed 'Il Piccolo' (Little One), meaning that it was not considered worthwhile entering him in the Italian Classics. Nevertheless, he steadily grew over the years into a highly muscular and powerful individual, 16 hands of deep girth, huge lung capacity, impressive eyes and good feet, and improving each year like a fine wine.

At two, running mainly in Milan, he started over five furlongs, winning the Premio Tramuschio by a length, before a two-length victory in the Criterium

Nazionale, finishing with a narrower victory in the Gran Criterium. He looked very useful.

Aged three, ambitions grew further, and he really began blitzing his opposition, first by six lengths in the Premio Pisa, and then officially by ten lengths back in Milan in the Premio Emanuele Filiberto, although the photos prove this to be an almost laughable underestimate. His summer campaign was rounded out over the 12 furlong Premio Besana, where he destroyed Derain by ten lengths – form which was franked a fortnight later when the latter won the Italian St Leger.

Ribot wasn't averse to demonstrating coltish behaviour – some of his entourage went so far as to call it rebellious. But as with so many other capricious geniuses, it took some observation and imagination to temper it. In Ribot's case, it was his groom who noticed how Ribot's difficult behaviour would suddenly change whenever he was in the proximity of his stablemate Magistris. The latter, an infinitely more chilled animal, had a wonderfully calming influence on Ribot, and so it was decided that they should hang out together wherever possible, including always being trained as a pair. It was an equine friendship that would last throughout the rest of his career. Indeed, whenever Ribot travelled to run abroad, Magistris would go with him, even though he wasn't running himself. It worked a treat.

Now proven over a mile and a half, connections then chose to test Ribot against Europe's best in the Prix de l'Arc de Triomphe. Starting at lengthy 9-1 odds, he duly beat the international field easily by three lengths under a hand-and-heels ride. Europe was impressed, and even more so when he returned to Milan for the 'Italian Arc', the Gran Premio Del Jockey Club, and ploughed through the mud to crush Norman, the winner of the previous two iterations, by 15 lengths. Ribot was already a great. And he would get better.

At four, and now a *bona fide* star in his homeland, Ribot again started his campaign in Group 1 company in Milan, winning three races of between ten and 12 furlongs by a combined distance of 24 lengths. Bookmakers had virtually stopped taking bets on his races. He was then tested over a longer 15 furlongs in Italy's premier weight-for-age race at the time, the Gran Premio Di Milano. It made no difference, with Ribot displaying his incredible versatility by trotting up by an official eight lengths, although witnesses swore that it was considerably further.

Ribot now travelled again, taking in England's top middle-distance weight-for-age race, the King George and Queen Elizabeth Stakes at Ascot. The ground was once again very deep and slow, and Ribot started at 5-2 on. Although shoved along by Camici from quite early on to get him going in the

RIBOT

unsuitable conditions, Ribot drew away from the Queen's horse High Veldt to win impressively by five lengths, his 14th straight victory.

He was already a champion, but after an easy nine-furlong victory back in Milan, connections were keen to seal his immortality with a rare second victory in the Arc. The 1956 running was of an even higher calibre than the previous year, with Irish Derby winner Talgo leading French three-year-old Tanerko, and the two top US middle horses, US Champion middle distance turf horse Career Boy and future Washington DC International winner Mister Boing all lining up to take their chances. And that was the order in which Ribot beat them, pouring it on in the muddy Longchamp straight to win by an official six lengths that photos and video evidence confirmed to be half as far again. It was both his final and his crowning glory, a performance to rank with any in the history of this prestigious race, and earning in the process one of the highest ratings in history.

To give some further context both to his reputation and his performance, not only did Ribot start odds-on, but Talgo – a *Classic winner* – was available at 100-1. Meanwhile, legendary US jockey Eddie Arcaro, confidently partnering Career Boy, was overwhelmed: 'I was going along there pretty good, fast enough to win it, I thought, when all of a sudden – whoosh! A horse took off from me so fast I couldn't recognise him.' It had eerie echoes of Charles Bouillon's experience during Pharis's Grand Prix de Paris at the same track 17 years earlier. Half the horses that Ribot trounced that day would go on to Group 1 glory in the next 18 months.

And thus this legend of European racing retired after 16 races in which, not only was he unbeaten, but he was never properly extended. That said, there was a final flourish. With his Italian public desperate to see him once more, two exhibition gallops were put on in Rome, allowing Ribot to sprint clear of – who else? – Magistris in glorious isolation. As the crowd roared their approval, Ribot came to a halt, paused, and then threw Camici off his back. Almost everyone saw the funny side.

His versatility was immense: whether over five furlongs or 15, whether on dry ground or in desperately sticky turf, he despatched his rivals effortlessly. Put together, his official total winning distance over those 16 races was 105 lengths – averaging out at six-and-a half lengths per race. Unofficially, of course, it was many more. Retiring to stud first in Newmarket and then Italy, it didn't take long for him to make his mark. Two offspring followed in their father's footsteps and won the Arc, Molvedo in 1961 and Prince Royal in 1964.

He was subsequently leased out for five years at the considerable sum of US$1.35 million to John Galbraith's Darby Dan Stud in Kentucky, becoming champion British and Irish sire three times in the 1960s. But he also became utterly cantankerous, with only one very tough stable lad able to get anywhere near him; he simply couldn't abide being near any other stallion. It was clear too that he loathed being confined to his stall, and would regularly jump up to place his front hooves on top of the wooden panel at the front of his barn, allowing him to gnaw at his favourite wooden beam. Although unproven, it might have been an undiagnosed brain tumour eating away at him. Or perhaps he just missed Magistris. With no insurance company wanting to cover his transport back to Europe, he remained in the States until his death at 20. A slightly ignominious end, perhaps, but ultimately insignificant compared to his untouchability on the track.

To say that he made Italy proud is to undercook his impact. The country daily sports bible, *La Gazzetta dello Sport*, held a poll at the end of the 20th century, and Ribot was named fourth greatest Italian athlete – not horse, note, but *athlete* – in the 20th century. It would be hard to find any other sports-mad nation ranking their favourite equine so highly alongside their human heroes. But that was the effect that Ribot still had, decades after his superlative performances.

It had always been the stated goal of Tesio – 'The Wizard of Dormello' – to boil down his ambition into one simple but highly challenging outcome: 'to breed and raise a racehorse which over any distance could carry the heaviest weight in the shortest time.' To that end, legacies don't come much better.

FACTFILE

Description: **Bay Colt**
Size: **16 hands**
Dates: **1952-72**
Racing seasons: **1954-56**
Where were they trained?: **Italy**
Trainer: **Ugo Penco**
Owner: **Lydia Tesio**
Jockey: **Enrico Camici**
Sire: **Tenerani**
Dam: **Romanella**

Damsire: **El Greco**
Record: **16: 16-0-0**
Most impressive victory: **Prix de l'Arc de Triomphe 1956**
Nickname: **Il Piccolo**

SWAPS

A young Willie Shoemaker aboard the mighty Swaps, The California Comet, 1956.

Much is often made of rivalries between horses from different nations during the big international races that attract a cosmopolitan field. It's mostly hot air, of course, but adds to the occasion. It is worth noting, however, that often there is an informal tension – artificial or otherwise – within a horseracing nation itself. In England, there is something of a north-south divide; in France, where things feel more centralised, you tend to be either 'Paris' or 'everywhere else'. In the US – perhaps more so in the past than now – it was all about East vs. West. Swaps happened to be West. But by the time he finished, the details of his origins had long been drowned out by the facts describing his relentlessly fabulous career.

Swaps was always likely to be slightly looked down upon by the East Coasters, as his breeder and owner Rex Ellsworth was a former cowhand, and trainer Mesh Tenney conditioned his horses differently to the norm – he was unapologetically a cowboy first and a trainer second. Both Mormons, they had been friends since third grade in Arizona. To East Coast traditionalists, this was material ripe for a good, sly tease. They would ultimately regret this.

Swaps' sire, Khaled, was another successful, inter-war Aga Khan-owned and British-trained horse sold to the US despite promises to the contrary. A striking chestnut, Swaps would memorably be described as '... a big gorgeous bronze statue of a horse', with a noticeably long back and an irresistibly light action that made him appear to float as others floundered. His very start, however, was possibly far less auspicious, as legend has it that he was foaled out of his dam, Iron Reward, with no assistance and in a rain puddle – a story that Ellsworth did nothing to deny. And his two-year-old career was frankly unspectacular. But the step change he would demonstrate over each of the next two years was extraordinary.

He started his three-year-old season by ripping up the San Vicente Stakes and the Santa Anita Derby, interspersed with some outrageously fast time trials. In the former race, however, he infected his right front hoof in the dirty mud, a situation that would quietly plague him for the rest of his career. Tenney, ever the resourceful cowboy, took to putting a leather cloth between hoof and shoe to alleviate the pain. But even so, the Californians decided to send their big hope to the Kentucky Derby, with Tenney not taking any chances and allegedly sleeping in Swaps's barn for a full two weeks before the big race.

The Derby at Churchill Downs would mark the start of one of the most famous rivalries in US racing, although one has to remind oneself that it consisted of no more or less than two races. With regular rider Bill Shoemaker on board, Swaps was to take on – amongst others – the big Eastern hope Nashua, trained by the affable veteran 'Sunny Jim' Fitzsimmons, and ridden by the omnipresent Eddie Arcaro. The Eastern press bigged up the differing origins of the horses, some straying into patronising the cowboys again. In the race itself Shoemaker, then still a 24-year-old youngster, found Swaps very keen and decided to dictate calmly from the front, against the trainer's instructions. As they rounded the home turn, Nashua made his challenge and the two drew clear, but Swaps was not for the taking, and determinedly beat his rival fair and square. Arcaro admitted later that he had underestimated his rival. The west coast press gloated, one writing the rapper-friendly header 'East meets West and Swaps is Best'. Swaps became the first horse who was both Californian-bred and trained to win the Run for the Roses.

In a normal year, two things would have naturally ensued: Nashua and Swaps would meet again in each of the remaining two legs of the Triple Crown, and Swaps would, by the law of averages, master his rival again. But there wasn't much normal going on that year. In a break with tradition, Ellsworth and Tenney decided to return their colt to California and take in the sun, the less pressured life and the impressive purses of the Californian races. For the newspapers, this was predictably a red rag to the bull, further exacerbated when Nashua, a fantastic horse by any standards, helped himself to both the Preakness Stakes and – in a nine-length drubbing of his rivals – the Belmont Stakes.

SWAPS

Swaps was doing his own thing, and doing it equally impressively. The Will Rogers Stakes he took by a huge 12 lengths, after which he won the Californian Stakes at Hollywood Park over eight and a half furlongs, breaking the world record for the distance. Incredibly, the official racecard comments, describing him as taking his victory 'almost casually', were not inaccurate. He was that good. He then polished off the Westerner Stakes and the American Derby, earning himself the nickname 'The California Comet' in the process.

But in the background, all the parties of these two top colts were keen for a rematch, yet couldn't find the right time or place to make it happen. The hubbub had turned into chatter, which itself turned into a raucous press-driven necessity. The whole situation stank of 'match race', and so it was – one of the most famous in US history. Bizarrely, the man who made it happen was Hollywood actor Don Ameche who, when he wasn't anachronistically inventing the telephone, was a keen race goer and knew the connections involved. A phone call here, a favour called in there, and the plan was all in place: Washington Park, Chicago – not East, not West, but somewhere in between. Ten furlongs, $100,000 winner-takes-all. Game on.

Every US race fan knows what happened next. Nashua won. Or perhaps, more accurately, Eddie Arcaro did. 'Old Banana Nose' was still the master, and young Shoemaker, who was himself to become a legend, was caught out from the start. As the flag went up, the crowd heard Arcaro roar, and start furiously whipping Nashua into the lead. He held the inner, better ground, having had the advantage of the better draw in the first place, and Swaps was clearly suffering from his infected hoof – Shoemaker hadn't wanted him to run but there was too much public investment to pull him out.

Nashua pulled away from Swaps – who couldn't even run straight in the home stretch, such was his pain – to win. It was that race that ended up deciding who would win Horse of the Year, with Nashua taking the honours even though, when the stakes had been fair and even at Churchill Downs, it was Swaps who proved himself superior. As Swaps's injury meant he couldn't run again that year, Ellsworth and Tenney believed that the lack of award for their colt was a travesty and knew what they had to do: keep him in training as a four-year-old and reveal the truth.

Swaps rose to the challenge with incredible ability. His four-year-old career was one for the history books. Sticking mainly to his beloved home track of Hollywood Park, taking many of the valuable handicaps head-on, and despite being burdened with colossal weight, he found a way to win almost every time, sometimes displaying impossible-to-believe splits. To mention but a few: in the Broward Handicap, heaving around lumps more weight than his competitors, he broke the world record for a mile and 70yds; in the Argonaut Handicap he broke Citation's mile world record; in the Inglewood Handicap, he broke the eight-and-a-half furlong word record, breaking his own new mile record along the way. In winning the Washington Handicap over a mile, he covered the first six furlongs in under 1min 8secs – which would have smashed the standing track record for that distance. Each time he was carrying at least 130lb – a weight that Nashua could never carry to victory once.

Further, Shoemaker wasn't pushing in any of them – on the contrary, he was holding his superstar colt so tight on some occasions that he claimed his arms were aching afterwards. And it was for a very good reason: only Ellsworth, Tenney and the jockey himself were aware that, thanks to that nasty on-going hoof infection, only three of Swaps's legs ever worked properly. Despite this, it was one of the most astonishing seasons of any horse anywhere, all assisted by that incredible pure action of his that seemed to carry the heavy loads on his back so much more effectively than others. This time there was to be no mistake as to who the Horse of the Year was in the US.

Swaps would retire holding more speed world records – five in all, from distances between eight and 13 furlongs – than any horse in history. His retirement came about in circumstances both sad and inspirationally poignant. On a training gallop in preparation for the Washington DC International, Swaps shattered his left hind leg, often fatal for racehorses. It needed a special sling in order for it to heal properly and there weren't many around. But one particular man had a spare one, and sent it quickly to Tenney: 'Sunny Jim' Fitzsimmons, trainer of Nashua, a fan of the mighty Swaps and a gentleman to the last. Despite losing 300lb as he fought for his life, the brilliant, courageous Swaps survived.

Hollywood Park wasted no time in commissioning and erecting a statue of Swaps and Shoemaker, as the racing world wondered what this beautiful colt could have done if *all* his legs had worked properly …

FACTFILE

Description: Chestnut Colt
Size: 16.2 hands
Dates: 1952-72
Racing seasons: 1954-56
Where were they trained?: USA
Trainer: Meshach 'Mesh' Tenney
Owner: Rex Ellsworth

Jockey: Bill Shoemaker, Dave Erb
Sire: Khaled
Dam: Iron Reward
Damsire: Beau Pere
Record: 25: 19-2-2
Most impressive victory: Sunset Handicap 1956
Nickname: The California Comet

TULLOCH

A clearly ecstatic George Moore returns to the winner's enclosure aboard Tulloch after the Victory Derby, Flemington, October 1957.

This tome deliberately shies away from asking the unanswerable question: who was the greatest? If, however, the question 'who was the most courageous?' was posed, you would be hard pressed to find any horse braver than Tulloch. And it isn't because of his size – he was as small as any in this book. It is because he proved himself a world-class champion, then spent nearly two years at death's door before coming back and, unbelievably, doing it again.

PUNCH A HOLE IN THE WIND

As with previous Australian immortals Carbine and Phar Lap, Tulloch was in fact foaled in New Zealand – in his case at Trelawney, the oldest stud in the country. He possessed a pedigree on his sire Khorassan's side that promised much. Bought as a yearling by trainer Tommy Smith for 750 guineas, he was quickly sold on to Evelyn Haley who liked his new purchase's intelligence and poise, despite also commenting, 'He's small, but if he's no good we can use him to round sheep.' Fortunately for world racing, that didn't come to pass, and he would go on to win 50 times his purchase price on the track. Haley named him both after his mother's birth town in Scotland and by extension his grandfather's cattle stud just outside Melbourne.

The 'tiny pony' only grew to 15.2 hands, and had quite a hollow back – or, in the delicious Aussie slang of the day, a 'swampy' back. But it didn't impede him; running 13 times as a two-year-old, he won seven and came second in the other six, and Smith thought the world of him, testing him in the very best company across New South Wales, Victoria and Queensland.

At three, he blossomed further. He immediately took on the older horses in the Warwick Stakes, easily defeating Melbourne Cup winner MacDougal and previous AJC Derby winners Monte Carlo and Caranna. When it was his turn to run the AJC Derby, he coasted home by six lengths, beating the mighty Phar Lap's 28-year-old track record by over two seconds. To show it was no fluke, he went to Melbourne, collected the Caulfield Guineas, and then took on the older horses in the Caulfield Cup.

Drawn on the extreme outside, a confident Smith told the press beforehand, 'He has to start from somewhere and he'll win it just the same.' Punters were also in no doubt, making him the shortest-priced favourite in Caulfield Cup history. With a field of 17 and Caulfield's bendy track to navigate, there was a moment of alarm when Tulloch found himself boxed in with only the short straight to negotiate. A cool Neville Sellwood pulled him wide and let the colt take over, with a predictably galvanic response. Tulloch was in the lead in the blink of an eye, finishing an easy two lengths clear of Mac's Amber.

The winning time of 2min 26.9secs was a turf world record – which wouldn't be beaten locally until the turn of the century – and the second-fastest ever for 12 furlongs. In an echo of Native Dancer in the US a few short years before, Tulloch's rise coincided with the birth of racing being broadcast to a wider audience, in this case to the lucky households of Sydney and Melbourne. As was so often the way, as soon as Australia had a new superstar on its hands, the US racing scene would look across the Pacific with envious eyes and bulging chequebooks, keen to see if they could make an offer that Haley couldn't refuse.

TULLOCH

The Australian press were certainly hailing him categorically as 'The Best in the World' and in 1957 he very likely was.

More immediately came Australia's most cherished race. Surely the Melbourne Cup would be a formality? But no. Haley shocked the racing public by scratching him from the Blue Riband event. One the eve of the race, he told the press, 'I love horses too much to run a three-year-old, any three-year-old, not only Tulloch, in the Melbourne Cup. I will not risk breaking the colt's heart.' There was much anger, likely from those who had placed ante-post bets, and it does beg the question as to why Tulloch was entered in the big race in the first place. Conversely, in retrospect, it is refreshing to see horse welfare taken so seriously by some at a time when there was plenty of evidence that not everyone did.

Regardless, Tulloch next trotted up in the VRC Derby, beating Prince Darius (who had come a neck second in the Melbourne Cup) by eight lengths, before running away with the Queensland Derby, becoming the first horse to win the Australian 'Derby slam'. It would therefore have been a seismic shock if Tulloch had run in the Melbourne Cup and not won. His winning distances in some of his subsequent races were so far that they bordered on the comic. Notwithstanding this story of 'What if?', he still finished the season with 14 wins, a second and a third from 16 races, with crowds of 40,000 or more regularly turning up to see 'Haley's Comet' run. At the time, the Group race system had not yet been introduced in Australia, but ten of those races he won that year are now well-established Group 1s. Connections excitedly planned an international four-year-old career like no other for their flying little colt, to take in big races in the US and UK.

But that is not how it panned out. In April 1958 Tulloch fell desperately ill to a mysterious stomach illness. Absolutely no one knew what it actually was – and they still don't. He kept catching infections, he could barely eat and lost a huge amount of weight. It went on, horrifically, for nearly *two years*. As Smith recalled later, 'He spent 22 months lying against a wall. I thought he'd die for sure.' It is almost inconceivable to imagine the physical and mental agony that Tulloch must have gone through for that interminable period, and the will to live he displayed was beyond measure.

Not knowing what was causing it all drove his connections to despair, and they couldn't bear seeing him in such pain for so long. But then the miracle occurred. A young English vet called Percy Sykes suggested that there might be germs in Tulloch's mouth that needed killing, so his oats were mixed with port and brandy to make a distinctly heady porridge. We might scratch our heads at the mere suggestion now – but, astonishingly, it worked. Even Sykes himself wasn't expecting great things: 'It seemed to be absolutely miraculous. I've tried it on other horses since and it hasn't worked. Yet within a matter of 72 hours, Tulloch was absolutely normal.' Tulloch, like an Antipodean Lazarus, recovered, having spent two of his prime years half-dead.

No one was sure how he would race again, but a return at the ten-furlong Queen's Plate at Flemington in front of a colossal 90,000-strong crowd proved a victorious – and highly emotional – one. Tulloch's absurdly brave home stretch run took him just past the highly rated Lord, and grown men made no apologies for crying. Smith had been vindicated for not retiring the glorious colt despite all the naysayers. Indeed, at age five and six, he won nine of his next 11 races, including the Cox Plate and the Craven Plate, the former in a sensational time. The only blemish came in the Melbourne Cup, celebrating its centenary that year, where regular rider Neville Sellwood gave him an utterly baffling ride, at one stage being held up a long way detached from the field – some claiming as much as 60 lengths behind the leader, although film evidence suggests that to be an exaggeration. He made huge progress in the home straight but could only finish seventh under top weight. Incredibly, it was his only time outside the top three in any of his 53 starts.

Nevertheless, more top-level victories came his way throughout Victoria, New South Wales and Queensland, with the popular little horse never again finishing worse than third, often handicapped to the tilt. He bowed out, a hero for the ages, with a victory at 1961's Brisbane Cup, under a huge weight, by just under two lengths. A reflective Smith shared his thoughts: 'The secret of his greatness is that he is a stayer who can go like a sprinter in the big races.'

Tulloch's stud career at Haley's Te Koona farm was, by comparison, a major let down, siring only a handful of stakes winners before he passed away in 1969. But no one judged him on that. They judged him instead on his consistently brilliant performances, and on the outcome of those two years of anguish, during which he battled with a transcendental courage seldom seen before or since.

FACTFILE

Description: **Dark Bay/Brown Colt**
Size: **15.2 Hands**
Dates: **1954-69**
Racing seasons: **1956-58, 1959/60**
Where were they trained?: **Australia**
Trainer: **Tommy 'T.J.' Smith**
Owner: **Evelyn Haley**
Jockey: **George Moore, Neville Sellwood, Arthur Ward, Bill Pyers**
Sire: **Khorassan**
Dam: **Florida**
Damsire: **Salmagundi**
Record: **53: 36-12-4**
Most impressive victory: **Caulfield Cup 1957**
Nickname: **Haley's Comet**

KELSO

'Once upon a time there was a horse called Kelso … but only once.' The evergreen Kelso with trainer Carl Hanford, October 1961.

US racing journalist Joe Hirsch wrote a poignant line about Kelso that no one, it seems, can better: 'Once upon a time there was a horse named Kelso … but only once.' To understand the meaning seeping through these simple words is to understand the power that a horse who comes back, year after year, trying his best – and he really was one of *the* best – can have over the public. As Kelso was a gelding, he would only ever get to do his talking and winning on the track and not subsequently in the breeding shed. And he did plenty of winning, becoming – over many seasons – not just a champion, but a folk hero.

Kelso's pedigree was far from blue-blooded, although Man O' War lurked further back in the bloodlines. By Your Host out of the little-known Count Fleet mare Maid of Flight, his sire was harshly nicknamed 'The Magnificent Cripple' because he had one eye clearly higher set than the other, meaning he had to carry his head sideways to see straight. Some of his sub-par traits were passed onto Kelso, who as a youngster was variously described as 'scrawny, runty and hard to handle'. Owned by Allaire DuPont, who named him after her good friend Kelso Everett, and trained initially by John Lee, they soon realised that he was a 'rig' – his reproductive organs had not properly developed, making him an understandably grumpy soul at the time. He was therefore gelded at two before running a race.

Another DuPont family friend Dickie Jenkins was right there holding the young horse while veterinarian George Rosenberger did what he needed to. The unkind cut completed, Jenkins grabbed Kelso's testicles and launched them onto the roof of his barn, claiming that this was supposed to bring good luck. Bearing in mind what was to follow, it would be wrong to question this. Kelso's career that year was good, if unspectacular, with a first and two seconds in some minor races, with little indication of the dream that would follow.

Passed onto Carl Hanford's stable over the winter, Kelso suddenly started filling out and developing a real focus to his running. He didn't run at three until the Triple Crown was done and dusted. But his first two races – won by ten lengths and 12 lengths – showed that this was a different and much-improved beast. A rare misstep in his next stakes race at Aqueduct was quickly amended for by a six-race winning streak, improving with each and culminating with victories against the older horses in the Jockey Club Gold Cup and Hawthorne Gold Cup, the former in a new US record of 3min 19.8secs. To place himself further in hallowed circles, he matched Man O'War's 13-furlong record in the Lawrence Realizations Stakes. In a rare change of tradition, the Horse of the Year award went to the increasingly popular gelding rather than the Triple Crown colts.

Yet still the best was to come. At four, in Eddie Arcaro's safe hands, Kelso was imperious, the highlight being his clean sweep of the Big New York Handicaps – The Metropolitan, Suburban and Brooklyn – a feat only achieved twice previously and only Tom Fool had ever carried such burdensome weights (Kelso lumped around a huge 136lb in the Brooklyn). Another Jockey Gold Cup followed, as did a second Horse of the Year award. By now he was a true star of the racetrack, but he had captured the wider public's imagination in a way that no horse, except perhaps Native Dancer, had done for decades. Part of this was because of his huge versatility as well as his consistency, and above all his incredible, never-say-die attitude. 'He was an extremely determined horse,' recalled Hanford. 'If he saw a horse in front, he wanted to get to him. You could take him back or send him to the front.'

By 1962, vast numbers of spectators were turning up to some of his races, and as often as not he didn't let them down, invariably wearing a yellow ribbon on the bridle around his almost Arabian-like head. Now partnered by Milo Valenzuela, his six wins included the Stymie Handicap and Woodward Stakes over ten furlongs then a third Jockey Club Gold Cup over six furlongs further.

Surpassing $1 million in winnings, he was a shoe-in for an amazing third Horse of the Year award, and usually now referred to as King Kelly.

Aged six in 1963, he showed no sign of slowing down, to his adoring public's immense pleasure. Winning three quarters of his races, some over as short as a mile, as well as a fourth in the Jockey Club Gold Cup over two miles – a distance that his lean musculature was clearly well suited to, as attested by his five-and-a-half length victory in front of a record 71,876 adoring fans. Unsurprisingly, an unprecedented fourth Horse of the Year award followed. He celebrated by being treated to his favourite snack: a chocolate sundae.

You would be hard pressed to find a horse as good aged seven as they were aged four. Yet if anything, Kelso was arguably at the height of his powers. He now had an immensely talented new rival, Gun Bow, with whom he swapped victories throughout the year – and with Kelso almost always carrying the bigger weight. The zenith of their rivalry came in the Aqueduct Handicap which, being held on Labor Day and with King Kelly always attracting a large following, meant that the crowd that day was immense.

The horses duly delivered. Gun Bow took off like a scalded cat with Kelso being pushed after two furlongs just to keep within six lengths. But then his mythical courage and pig-headedness kicked in. Kelso utterly refused to be defeated that day, gradually reduced the gap, and finally broke his rival in a titanic home stretch match-up, getting up by less than a length. Writer David Alexander wrote after, 'I think it can be stated beyond dispute that the ovation Kelso received after his triumph on Labor Day at Aqueduct was the greatest ever given any horse in the history of the American turf,' while *Daily Racing Form* correspondent Charles Hatton described it as a 'Niagara of Sound'.

The finale was in the Jockey Club Gold Cup, the race that he had made his own for half a decade, and to prove his superiority he not only won by nearly six lengths but broke the US dirt record for two miles in the process.

It didn't end there. A mere 11 days later, seemingly unfazed by his considerable exertions, he laid an extra ghost to rest. Having come second three times in the Washington DC International, he now went one better, scorching to victory breaking the US turf record for 12 furlongs, registering 2min 23.8secs. It came as a surprise to no one that he was crowned Horse of the Year for an inconceivable fifth time – no other horse had more than three, and it is a record that will likely remain untouched forever.

The US may have been going through the upheaval and optimism in the early 1960s but, as much as anything, it was also the 'Era of Kelso'. David Alexander captured this perfectly when he reflected: 'If asked to state the reason why Kelso was the greatest racehorse we have ever known, I'd simply tell you that I think he's done more things better on more occasions over a longer period of time than any other horse in history. Or maybe I'd say it's just that I love him.' Eddie Arcaro called him the best of all his rides 'without question', although he was also on record as saying the same about Citation.

Kelso's age began to catch up with him at eight, but he still managed top-drawer wins in the Witney Stakes and Stymie Handicap. But then, just as he turned nine, he fractured a sesamoid bone and his adoring owner and trainer had no hesitation in immediately retiring him. A shocked public fully understood but struggled to adjust to a racing life without him. Of course, the breeding shed was out of the question, but he adapted to life as DuPont's hunter for a few years where his constant companions were an old hunter called Spray and a dog called Charlie Potatoes, who slept pretty much on Kelso's neck every night until he was run over by a truck. Kelso was in mourning for days and refused to eat.

He still made plenty of public appearances to satisfy his adoring public. On 15 October, 1983, aged 26, he led the parade before his beloved Jockey Club Gold Cup. The following day, he succumbed to a bout of colic. His death was back page news, pushing all other sports off. That was the hold that Kelso continued to have.

'Kelso was one of a kind,' said Hanford on his inauguration into the Hall of Fame in 2006. 'The way the game is today we will likely never see a horse have that kind of success for that long.

'They don't make them like that anymore. In fact, they never did.'

FACTFILE

Description: Brown Gelding
Size: 16 Hands
Dates: 1957–83
Racing seasons: 1959–66
Where were they trained?: USA
Trainer: John Lee, Carl Hanford
Owner: Bohemia Stables/Allaire DuPont
Jockey: Ismael Valenzuela, Bill Hartack, Eddie Arcaro, Jon Block, Bill Shoemaker

Sire: Your Host
Dam: Maid of Flight
Damsire: Count Fleet
Record: 63: 39-12-2
Most impressive victory: 1964 Washington DC International
Nickname: King Kelly

'It was his simple excellence to be the best': the magnificent Phar Lap, under the shortest of reins, strides out to victory, 1930.

Windsor Lad enters Epsom's hallowed winner's enclosure in June 1934 after the Derby, the race that would set him off on his path to greatness.

Count Fleet (Johnny Longden up) completes the US Triple Crown with a victory in the Belmont Stakes by officially 25 lengths – but in fact considerably more.

Two years after his fabulous three-year-old campaign, Citation (Steve Brooks up) breaks the mile world record at Albany, California, March 1950.

Native Dancer - seen here in training at Santa Anita, January 1953 – had a huge following in person and on TV, with most fans oblivious to his appalling chacracter.

Poetry in Motion: Swaps (Willie Shoemaker) defeats Nashua in the Kentucky Derby, May 1955.

Kelso – five times US Horse of the Year – wins the 1961 Woodward Stakes under Eddie Arcaro.

Vaguely Noble, with joint owner Robert Franklin and jockey Bill Williamson, can afford to mess around after his brilliant victory in the 1968 Prix de l'Arc de Triomphe, October 1968.

Two greats in one race: Brigadier Gerard, the consummate miler, defeats Mill Reef – who would come into his own over middle distances – in the 2,000 Guineas at Newmarket, May 1971.

Secretariat and Ron Turcotte come home alone in the Kentucky Derby at Churchill Downs in a record time for the race that still stands, May 1973.

The stunning Ruffian (Jacinto Vazquez up) stretches clear to win her tenth consecutive race, the American Oaks at Belmont, June 1975.

Argentine trainer Angel Penna soothes the capricious Allez France, 1975.

Seattle Slew and Jean Cruguet on their way to victory in the 1977 Kentucky Derby, May 1977.

'He was a super intelligent horse, smart and willing': the small but powerful Affirmed in training prior to the Kentucky Derby, April 1978.

'Kingston Town can't win.' Except he did. Despite a seemingly hopeless position just 300m from the line, Kingston Town (in the middle of the pack with jockey's whip in the air) still won a third Cox Plate, Moonee Valley, October 1982.

Spectacular Bid and Ronnie Franklin scoot to victory in the Kentucky Derby, May 1979.

Despite running the fastest single furlong ever recorded in the Epsom Derby, the post comes three strides too soon for Dancing Brave and Greville Starkey, with Shahrastani and Walter Swinburn just holding on, June 1986.

Shergar and Waler Swinburn on their way to post for the King George and Queen Elizabeth Stakes at Ascot, July 1981.

Ordinary on turf, a legend on dirt: Cigar (Jerry Bailey up) in splendid isolation at the Hollywood Gold Cup, July 1995.

The 'Eccentric Genius' Montjeu, with his favourite exercise rider Didier Follope aboard, in training for the Breeders' Cup Turf, November 2000.

Another pulverising victory for Silent Witness and Felix Coetzee at Sha Tin, January 2003.

'The horse that Japan had been waiting for': Deep Impact and Yutaka Take win the Japan Cup, November 2006.

Zenyatta and Mike Smith notch up yet another victory in the Lady's Secret Stakes at Hollywood Park, October 2010.

The start of a season for the ages: Sea the Stars and Mick Kinane comfortably take the 2,000 Guineas at Newmarket, May 2009.

A young Black Caviar (Luke Nolen) makes it all look so easy in the Arrow Services Training Plate, Moonee Valley, August 2009.

The amazing Frankel, with Tom Quealley aboard, destroys the opposition yet again in the Queen Elizabeth II Stakes at Ascot, October 2011.

The inimitable Winx (Tommy Berry) streaks clear in the Phar Lap Stakes, Rosehill Gardens, March 2015.

'American Pharoah is finally The One!' With Victor Espinoza up, American Pharoah trounces the field in the Belmont Stakes to become the US's first Triple Crown winner in 37 years, June 2015.

SEA-BIRD

A hard-held Sea-Bird under Pat Glennon wins the Epsom Derby, June 1965, putting up the easiest and most sublime victory in the history of the venerable race.

There were a few horses over whom I agonised about their relative merits and whether or not they reached the threshold for inclusion. Sea-Bird was not one of them.

Do I mean Sea-Bird? Or Sea Bird II? Let's clear up this minor distraction now. Sea-Bird is the name he ran under in France, yet when he ran in the UK, for obscure precedent reasons, he needed to be called Sea Bird II. When he went to be a stallion in the US, they decided to go along with the Anglo-Saxon version. It ultimately doesn't matter: He was, in any case, more than just a horse; he became a near-mythical benchmark.

Owned by textile manufacturer Jean Ternynck, his breeding suggested that he would never get anywhere near such a list of great horses, let alone vie for the top of it. His sire Dan Cupid may have come second in the Prix du Jockey Club (French Derby), but he was hugely inconsistent, and on his mother Sicalade's side, there were no female winners for four generations. Further, Sicalade had a traumatic time foaling Sea-Bird, as well as his siblings before and after, leaving Ternynck with little choice but to sell the mare to the butcher in nearby Andelys for the princely sum of 1,000 francs before Sea-Bird ever ran.

Ternynck had no hesitation as to where his horse should be trained: the stable of the outstanding Etienne Pollet, a highly regarded, multiple Classic-winning trainer whose medium-sized set-up never got beyond 50 thoroughbreds and who was, in any case, the owner's cousin. Ever astute, Pollet spotted something early on in the tall, initially gangly two-year-old: an amazing, elastic stride. He eventually ran on 2 September 1964 in the Prix de Blaison at Chantilly, running very green but getting up to win over an inadequate seven furlongs. He followed up well in the Criterium de Saint Cloud before being given a shocking ride in the Grand Criterium by Maurice Larraun and, despite making up a staggering amount of ground in the last 300 yards, couldn't get to his stablemate Grey Dawn. Pollet didn't mind as he had seen that day the colt's potential for middle distance glory. He would never lose again.

At two he showed great talent, but at three Sea-Bird was borderline supernatural in his abilities, and he once again had on his back the dependable Aussie Pat Glennon, who had moved from Ireland to France specifically to work with Pollet. Warming up effortlessly in the Prix Greffuhle, displaying his strangely high head carriage, he then won France's main Derby trail, the Prix Lupin, by a huge six lengths, destroying the hitherto unbeaten Diatome, who would act throughout his career as a dependable yardstick to measure Sea-Bird's true greatness.

Pollet chose to cross the Channel to take on the Brits and Irish at the Epsom Derby where, post-Lupin, his reputation had caught up with him and he started a short-priced favourite. Everyone who was there that day found himself or herself using the same phrase: 'It had to be seen to be believed.' It started inauspiciously as Sea-Bird was side-on when the tape went up – not that Glennon lost any sleep over it. The ease with which he beat his 21 rivals, without ever coming off the bit, made a mockery of this Blue Riband event. Glennon was barely touching him; the winning margin of two lengths could easily have been eight if the jockey had shaken his reigns just a tiny bit. In fact, he was under strict instructions. Pollet was aware of a road crossing the course soon after the finish line and didn't want his charge to damage his legs by running fast over it, so Glennon was pulling him up fully *a furlong* from the finish line. Sea-Bird was seen to barely breathe after his efforts. He hadn't really galloped; he had sauntered.

Be under no illusion as to the quality of the field: Meadow Court, in second place, went on to win the Irish Derby and King George in the ensuing weeks, I Say in third won the following year's Coronation Cup; Silly Season would win the St James Palace Stakes at Royal Ascot. There have been longer Derby-winning distances, but there has surely never been an easier victory. The man who got the best view, in fact, was Lester Piggott, doyen of British jockeys at the time, and riding Meadow Court. As parsimonious in his words as he was with his finances, he was asked in 2015 who the greatest horse was that he had seen (in Europe): 'Sea Bird, Ribot and Frankel were the best, in that order,' he responded. Just one man's opinion, but insightful nonetheless.

Sea-Bird repeated this trick back in Paris against the older horses at the Grand Prix de Saint-Cloud, again without coming off the bit, and again being given a ride of supreme confidence by Glennon. From there, all roads led to an October date at Longchamp for the Prix de l'Arc de Triomphe, already acknowledged as Europe's supreme middle distance race. There will never be agreement over which post-war race had the greatest-ever assembly of thoroughbreds at the peak of their game, but the 1965 edition of the Arc would surely be in any sensible person's top three. Aside from Sea-Bird, Diatome was back, unbeaten Prix du Jockey Club winner Reliance was there, Meadow Court too, as well as US Champion Tom Rolfe and even the greatest horse to ever come out of the Soviet Union, Anilin. And there were plenty of other Group 1 winners too in the 20-strong field, and as usual Sea-Bird sweated freely in the preliminaries.

It is thought that almost every horse that day ran close to its full ability, but the result wasn't even close. Entering the straight, lit by bright autumnal sunshine, and whilst most of the horses galloped, one horse appeared to be cantering, his head as usual held unusually high. Sea-Bird and Reliance pulled away… but only until Glennon decided it was time ('I thought it pointless to wait any longer,' the phlegmatic Antipodean said after). By the post, Sea-Bird was six lengths clear, despite veering bizarrely from the rails to the centre of the track, and Glennon easing up to pat his beloved ride well before the end. Reliance in turn showed his excellence by beating Diatome by another five lengths. The superlatives – first heard at Epsom – now went into overdrive. His performance that day was the highest *Timeform* rating achieved by any horse until Frankel in 2012.

Although retired at his peak the following week, the strength in depth of Sea-Bird's Arc was confirmed soon after by Anilin (who came fifth) winning the Grosse Preis Von Europa in Cologne and Diatome crossing the Pond to win the US's top international race at the time, the Washington DC International. But by then, everyone already knew that the effortless contempt with which this lanky chestnut always dispatched his top-drawer rivals was something utterly out of the ordinary.

Already, and despite his dubious breeding, the studs were salivating at the prospect of this wonder horse as a stallion, sadly ensuring that he wouldn't run at four where, whisper it, he could well have been even better. There was

European disappointment when an American syndicate led by John Galbraith's Darby Dan Stud in Kentucky made Ternynck an offer he couldn't refuse, initially for a five-year lease but it ended up being seven. Sea-Bird was far from disgraced at stud, producing one of Europe's greatest-ever fillies Allez France, as well as the hugely popular dual Champion Hurdler Sea Pigeon, before his tragic early demise aged only 11 of intestinal blockage, just six months after returning to France. Such were his standards on the racetrack that his stud career would always seem comparatively underwhelming. Yet with those performances at Epsom and Longchamp preserved for eternity, he had absolutely nothing to prove.

Perhaps the final word should be left to an unnamed Arc spectator. In the sizeable crowd that day was a 28-year-old doctor from Mauritius, resident at the American Hospital in nearby Neuilly, and known as Pierre – although to me he was simply 'Pap' or 'Dad'. Beside him stood an old French race-goer, repeatedly shouting 'Mais, arretez-le! Arretez-le!' ('Stop him! Somebody Stop him!') as Sea-Bird's sublime stride stretched him away from that incomparable field. As Ternynck's colt-in-a-million crossed the line, my father turned to his neighbour in the stands and asked why he wanted Sea-Bird to be stopped. 'Because if they don't catch him, he'll take off.' No horse in recorded history has yet been seen to fly, but on that sunny autumnal day in the Bois de Boulogne, one feels that the aptly-named Sea-Bird came closer than most.

FACTFILE

Description: Chestnut Colt
Size: 16.1 hands
Dates: 1962-73
Racing seasons: 1964-65
Where were they trained?: France
Trainer: Etienne Pollett
Owner: Jean Ternynck
Jockey: Pat Glennon, Maurice Larraun
Sire: Dan Cupid

Dam: Sicalade
Damsire: Sicambre
Record: 8: 7-1-0
Most impressive victory: Prix de l'Arc de Triomphe 1965
Nickname: L'Empereur

DR FAGER

'He could punch a hole in the wind': Dr Fager strides out under Bill Boland, September 1967.

Do racetrack course records matter? Usually not – there are so many extenuating factors affecting the time that a race is completed in, that it is clearly not a science when deciding the quality of one horse over another. But when a record is set by a horse like Dr Fager, then we take notice. Over 50 years on, his one-mile dirt world record still holds. And that's for the simple reason that Dr Fager was a machine like few others.

A son of Rough n' Tumble, Dr Fager was foaled at Tartan Farms in Ocala, Florida, whose principal trainer was Nebraskan John Nerud, a World War Two veteran who moonlighted as a rodeo cowboy. Falling off a pony one day in October 1965, Nerud gradually felt worse before travelling to Boston to consult renowned neurosurgeon Dr Charles Fager, who immediately saw that a subdural haemorrhage was on the verge of killing Nerud. He operated immediately, saved Nerud's life, and the grateful trainer soon found a perfect way to thank his surgeon.

Although only then a yearling, Dr Fager (the horse) would grow into a strong 16.2 hand bay, with an uncommonly large head and uniquely fluid stride, Dr Fager was wilful yet sensitive from the outset. Nerud remarked: 'He didn't want you to raise your voice to him, and he didn't want anyone whipping him. If something didn't suit Dr Fager, he would let you know immediately.' There was something gloriously wild about him, being memorably described by one admirer as '… like some malevolent wind blowing around American racetracks, charging the air with the crackle of positive ions.'

In 1966, at two, he was more than good, winning four out of five races at various east-coast tracks under regular partner Braulio Baeza, only coming up short when second to Successor in the Champagne Stakes at Belmont. But it augured well.

The following spring, his season started with a brutal challenge. In Aqueduct's Gotham Stakes, in front of over 50,000 spectators, he would be squaring off in front of one of the Kentucky Derby favourites, Damascus, with the legendary Bill Shoemaker up. Dr Fager that day had Manuel Ycaza on top. It would be the first spark of a rivalry like no other in US racing in the 1960s. As joint-favourites, the two colts proceeded to inexorably draw clear of the rest of the field in the home stretch. Dr Fager and Ycaza, pinning their rival firmly but fairly against the rail, prevailed by half a length. The crowd bayed more, and they would get it.

For reasons that remain hard to fathom, other than Dr Fager not having the toughest knees around, Nerud opted out of the tried-and-tested Triple Crown route for his top three-year-old. He next went instead for the Withers Stakes, where he demolished all by six lengths, and then the Jersey Derby where, despite a seemingly innocuous ride by Ycaza to again mince the opposition by six lengths, he was controversially disqualified for 'crowding the clubhouse turn'.

Several more top-rank races over a mile or just over followed, each with an easy victory, and often with a track record for good measure. Despite side-stepping the Triple Crown races, his reputation was sky high. He was then all set for the Woodward Stakes at Aqueduct, and another showdown with Damascus as well as the 1966 Horse of the Year, four-year-old Buckpasser. But a trap had been set for him, and he fell for it like a bear to honey.

The other two colts were accompanied by pacemakers, who both hared off, and the headstrong Dr Fager felt he absolutely had to go with them; Damascus and Buckpasser, meanwhile, sat ten lengths back. By the home turn, Dr Fager had exhausted himself and fell back with the 'rabbits', with the others overtaking him. He would not fall for it again, and it would be the only time he would finish a race outside the top two.

Completing the season by first cruising to victory in the Hawthorne Gold Cup, he then won the seven-furlong Vosburgh Stakes against older horses, to whom he conceded considerable weight. This performance alone was enough to make him Champion Sprinter for the year – not bad for a horse who was so much more than a sprinter.

DR FAGER

He had been superb at three, but at four Dr Fager was mesmerising. US aficionados believe to this day that the Good Doctor's 1968 season ranks as one of the greatest by any US horse in history. From May to November, he won seven of his eight races, carrying huge weights, at between seven and ten furlongs, on east coast, west coast, and in between. He was only beaten into second once by old rival Damascus, who he in turn beat on more level terms.

His rare foray to the west coast was diverting. One story, possibly embellished, is that Nerud believed his great colt had been allotted a little less for the California Stakes at Hollywood Park, only to be told on the morning of the race that there had been a miscalculation and that he would be carrying 130lb after all. Nerud let the red mist rise, as he was prone to do, but allowed his charge to run. By winning easily regardless, he made an impression on the Californians as he had elsewhere. Racing journalist Barry Irwin was there that day: 'He looked like a movie star of a horse. I remember reading in The Blood-Horse someone described Man O'War as the closest thing to flying he's ever seen, and that's what this horse reminded me of. He was just so fast, it was unbelievable. I got goosebumps.'

Later in the summer, at the Whitney Handicap at Saratoga, where he cantered to victory by eight lengths, author Steve Haskin recounts: 'He looked like no other horse, seemingly taller than his 16.2-hands frame and with a wild, untamed look about him. Off the track he was a gentle soul who did not like being scolded or yelled at, but on the racetrack he ran with a reckless abandon, a force of unharnessed energy.'

Yet this was all the prelude to a hot August day in Chicago, when Dr Fager was allotted a whopping 134 pounds top weight for the Washington Park Handicap at Arlington. Do yourself a favour and watch it, complete with commentator Phil Georgeff's idiosyncratic and inimitable delivery. Three things stand out. Firstly, the second quarter-mile. The half-mile was completed in a stunning 44 seconds flat, after a slightly tamer opening quarter. But allowing for Dr Fager's move in those two furlongs from sixth to first, it has been calculated that he completed furlongs three and four in a barely comprehensible 20.6 seconds – which out-and-out sprinters usually can't come close to when running over far shorter. There are no reliable records for the length of Dr Fager's stride, but it was clearly enormous. Second, the home straight. Dr Fager sprouts wings. Baeza does little more than nudge him and the picture almost doesn't seem to make sense as the others appear to be fixed to the spot. Third, listen carefully to Georgeff after the finish. He goes utterly silent for a full ten seconds, in shock, before uttering, off-mic, 'Wow … THIS is a racehorse.' And then he spots the time …

PUNCH A HOLE IN THE WIND

It was a beasting of the first order, a jaw-dropping new world mile record of 1min 32.2secs. One can only imagine what time he would have done if Baeza had bothered to either push him or not pull him up well before the line. ('If I knew he was setting a world record, all I had to do was chirp to him and he would've lowered the record even more.')

The following month, he ran for the one and only time on turf in the United Nations Stakes at Monmouth Park, clearly hating it, but still getting up to win 'on class and heart alone,' according to Nerud. His season, and career, was completed again in the Vosburgh, where he was allocated 139 pounds – the highest ever in a US stakes race, such was his reputation. Mighty to the last, he shouldered the crippling weight to a six-length victory, just 0.2 seconds off the seven-furlong world record.

On retirement, Dr Fager was given the ultimate accolade of winning four categories of the America horse titles: champion grass horse, champion sprinter, champion handicap horse and, of course, Horse of the Year. It is hugely doubtful that any horse will ever achieve this again. He was champion sire once, posthumously in 1977, but it is his remorseless combination of speed and strength for which he will always be remembered.

As Baeza once marvelled: 'He could punch a hole in the wind.'

FACTFILE

Description: Bay Colt
Size: 16.2 hands
Dates: 1964-76
Racing seasons: 1966-68
Where were they trained?: USA
Trainer: John Nerud
Owner: John Nerud/Tartan Stable
Jockey: Braulio Baeza and Manuel Ycaza

Sire: Rough n' Tumble
Dam: Aspidistra
Damsire: Better Self
Record: 22: 18-2-1 (1 DSQ)-3-2
Most impressive victory: Washington Park Handicap 1968
Nickname: The Good Doctor

VAGUELY NOBLE

A two-year-old Vaguely Noble on the day of his record sale at auction, December 1967.

Horses sold for record prices at auction have something of a mixed record. Seattle Dancer, who sold for over $13 million in the mid-1980s, was a Group 2 horse at very best. And few will forget the farce that was Snaafi Dancer, bought for over $10 million in 1983, but so appallingly slow on the training grounds that it was deemed too embarrassing to ever race him. Fortunately, it wasn't always that way. When two-year-old Vaguely Noble was sold at auction for a then-record $342,500 in 1967, it actually turned out to be a bargain, as he would prove himself to be unquestionably one of the greatest middle-distance horses to run in Europe since the war.

The reason for his going to auction in the first instance had a deja-vu ring to it – namely the breeder of a great horse tragically dying before they ever get to see their hero become a champion. Consider the 1st Duke of Westminster passing away in 1899 before his great filly Sceptre ran; or perhaps, even more poignantly, when one-off Italian legend Federico Tesio died before his masterpiece Ribot ever saw the starting gate. So it was with Vaguely Noble, bred by quirky textiles magnate and unrepentant Yorkshireman Major Lionel Holliday. Even his friends called him irascible, grumpy and vinegary. Nevertheless, he knew his horses, and spent two decades building up an old-school breeding empire similar in scale to Lord Derby and the Aga Khan earlier in the century. Petulant yet wily, he once stood up for himself when challenged as to why he dispensed with his trainer so quickly: 'They come to me on bicycles but they all leave in Bentleys.'

Yet none of us is immortal, and when the Pearly Gates beckoned Major Holliday in 1965, the huge death taxes meant eventually selling most of his bloodstock in 1967. But by then Vaguely Noble had already caused a significant stir. Sent into training with Walter Wharton, he initially turned few heads either in looks or on the gallops. Coupled with his unfashionable pedigree (by Sir Winston Churchill's Vienna out of Nearco mare Noble Lassie), no one bothered to enter the rather plain colt into the Classics. He ran very green but promisingly on his first two races, running a close second in maidens at Newcastle and at Doncaster. But then something clicked, and connections realised that he liked to run on quite soft ground. It didn't just improve him – it transformed him into a world-beater.

With top Australian jockey Bill 'Weary Willy' Williamson on board, they decided to try him out in the seven-furlong Sandwich Stakes on soft ground at Ascot. This was not the kind of race usually won but 12 lengths. But somehow Vaguely Noble did and the British racing scene sat up and took notice. A fortnight later he stepped up in class again, this time for the Group 1 Observer Gold Cup at Doncaster, England's top two-year-old race over a mile. Despite being boxed in on the home straight, the massively improving colt made light of the yielding ground and produced a 'devastating run' to win as he pleased by seven lengths. This was a juvenile of very rare ability.

It was at the end of the year that he was sold at auction, where anticipation was sky-high, with the *Sporting Life* newspaper asking the simple question, 'What Price Runaway Vaguely Noble?' as its headline. The record UK auction price at the time had stood since 1932, when Solario went for just under £45,000, yet here the bidding *started* at £76,000, with the gavel eventually knocking down at £129,000 to American couple Robert and Wilma Franklin. There was something quite bizarre about it, as Robert Franklin, who had made his fortune as a plastic surgeon to evergreen Hollywood stars, had only bought his first racehorse four months previously. To call it a gamble was an understatement. Amid fanfare, the superhorse was sent into training with Paddy Prendergast in Ireland, but that lasted only a matter of days. Behind the scenes, the under bidder at the auction, oil billionaire Nelson Bunker Hunt, had smoothly talked the Franklins into selling him a half share. They acceded, and agreed in the process to have him sent over to be trained by Etienne Pollet in France.

VAGUELY NOBLE

The rationale was no slight on top trainer Prendergast, but more an indictment of the realities of prize money. With such a huge outlay paid for the colt, only France amongst European countries offered the winnings that could help recoup the cash. Comparable races in France at each level were worth on average four times more than in the UK. More specifically, with no UK or Irish Classics having been entered, there was only one race that his year was to be geared at: the Prix de l'Arc de Triomphe. Pollet, who had masterminded Sea-Bird just three years earlier to immortality, must have thought all his Christmases had come at once.

Pollet plotted a long but easy season for the colt – now a tall, strong bay – starting in April with a facile victory in the ten-furlong Prix de Guiche at Longchamp. They then needed to prove that he definitely stayed the 12 furlongs so he was tried in the Prix du Lys at Chantilly, where he hacked up by eight lengths against an above-average field. Connections were feeling confident that their gamble had paid off, so decided to next pitch him against older horses over the extended 12 furlongs of the Grand Prix de Saint-Cloud. It was clear to all that he should have won, but his jockey for the race, Jean Deforge, was going through a period of exaggerating his waiting tactics and misjudged badly, leaving Vaguely Noble far too much to do. He still came a close third behind very useful older horses Minamoto and Hopeful Venture.

Not too put out, Pollet gave his charge a short break before returning for his Arc warm up in the 11-furlong Prix de Chantilly at Longchamp, this time with Bill Williamson back on board. Despite being a trial, it had the line-up of a championship race, with eight-length Prix D'Ispahan winner and French Guineas hero Zedaan setting a strong pace round the turn. But Williamson's cool tactics saw him breeze past and pass the post four lengths clear, easing up, with top-class horses toiling behind.

The stage was set for the Arc, but Vaguely Noble wasn't going to have it all his own way. As he had prepped his way in France towards the Autumn showdown in Paris, across the Channel another colt had been setting the courses alight. Sir Ivor, trained by Irish master Vincent O'Brien, had taken both the 2,000 Guineas and then, with a show-stopping late burst, the Epsom Derby. Despite close tactical defeats in both the Irish Derby and the Eclipse Stakes, he was rightly considered a major threat to Vaguely Noble's claim to the European throne.

Two top horses therefore met, with a no-excuses backdrop. Indeed, it was a stellar line-up all through, with seven winners of 11 Classics taking their chance. With the cut in the ground that he liked, Vaguely Noble was made marginal favourite, and two and a half minutes later confirmed it spectacularly. With two furlongs left to go, Williamson asked for his effort, and his colt bolted clear. Sir Ivor was right there, quickening as usual under the whip, and was the only one who was close to keeping up with Vaguely Noble's remorseless hands-and-heels gallop, but at the post they were separated by three lengths, well clear of the others. In most other seasons, Sir Ivor ('the best I've ridden,' according to jockey Lester Piggott after the Epsom Derby) would have been a worthy champion, and he went on to frank the form emphatically by winning both Newmarket's Champion Stakes before crossing the Atlantic and ploughing through the mud to win an incredible Washington DC International. But there was just no escaping the fact Vaguely Noble had defeated him fairly, acknowledged by Sir Ivor's owner Raymond Guest: 'Sir Ivor ran the best race of his life and was beaten by the best horse in the world.' There were few arguments.

Thus the gamble to buy this electrifying two-year-old had paid off handsomely, with the owners sadly – but understandably – deciding to cash in their chips and lead him to a lucrative life at stud in Kentucky rather than risk his star aged four. Syndicated for a world record of $5 million, he continued to show what a sound investment he had been, providing globetrotting champions Dahlia and Exceller amongst over 70 graded stakes winners.

Perhaps more than any horse here, Vaguely Noble makes a mockery of the continued insistence in some circles to assert a 'nationality' on a racehorse – as though this splendid breed has any concept of passports. Bred in Ireland, trained in England and then in France, owned by Americans and ultimately ridden by an Australian, all this was some time before the truly global age of flat horseracing. He may have stamped his authority as an all-time great in Europe's biggest race, but ultimately – as with so many heroes in this book – the fabulous feelings Vaguely Noble sparked from his magnificent victories belong to all of us.

FACTFILE

Description: Bay Colt
Size: 16.2 Hands
Dates: 1965-89
Racing seasons: 1967-68
Where were they trained?: France, UK, Ireland
Trainer: Etienne Pollet, Walter Wharton, Paddy Prendergast
Owner: Major Lionel Holliday, Nelson Bunker Hunt, Wilma Franklin

Jockey: Bill Williamson, Jean Deforge
Sire: Vienna
Dam: Noble Lassie
Damsire: Nearco
Record: 9: 6-2-1
Most impressive victory: Prix de l'Arc de Triomphe 1968

NIJINSKY

Lester Piggott comes close to a smile on board the striking Nijinsky, a horse whom he nevertheless still struggled to understand.

Shortly before he died in 1950, feted ballet dancer Vaslav Nijinsky stated unequivocally that he would one day be reincarnated as a horse. Absurd, yes, and yet … less than two decades later a horse carrying his very name – and his indefinable elegance – would launch himself into equine immortality. Horses don't have to be supermodels in order to be great. But when, like Nijinsky, they are almost ridiculously handsome, it certainly adds something to their lustre. The fact remains that, gorgeous or not, Nijinsky staked a realistic claim in 1970 to be the greatest horse trained in Ireland in the 20th century.

Bred in Canada, Nijinsky was the first European-trained horse to really put the all-conquering Northern Dancer line on the map, even though his powerful 16.3-hand frame was more reminiscent of his dam Flaming Page than of his undersized sire. But it was only the eagle eye of master Irish trainer Vincent O'Brien that brought him there in the first place. O'Brien had been asked by mega-wealthy

PUNCH A HOLE IN THE WIND

mining magnate and breeder Charles Engelhard to hot-foot it to Toronto as there was a yearling by Ribot on which he wanted an expert second opinion. O'Brien was underwhelmed by what he saw, but another caught his eye and he suggested that his benefactor bid for that one instead. Engelhard trusted the guru's sixth sense and paid a Canadian-record $84,000 to secure him at the sales.

He was a striking rich bay, with a white forehead star and a fiercely intelligent eye. Soon to be named Nijinsky, he would also develop a poetic stride fitting of his namesake. O'Brien initially raced him only at The Curragh, just outside Dublin, as a two-year-old, including the Railway and Beresford Stakes. From the outset he usually started odds-on, as word had got out of his abilities. Ridden in all his Irish races by Liam Ward, he duly obliged in each, before O'Brien sent him to take on the England's best in the Group 1, seven-furlong Dewhurst Stakes in Newmarket. Ridden by Lester Piggott, he was held up before weaving through the field to win comfortably. He promised much.

At three, after an easy warm up in the Gladness Stakes at the Curragh, he took on the best of his peers in Newmarket's 2,000 Guineas, delivering the prize with a mixture of grace and power, although he appeared also to be crying out for further. All eyes then turned to the Epsom Derby. For once he started odds against, mostly due to the presence of the gangly but hugely talented French colt Gyr, a son of the legendary Sea-Bird. Etienne Pollet, respected trainer of both father and son, had chosen to delay his retirement specifically to train him. Halfway down the cambered Epsom straight, Gyr was moving ominously well in the lead, and about to go clear, which was when Piggott lifted his whip and got an immediate response from Nijinsky, who sped past to win by two and a half lengths in a quick time. His penultimate furlong was timed at 10.6 seconds – only Dancing Brave would ever cover a Derby furlong quicker.

He repeated the trick three weeks later in the Irish Derby, with Ward back on board, beating Meadowville effortlessly by three lengths. It was then time to take on the older horses at the King George and Queen Elizabeth Stakes in July at Ascot. The international field was small but very select, including the Group 1 winners of the 1969 Epson Derby (Blakeney), the Washington DC International (Karabas), the Prix de Diane (Crepellana) and the Coronation Cup (Caliban). You will be very hard pushed to find a Group 1 race being won with a jockey as immobile as Piggott was that day, toying with Blakeney in second. It was sublime, and reinforced Piggott's view, expressed later, that in the summer of 1970 Nijinsky was utterly unbeatable.

Much is made of jockey's relationships with certain horses. Some seen to have an understanding that borders on the telepathic; it is testament to their intelligence as well as the expertise of the jockeyship. But if you thought that Piggott and Nijinsky possessed that mutual language, you would be mistaken. Piggott was in awe of his mount, but he nevertheless found Nijinsky highly mysterious: 'He wouldn't talk to me. He never talked to me. Nijinsky had that far off look in his eye from the first time I saw him ... it was like he was looking right through you.'

All was looking so rosy, but then illness struck in the form of ringworm, with weeks of training lost. Engelhard was keen for Nijinsky to take in the 14-furlong St Leger and become the first winner of the English Triple Crown since Bahram in 1935. It was touch and go, but he just recovered in time. Tenderly ridden by Piggott, he did what he had to and beat Meadowville again, by just a length. The Triple Crown was won and he was further hailed as a great.

It was clear, though, that it was only his outrageous class that got him there, and that he was likely still suffering. It had taken far more out of him than was initially apparent. The traditional October championship target of the Prix de l'Arc de Triomphe at Longchamp came next. It was a strong, but beatable, field. In the straight, Nijinsky was baulked twice when making his move on the outside, although it did not unduly affect him. He passed Miss Dan and then French champion jockey Yves Saint-Martin on Prix du Jockey Club winner Sassafras ... but then could find no more, and Sassafras, running the race of his life, found extra. They flashed pashed the post together, with many in the crowd unsure who had won.

It was only as the horses returned to the paddock that it became clear: Piggott – never the world's champion smiler – was even more hangdog than usual, whilst his great rival Saint-Martin, with whom he shared enormous mutual respect, beamed joyously. Nijinsky had lost for the first time. It is hard to overstate the shock of racegoers that day. It simply wasn't in the script, and the finger pointing started almost immediately.

The inquest initially blamed Piggott for leaving his horse too much to do, although a study of the race shows that he rode the fiery colt exactly the same as he always had. Saint-Martin had just kept with the pace better. It was likely that he was still feeling the effects of the ringworm, as well as running in the Leger; the horse had every right to feel tired after a long season. Respected racing writer Arthur Fitzgerald suggested an altogether different reason: Perhaps Nijinsky wasn't a true mile-and-a-half horse in the first place, with the stiff Longchamp test exposing the limits of his stamina. Nijinsky, he argued, had essentially burgled the other 12-furlong races because they were on more forgiving tracks where he could simply recharge during the downhill sections.

Whichever the reason, amends were sought a mere fortnight later over the straight ten furlongs of Newmarket's Champion Stakes, but the electric acceleration was again missing, with Nijinsky beaten two lengths by the patently inferior Lorenzaccio. Nijinsky had had enough. His owner, Charles Engelhard, would pass away just five months later.

At stud in America, Nijinsky cemented his sire's line and produced 155 stakes winners, becoming the only horse to sire the same season's Kentucky Derby and Epsom Derby winners. Piggott – winner of 30 English Classics – would still claim many years later that Nijinsky was one of the two most brilliant horses he had ever ridden (the identity of the second would change with the seasons).

Are there lessons learned from Nijinsky's brilliant career? Perhaps. We see the inferior horse that Nijinsky became after his tiring Leger win, and – much as the more traditionally minded Brits would hate to admit it – the race has undoubtedly lost some of its glamour since as a direct consequence. It is now very much the exception rather than the rule that Epsom Derby winners even consider taking in this hard, long race when so many end-of-season championship races – The Arc, the Breeders' Cup and more – offer so much more in terms of honours, stud value, as well as considerable immediate riches. It is telling that both Ireland and France have opened up their equivalents to older horses, recognising that times – and the very make-up of the thoroughbred – have changed.

Nijinsky could therefore be not just the greatest English Triple Crown winner, but also its last. Either way, this capricious, haughty, whimsical soul of a horse entranced the racing scene in a way that a dancer of the same name had, a few decades before, similarly enraptured crowds. Perhaps Vaslav Nijinsky had had the last laugh after all.

FACTFILE

Description: Bay Colt
Size: 16.3 hands
Dates: 1967-92
Racing seasons: 1969-70
Where were they trained?: Ireland
Trainer: Vincent O'Brien
Owner: Charles Engelhard Jr
Jockey: Lester Piggott and Liam Ward
Sire: Northern Dancer
Dam: Flaming Page
Damsire: Bull Page
Record: 13: 11-2-0
Most impressive victory: King George VI and Queen Elizabeth Stakes 1970

BRIGADIER GERARD

Brigadier Gerard, with Joe Mercer on board, canters down to post before another facile Group 1 victory, July 1971.

Most champions these days, it must be said, have a regal breeding, which in turn means some eye-watering sums were spent to bring them into existence in the first place. While £250 is clearly not a large sum now, frankly neither was it in 1967 when amateur rider and breeder John Hislop, armed with that paltry sum, sent his mare La Paiva (who had never won) to Queen's Hussar, a decent racer but hitherto an underwhelming sire. They produced Brigadier Gerard, and his stunning record in the early 1970s shows, perhaps better than any horse in this book, just how much a big dollop of chance is involved in this sport.

Trained by Dick Hern and always ridden by Joe Mercer, he ran four times as a two-year-old, progressing from a maiden to the Group 1 Middle Park Stakes, and winning each more comfortably and stylishly than the last.

That he wasn't favourite for the next Spring's 2,000 Guineas was for no other reason than 1970 saw perhaps the best crop of two-year-olds ever seen in the country. Top was My Swallow, undefeated in seven, including four Group 1s in France. Then came Mill Reef, who was winning all manner of other big races by large distances, and had only just been pipped by My Swallow in the Prix Robert Papin at Maisons-Laffite after a terrible cross-channel journey to get there. What a joy it must have been to have gone racing in 1970 on Europe's courses, with these outstanding juveniles tearing it up and a three-year-old Nijinsky crushing (almost) all before him.

Brigadier Gerard had no warm-up race and started as third-favourite at Newmarket that day in what many consider the best-quality Guineas field in its history. My Swallow and Mill Reef again battled out closely in the final two furlongs, suggesting that they were running up to form. The difference was, at the finishing line, Brigadier Gerard was three lengths ahead of both of them, having unleashed a devastating turn of foot and bolted up in the last furlong. Over a mile, both that day and in the future, he was unbeatable – although Mill Reef clearly wanted and needed further. Mercer was almost scared when he jumped off afterwards: 'My God, did he pick up!' he uttered. John and his wife Jean (in whose purple silks The Brigadier always ran) were extra happy as it more than upheld their decision to keep their special colt after they had turned down a £250,000 offer for him in the latter part of the previous year.

A glorious summer and autumn ensued, The Brigadier taking on peers and older horses alike over a mile, and always at Group 1 level, at Royal Ascot, Glorious Goodwood and more. He would never again start at odds against, despite the quality of the competition, and that year the result was always the same: he won – sometimes leading from the front, other times streaking from behind, sometimes on firm ground, sometimes in the mud.

He trounced his rivals in the Sussex Stakes, winning by five lengths from Faraway Son, the Queen Elizabeth Stakes was a cakewalk, and in the Goodwood Mile he put ten lengths between himself and Gold Rod. Finally, Hislop decided that he could be tested over ten furlongs in the Champion Stakes back at Newmarket, where in shocking weather and horrid ground he just beat Rarity. The jury was out about whether it was his distance, although connections ultimately had no such concerns – they believed he was just tired after a very long season.

There was an interesting coda to the season, though, when the votes for Horse of the Year went largely to Mill Reef rather than The Brigadier, even though the latter had won well in their only meeting. Whilst the acceptance that Mill Reef was clearly better over middle distances was a factor, one also suspects that voters were still more susceptible to the exotic background of Mill Reef when compared to the anything-but-glamorous Brigadier Gerard. Whatever the reasoning, the dream for the public now was for the champion miler Brigadier Gerard to meet the best 12-furlong horse Mill Reef over the intermediate distance of ten furlongs. The Eclipse Stakes the following summer was earmarked.

Brigadier Gerard may have been even better at four. Bloodless victories in the Lockinge Stakes and Westbury Stakes kicked off his season, before he pulverised Steel Pulse by five lengths in the Prince of Wales Stakes at Royal Ascot in course-record time. That, for Mercer, was his mount's greatest day, but nor for the most obvious reasons. As he later recalled: 'I'd been involved in a light-aircraft accident two days before. I was in a lot of pain and the big fella did it all for me. I'm convinced the horse knew I wasn't feeling well. He never put a foot wrong the whole way.'

But the showdown in the Eclipse never happened, with Mill Reef having injured himself in training. The Brigadier won regardless in workmanlike fashion before being tested over the 12 furlongs of the King George and Queen Elizabeth Stakes, and against top-quality challengers. It was clearly not his distance, and he hung right towards the end, but a patient ride from Mercer – not to mention the horse's brilliance – saw him win by a length-and-a-half from Parnell. He was all-conquering, and seemed truly invincible. The next stop was the newly inaugurated Benson and Hedges Gold Cup over an extended ten furlongs at York's Ebor meeting, facing top three year-olds Roberto and Rheingold, Mill Reef being still injured.

But that day the impossible happened, and the Brigadier was beaten for the only time. Roberto had just won the Epsom Derby from Rheingold under a possessed ride from Lester Piggott, but then flopped in the Irish Derby. He was utterly unpredictable. At York, Piggott ditched him for Rheingold. Roberto's owner John Galbraith, despite the options available to him locally, persuaded trainer Vincent O'Brien to fly over one of the top jockeys in the US, Panamanian Braulio Baeza, to take just this one ride. On rock-hard ground, Baeza rode Roberto like he had never been ridden before, charging from the gates and playing catch-me-if-you-can. And The Brigadier couldn't, coming up three lengths short.

A distraught Mercer claimed that his mount was ill, with mucus dripping out of his nose later that day, but in fact the evidence didn't stack up. He had thrashed

Rheingold and Gold Rod by the same distance as he had previously, and actually beaten the course record himself. It was just that Roberto ran a freakish, outlier race that he would never get close to repeating. John Hislop's wife Jean was heard to utter 'Roberto must have been stung by a bee,' although it was hard to work out if she was being frivolous or catty, but all the Brigadier's connections were undoubtedly crestfallen.

Baeza's tactics deserved a lot of the credit, and perhaps acted as something of an eye-opener to the British jockeys, more used to pacing a race differently and adopting a different style to the US crouch. That said, Mercer himself was universally regarded as one of the most stylish British jockeys of the century. With the crowd stunned that their 3-1 on favourite had been dispatched by the 12-1, unloved Roberto (one reporter even called him an 'upstart villain' for deigning to defeat the King), there was another victor that day: York racecourse. With such a high-profile start, their new ten-and-half furlong mid-August race, now called the Juddmonte International, has grown to become a centrepiece of British racing.

Picking himself up, The Brigadier returned for a second crushing victory in the Queen Elizabeth II Stakes at Ascot in a huge course record, despite missing the break. Beforehand in the paddock, owner Hislop asked Mercer what his planned tactics were for the race. A steely Mercer replied, 'I'm going to go out there and break the track record.' And he did. He then rounded off his career with another Champion Stakes, comfortably defeating Riverman. He was still utterly awesome.

Despite his unfashionable pedigree, Brigadier Gerard still managed to produce a St Leger winner, but he was never going to light up the stallion scene as he had the racecourse. By the end of his career, his official rating with some organisations was the highest achieved by any British horse in the 20th century, and no one ever felt the need to question it.

FACTFILE

Description: **Bay colt**
Size: **16.2 Hands**
Dates: **1968–89**
Racing seasons: **1970–72**
Where were they trained?: **UK**
Trainer: **Major Dick Hern**
Owner: **John Hislop**
Jockey: **Joe Mercer**
Sire: **Queen's Hussar**
Dam: **La Paiva**
Damsire: **Prince Chevalier**
Record: **18:17-1-0**
Most impressive victory: **Queen Elizabeth II Stakes 1972**
Nickname: **The Brigadier**

MILL REEF

Even at two, Mill Reef was a star, seen here wining the Coventry Stakes at Royal Ascot by eight lengths with Geoff Lewis aboard, June 1970.

Only the best and most popular horses that prove their timeless brilliance on the course even get *considered* to be the subject of a life-size bronze statue, let alone have that project seen through to completion. That Mill Reef has not one but *three* full-size statues – at Rokeby Stables in Virginia, as well as Kingsclere stables and the National Stud in the UK – in many ways tells you much of what you need to know about how this superb colt captured not just the top prizes across Europe, but the hearts of millions too. As racing journalist Julian Wilson so simply put it: 'To know him was to love him.'

Part of that was to do with his size. Whilst not tiny, he was not much more than 15.2 hands, and aptly fitted that hackneyed description 'small, but perfectly formed'. Bred by American Paul Mellon at Rokeby Farm and named after a stretch of coastline in Antigua, and the exclusive local club where Mellon was a member, he soon developed a light, fluid action that suggested he would suit European turf tracks more than dirt, and thus he was sent to the stables of Ian Balding at Kingsclere – the first offspring of Never Bend to run in the UK.

He showed great maturity as a yearling, getting Balding quietly excited, but it was not until his first proper work at two that he truly saw what he had. Journalist Andy Stephens describes beautifully what happened next: '[Balding's] instruction to John Hallum, Mill Reef's work rider, was to merely get upsides his lead horse and then "just let him go a stride faster". Everything went perfectly to plan, apart from the part where Mill Reef moved alongside his companion and then breezed 20 lengths clear. "John, I told you to just go a stride faster." "Guvnor, I promise you, that's all I was doing," Hallum replied.'

And so it was. His first race at Salisbury was an easy four-length romp. He then went straight to Royal Ascot and won the Coventry Stakes by eight lengths – pretty much unheard of for a two-year-old in that company. He was next sent to Maisons-Lafitte for the Prix Robert Papin but had a nightmare journey just to get there, and only failed by the shortest of heads to beat My Swallow who, although trained in England, would go on to win all of France's top juvenile races. It was no disgrace. Back in England, he was ready for the Gimcrack Stakes at York but the Knavesmire was a quagmire after lashings of rain. Balding had doubts about the little colt in such conditions, but a serene Mellon – who had flown over especially to see his colt run – was far more optimistic and insisted on running. Mill Reef, with perennial rider Geoff Lewis not budging a muscle, destroyed the field by ten lengths, and now there was no hiding his wondrous ability.

A bloodless win at Kempton, followed by victory in the Group 1 Dewhurst Stakes at Newmarket, saw The Reef sandwiched in the end-of-year ratings between My Swallow and Brigadier Gerard. It was a two-year-old crop like no other, and when, after a simple warm-up in the Greenham Stakes, Mill Reef faced his rivals in the 2,000 Guineas, there was much confidence. Yet The Brigadier won fair and square by three lengths on their only meeting, showing that he was the superior miler. But that told only half the story. Despite his pedigree, Mill Reef was no miler. Lewis, once a London hotel page boy, but now smelling stardom, promised Balding that he would thrive over further. Mill Reef's apologists also pointed out that the little colt had been visibly frightened in the parade ring by his huge and intimidating opponent Minsky.

As a consequence, he was surprisingly easy to back in the Epsom Derby where, demonstrating again his wonderful floaty stride, he skated away for an easy victory from Linden Tree, before reverting to ten furlongs in the Eclipse Stakes and despatching top French colt Caro – who had just won the Prix Ganay in record time – by four lengths. Caro's trainer Albert Klimscha knew how good his own charge was, and reflected: 'It is no disgrace to be beaten by a good horse, and Mill Reef is a great horse, better than Nijinsky.'

Back to 12 furlongs and he cruised to a six-length romp in the King George and Queen Elizabeth Stakes, leaving Italian Derby winner Ortis toiling in his serene wake. To further confirm his middle-distance credentials against the best Europe had to offer, he went to Longchamp for the Arc. This time, however, there would be no hellish journey to get there. An organised Balding was granted permission from the US Embassy to fly from Greenham Airbase, a stone's throw from his stable, and under lease to the US Air Force. Mill Reef was treated impeccably as he became one of the few thoroughbreds ever to fly with the United States Air Force. He touched down at Le Bourget just two hours after leaving his barn, and infinitely more refreshed than he had been for his last race in the country.

In front of a huge crowd that included President Pompidou, Mill Reef delivered, and then some. Not only did he unleash his electric acceleration once more to beat French filly Pistol Packer by three lengths, but he beat the course record in the process. Yet it was clear that the French loved the indomitable and kind little colt as much as the English did, with their press the next day comparing him to Sea-Bird.

It had been one of the most impressive European three-year-old middle-distance campaigns in history, and in the process he had become the first American-bred, American-owned winner of Europe's most prestigious middle-distance race, and the first British-trained winner since 1948. Balding's love of the colt was shamelessly obsessional. As his daughter Clare – herself a respected racing expert – would later claim: 'My father does not remember the fact that his first child was born in 1971, because all that year means to him is Mill Reef.'

Mill Reef, somehow, improved further over the winter. He went back to France to open his campaign in the Prix Ganay, where new superlatives were sought as he effortlessly sauntered to an officially ten-length (and unofficially 15-length) win over useful older horses. Back at Epsom's Coronation Cup in June, he could suddenly only scramble home by a head and it was revealed that he had a nasty virus and had missed several key training gallops in the run up due to appalling weather – making his victory all the more remarkable. It was his sixth Group 1 victory in as many races, a record for a UK-based horse that would stand for over 30 years.

This illness, however, meant there would be no rematch with The Brigadier over ten furlongs, either at the Eclipse Stakes at Sandown (which Brigadier Gerard duly won) or the inaugural Benson and Hedges Cup (where his rival was sensationally beaten). Instead, Mill Reef was prepared for an Autumn campaign centred on retaining his Arc crown – a rare feat then as it still is now. But plans came crashing down when, during a routine training gallop near Watership

Down, the little colt's cannon bone in his left foreleg suddenly shattered, the ghastly snap heard by all present.

His racing career was over, but a quick-thinking Balding, experiencing 'the most awful moment of my whole life', quickly called in vets Charles Allen and Jim Roberts where, in a room at the stable, they practised pioneering six-hour surgery to save the courageous colt's life, helped by the colt's incredibly calm temperament. Showing limitless devotion, John Hallum essentially lived with and nursed his charge around the clock for three months. The stable lost count of how many 'get well' cards they received.

Such love proved worth it. Syndicated to stand at the National Stud at Newmarket for a record £2 million, Mill Reef was a titan as a sire, with offspring winning English, Irish, French and Italian Derbies, other European Classics, Breeders' Cup races and so much more. His pedigree tentacles are still evident throughout the bloodlines of so many top horses. There were tears around the racing world when the hugely popular little horse passed away in 1986. British racing journalist John Oaksey stated boldly: 'Mill Reef had achieved in two racing seasons what most men do not achieve in a lifetime,' which felt entirely appropriate. At a time of almost unparalleled riches in UK Racing, he was the little horse that could.

FACTFILE

Description: **Bay Colt**
Size: **15.2 hands**
Dates: **1968-86**
Racing seasons: **1970-72**
Where were they trained?: **UK**
Trainer: **Ian Balding**
Owner: **Paul Mellon**

Jockey: **Geoff Lewis**
Sire: **Never Bend**
Dam: **Milan Mill**
Damsire: **Princequillo**
Record: **14:12-2-0**
Most impressive victory: **Prix Ganay 1972**
Nickname: **The Reef**

SECRETARIAT

Owner Penny Chenery offers a treat to her horse of a lifetime Secretariat.

The date was 9 June 1973, and the race was the Belmont Stakes, the third leg of the US Triple Crown, and open to the best three-year-old horses that the US had to offer. A mere five colts turned out, largely because many others had been scared away by the horse that had won the Kentucky Derby and the Preakness Stakes, the first two legs of the Triple Crown. That colt's name was Secretariat.

In retrospect the non-runners were right. To enjoy this race – if 'race' is indeed the right word – you don't need to be a horseracing fan. Arguably, you don't even have to be a fan of sport *per se*. What you would ideally need to possess is an appreciation of beauty and awe, because watching the grainy footage of this race now through the hazy prism of history, we still experience what the large New York crowd doubtless felt that day: we can't quite believe what we're watching.

But let us rewind three years to see how we got there. Secretariat came from decent stock (his sire Bold Ruler had himself won the Preakness Stakes) and he stood out from the day he was foaled, 30 March 1970 at Meadow Stable, Virginia. Nicknamed 'Big Red' because of the vibrant hue of his chestnut coat, he was a leader and a clown in the paddock from early days, closely guarded by his dam, Somethingroyal. When his owner Penny Chenery first visited the foal when he was merely days old, she made an entry in her notebook. The message simply said, 'Wow!'

Initially he was to be known as Scepter, but that was rejected by the Jockey Club registry as having been taken, as were Chenery's follow-up suggestions of Game of Chance, Something Special and Royal Line. Only a diplomat family friend's suggestion of Secretariat passed Jockey Club muster, and a legend was christened.

Sent into training under Quebecois Lucien Laurin, his first race – a five-and-a-half furlong Aqueduct maiden – was something of a baptism of fire, as another juvenile running very green, Quebec, cut up the field causing all manner of bumping, with Secretariat stumbling badly. His jockey that day, Paul Feliciano, remarked afterwards that it was only his horse's abnormal strength that got him back up to fourth that day. He ran eight further times that year, winning seven and only coming second in the Champagne Futurity after being demoted from first by the judges for a minor infringement. Such had been his electric performances that, in a rare turn of events for a two-year-old, he was awarded Horse of the Year. By now Ron Turcotte was his regular rider.

During the winter, Secretariat eventually grew to an imposing 16.2 hands, but of true note were his exceptionally powerful hindquarters and his massive chest; no one could recall any racehorse having to have a specially made girth, as he did to fit his barrel-like 76-inches. An admiring Australian trainer once saw him and said simply, 'He is incredible, an absolutely perfect horse. I never saw anything like him.' But Chenery now had a problem. Already in a minority as a strong woman in a man's world, her father Christopher passed away in January 1973, leaving her with a monstrous tax bill on the estate. Left with little choice, she had to syndicate Big Red's breeding rights to a consortium of very willing buyers, with the understanding that this would start at the end of his three-year-old season. Such was his reputation already, however, that they paid a record $6.08 million for him, which, in 1973, meant that pound for pound Secretariat was officially worth more than his weight in gold.

After a succession of warm-up races, and always wearing his distinctive blue-and-white checked hood to match the silks worn by jockey Ron Turcotte, he won the Kentucky Derby in the still-standing record time of 1min 59.4secs – the first ever under two minutes. He beat the highly regarded Sham, who again came second to him in the Preakness, where once more Secretariat beat the track record. When analysis was done after both races, something strange emerged: he had run each quarter-mile quicker than the last. Horses just weren't meant to do that. He didn't just look different; he ran differently too.

SECRETARIAT

And then to the Belmont. Unlike his previous tactics of being settled further back and then working his way gradually to the front, Turcotte chose to surprise his rivals and, as soon as the gates slammed open, nudged him to the front. Together with Sham, they rapidly drew ten lengths clear of the others, going absurdly quickly for a 12-furlong race.

Halfway through, the luckless Sham realised that he couldn't keep up with the remorseless, gut-busting gallop that Secretariat was maintaining – his spirit, one senses, finally broken. But perhaps Big Red had himself set off too quickly? At that halfway point of six furlongs, Secretariat was timed as having gone two seconds faster than the track record for an actual six-furlong sprint at Ascot racecourse at the time.

But stop he didn't; instead of gradually succumbing to his exertions, he relentlessly pulled away, appearing to be slowly morphing into Pegasus. As he flashed passed the post, a barely comprehensible 31 lengths separated this mighty thoroughbred from the very best of his contemporaries. This simply never happens in any flat races, let alone a Classic. He had beaten the 12-furlong track record by two and a half seconds. Turcotte, who had been nothing more than a barely moving passenger throughout, had trouble stopping the eager colt, so Secretariat ended up beating the 13-furlong world record too for good measure, even though the race had long finished.

Years later, an ever-mesmerised Turcotte recounted, 'I never experienced anything like it. Faster, faster, faster. Enemy hoofbeats soon disappeared; too far behind us on the track for me to hear. What a race. What a memory.' Secretariat now went one step better than Native Dancer and others, gracing not just the covers of *Time*, but also of *Newsweek* and *Sports Illustrated*. He was a phenomenon, but his timing was also prescient. With the backdrop of Watergate and Vietnam on the airwaves, writer George Plimpton pointed out that 'Secretariat was … the only honest thing in the country at the time … Where the public so often looks for the metaphor of simple, uncomplicated excellence, the big red horse has come along and provided it.'

You would think such an extraordinary horse would never get beaten. But although he easily won several more races that year – including the Canadian International and Marlboro Cup – before retiring to stud, he was also beaten into second a couple of times, first in the Whitney Stakes in Saratoga, and then in the Woodward Stakes, by horses demonstrably inferior in the scheme of things. It is inexplicable at one level, but racing is a capricious game, and the thoroughbred – forever skittish – has to be in the right mood to run. Then again, he might just have been ill or left a couple of gallops short in training.

At stud, he was a moderate success, confirming what breeders will often tell you: that when you breed the best with the best, you can still only *hope* for the best. In fact, the start was nerve-racking for the syndicate as his sperm showed immaturity, so he was first tested, with less risk attached, on three non-purebloods. Fortunately, they all fell pregnant. His greatest success thereafter was undoubtedly as a sire of excellent broodmares. After he was euthanised in 1989 following a very painful month-long bout of untreatable laminitis, it was discovered that his heart was gigantic – at an estimated 22lb, fully 2.5 times bigger than average. Maybe this x-factor mutation made the difference between very good and great. He was buried at Clairborne Farm in Kentucky, next to his sire Bold Ruler and his grandsire Nasrullah. In a break with tradition, connections decided not to just bury his head, heart and hooves but the entire body. Perfection, they felt, needed to stay that way.

Secretariat's legacy remains mind-boggling. Aside from the five statues of him dotted around the world, memorabilia associated with him goes for prices that dwarf that of others horses. One of his horseshoes from his Kentucky Derby success went at auction for over $80,000; one of the *nails* from one of his Belmont Stakes horseshoes sold for over $6,000. Everyone still wants a link to Big Red, and especially that Belmont Stakes.

But there is, perhaps, a more telling coda to the events of that balmy June day. As the crowd eventually drifted away, doubtless still shaking their heads in uncomprehending wonder, the on-track bookmakers started reporting something unusual. A huge portion of the winning tickets weren't cashed in that day – or any subsequent day – and gradually it dawned on everyone as to why. This otherworldly performance had had such a telling effect on so many spectators that they had instead chosen to keep their winning betting slips as mementos. To them, being up a few dollars was nowhere near as important as being able to later proudly show a scruffy piece of paper that proclaimed, quite simply, 'I was there'.

FACTFILE

Description: **Chestnut Colt**
Size: **16.2 hands**
Dates: **1970-89**
Racing seasons: **1972-73**
Where were they trained?: **USA**
Trainer: **Lucien Laurin**
Owner: **Helen 'Penny' Chenery (Tweedy)**

Jockey: **Ron Turcotte, Eddie Maple, Paul Felliciano**
Sire: **Bold Ruler**
Dam: **Somethingroyal**
Damsire: **Princequillo**
Record: **21: 16-3-1**
Most impressive victory: **Belmont Stakes 1973**
Nickname: **Big Red**

ALLEZ FRANCE

Daniel Wildenstein leads in his fabulous filly Allez France after her victory in the Prix de l'Arc de Triomphe, October 1974. Jockey Yves Saint-Martin would collapse soon after.

When renowned art dealer Daniel Wildenstein started buying horses, one of his first purchases in 1971 was a filly by the legendary Sea-Bird, out of Priceless Gem, who had beaten the wonderful Buckpasser fair and square in the 1965 Futurity Stakes. Sent initially into training with Albert Klimscha in France, Wildenstein could have called her anything he liked. But with almost fatalistic prescience, he chose Allez France ('Come on, France!' or 'Let's Go, France!'). And she didn't let him or her country down, becoming one of the great post-war fillies to grace the European turf.

Was 'grace' the right word? Opinion was oddly divided. Some critics called her 'charming and most feminine' and there are plenty of close-up portraits that back this up. Conversely, others called her 'ugly and masculine', which all goes to show that beauty is in the eye of the beholder. Wildenstein's broker, at least, was sure. When she came up for auction in the US in 1971, and Wildenstein saw her sumptuous pedigree, he passed on clear instructions: 'if that filly is pretty and looks like her mother, you have to buy her. If she looks like father, forget about her!' Ouch. Poor Sea-Bird. But $200,000 was a big sum for a filly at the time.

No matter. What she unquestionably did have was bags of class. Even though she was a very late foal, born in late May, she was already destroying her male peers on the training grounds. Stable jockey and 15-time *Cravache d'Or* winner Yves Saint-Martin rode her on the gallops, and hopped off one day, saying, 'It's money well invested.' She first demonstrated it at the racecourse at two in the eight-furlong Criterium des Pouliches. Unleashing a monstrous sprint in the straight, Saint-Martin was effusive afterwards: 'She was amazing. I had the impression that she was going three times faster than the others. She passed her opponents as though they had already stopped.' He wasn't the only one bowled over, as it was enough to make her champion two-year-old French filly.

At three she developed into a machine, but there was initially a problem. Noting that Allez France would quickly get anxious and sweat until she had soaked her blanket when left alone in her box, Klimscha realised that she needed company. He plumped for a rabbit but it ended up very unfortunately for the poor bunny, who didn't last the night under the tetchy filly's hooves. This was attempted twice more with predictably similar results. What she needed, they figured, was a sheep.

Enter Bastian – although for some reason, when the UK and US press found out about this, they called him Steve. Regardless, her fluffy companion would sleep in her stable and travel in her horsebox to every race. They were inseparable, even if on occasion Allez France let her complexities get the better of her and lift the poor beast in her teeth and throw him against the (fortunately padded) stable wall. Now a more relaxed filly, she cruised to victory in the Poule d'Essai des Pouliches (French 1,000 Guineas) and Prix de Diane (French Oaks), as well as the Prix Vermeille as her warm up for her first tilt at the Prix de l'Arc de Triomphe. Each time she revealed a devastating turn of foot, even on her preferred softer ground, which her rivals couldn't compete with. Starting favourite for the Arc, she came a creditable second to the unpredictable and mercurial Rheingold, before rounding off with another second on her first foray abroad at the Champion Stakes at Newmarket.

Wildenstein, meanwhile, had to deny rumours that the only reason he had called her 'Allez France' was purely to confuse the English and their loyalties when she ran there and they bet on her. Regardless, she was again top of the French filly rankings for the year. Saint-Martin noted something interesting about her running style: 'Riding Allez France generates a unique sensation. When she accelerates, she lowers herself by a good 30cm, as though streamlining herself to the turf.'

By this stage, a rivalry had already built up in the press between the two top French fillies, Allez France and Dahlia. Yet 'rivalry' felt like a very forced word. Over their careers, the two fillies met six times and Wildenstein's filly came out top every time. Yet they were chalk and cheese. All their meetings were in France, and whilst Allez France hated travelling – not least as Bastian/Steve wasn't allowed to come with her – Dahlia seemed to sprout wings only when she was abroad and would proceed to win a host of big races in the UK and the US, pioneering the globe-trotting campaigns of top horses that continues strongly to this day.

Meanwhile, as with so many horses, Allez France got even better at four. She had also moved to the stables of Argentine-born trainer Angel Penna, whose Horse Whisperer ability with fillies were tested by the ever-jumpy Allez France. Even so, the filly showed she had lost none of her class by pulverising a good quality field in the Prix Ganay by five lengths, and also trotting up in both the Prix d'Ispahan and the Prix d'Harcourt. There were no problems either in her Arc prep race, the Prix Foy.

The 1974 Arc was immortalised not just by the filly's courage but by that of her jockey, Yves Saint-Martin. He had fractured his foot and hip badly in a fall just a week before the big race. Doctor's orders: three weeks in bed. In normal circumstances he wouldn't have considered riding. He was still walking around on crutches on the day of the race, making sure to hide them before Wildenstein saw him. But this was his beloved filly – the greatest he ever rode – and it was the Arc. Further, he knew that if he didn't ride her, the mount would very likely be offered to his friend but also great rival Lester Piggott, who had been circling Wildenstein like a humourless vulture since Saint-Martin's fall. The French champion spent the week pumping himself full of xylocaine, up until 20 minutes before the race, trusting that Allez France wouldn't need to be hard ridden.

In the event, as 2-1 on favourite and against a top-drawer European field, she exploded clear two furlongs from home, only to be remorselessly hunted down by leading filly Comtesse de Loir. Saint-Martin, in agony and with no strength in his leg, pushed through the pain barrier, and she prevailed by a head. He always claimed that he never whipped Allez France because he knew how hard she was already trying. That day, he couldn't have even if he'd wanted to, as after the adulation, he gulped two glasses of champagne and then collapsed into his doctor's arms. But, unbeaten that season, Allez France was the darling of Europe, and her *Timeform* rating in 1974 remains the highest ever achieved by a European filly since the war.

Kept in training at five, Things started promisingly, with another easy victory in the Ganay and the Prix Dollar. By the autumn, however, she wasn't happy and in the Arc – starting as favourite for the third year in a row – she could only manage fifth to the rank outsider Star Appeal. A second attempt at the Champion Stakes in Newmarket again ended with a second place, even though she was clearly not comfortable on the ground.

There her wonderful career should have been wrapped up but connections, perhaps seeing the immense success that Dahlia was having in the US, thought it would make sense for Allez France to try her luck there too. But they should have paid more attention to Bastian/Steve. As Allez France was being boarded to North America, it was not possible to procure the right papers for the sheep, and both he and the great mare had a heartbreaking tantrum as it became clear to them that they were being separated. She hated travelling anyway and now she was miserable, so ran only once – poorly, in the National Championship Handicap at Santa Anita – before finally being retired.

Allez France was a moderate success as a broodmare in Kentucky, her two best offspring being the Group 3-winning colts Air de France (by Seattle Slew) and Action Francaise (by Nureyev). Always one to do things her way, she only foaled standing up. On her passing, there was no hesitation in burying her next to Man O'War, one great next to another.

FACTFILE

Description: Bay filly/mare
Size: 16.1 hands
Dates: 1970–89
Racing seasons: 1972–76
Where were they trained?: France
Trainer: Angel Penna and Albert Klimscha
Owner: Daniel Wildenstein

Jockey: Yves Saint-Martin
Sire: Sea-Bird
Dam: Priceless Gem
Damsire: Hail to Reason
Record: 21: 13-3-1
Most impressive victory: Prix Ganay 1974
Nickname: La Reine de Paris

RUFFIAN

One of the last photos of the remarkable Ruffian before her tragic match race against Foolish Pleasure at Belmont, July 1975.

When a talent sadly passes away too young in the performing arts, there is sometimes a tendency to overly eulogise the output and skill that they had displayed before they died, so that their potential, at least, is not forgotten. It is completely understandable. In the competitive world of sport, by contrast, we can instead look at the cold, hard reality of competition, and therefore judge one who leaves us too soon more realistically. To that end, we should ensure that Ruffian's utterly tragic end should never detract from the fact that, until then, she had already displayed more than enough to prove herself a true great, and should not simply be remembered as a ghastly footnote to the fragility of the racehorse.

But who was this incredible filly, who exploded supernova-like onto the racing scene? Plum in the middle of the US's golden decade of racing, with the fall of Saigon and a movie about a huge killer shark keeping the people occupied, along came a queen the public could rally around. Yet as time has passed, more and more the enigma has grown. A daughter of Reviewer by Native Dancer dam Shenanigans, Ruffian was always huge in stature as well as performance. Nearly jet-black, built like a stallion, yet still quite feminine – 'legs of a supermodel, muscles of a gladiator' – no one could recall any other filly standing at 16.2 hands as a two-year-old. Fiercely independent in spirit and business-minded to the last, it was often said that she had defeated her competitors before they had even started racing, such was her intimidating demeanour.

PUNCH A HOLE IN THE WIND

Trained by Frank Whiteley and owned by Stuart and Barbara Janney, she didn't enter the yard like a future champion. A distinctly fat yearling, she was called 'Sofie the Sofa' by the more cruel-minded stable hands. That didn't last though. Once she started racing, she would never be beaten – not in a 'real' race, at least. Taken to a Belmont Park maiden in May 1974, she started as she would carry on – in utterly dominant style. Even over an inadequate five-and-a-half furlongs, she burst out of the gate, and finished an incomprehensible 15 lengths ahead of her nearest pursuer.

The pattern was repeated, again and again. Whether at Belmont, Aqueduct or Monmouth Park, she wasn't beating her rivals, she was destroying them. Finishing off her season at the Spinaway Stakes at Saratoga with a scintillating annihilation of her opposition, she only took 1min 8.6secs to complete the six furlongs, and her nearest pursuer was toiling 12 lengths away. Sadly, she sustained a hairline fracture of her right hind ankle, probably during a morning gallop in late September of that season, so would be put away for the season to heal. The champion two-year-old filly title was already long hers.

Once recovered by the following spring, she carried on her rewriting of the record books. Indeed, crushing wins would be a feature of all her ten completed races, spread over her two-year-old and three-year-old career. She won them all with an average winning distance of over eight lengths. She was never even headed in any of them. And neither did she keep to the sprints, with all distances up to a mile and a half tried and conquered. She was a beast.

These were not run-of-the-mill races. Half of Ruffian's successes came at Grade 1, including the Fillies Triple Crown ('Triple Tiara') of the Acorn Stakes, the Mother Goose Stakes and the American Oaks. Further, and incredibly, she either beat or tied the track record in *every single one* of her races – utterly unheard of. Her principal jockey throughout was Jacinto Vasquez, who had only ever once felt the need to slap her with the whip, stating calmly: 'Ruffian sets her own pace.' In the Mother Goose, she won by 13 lengths and in a time that would not be beaten for 34 years.

The US racing scene was clear: here, surely, was the greatest filly to have graced the American racetracks. 'As God is my judge, she might be better than Secretariat' – powerful words coming from anyone, but given a whole new resonance when uttered by Big Red's actual trainer Lucien Laurin. But in 1975, sport was still sport, and not business, and public clamour grew for a match race between the newly crowned Queen, and the Kentucky Derby victor Foolish Pleasure. Such was her profile beyond racing circles that it became one of the most talked about sporting events of the year Stateside, and was to be shown on Live TV.

RUFFIAN

Initially, Whiteley and owners Stuart and Barbara Janney weren't keen, as it seemed an unnecessary distraction, but there was pressure both from the media keen to keep the public's interest high in a post-Secretariat world, and from an adoring public; the $125,000 winner's purse wouldn't hurt either. Once the race was switched to New York's Belmont Park rather than California, they relented. Vasquez, the regular rider of both Ruffian and Foolish Pleasure, was offered the ride on both. Despite misgivings over the whole enterprise, he picked the filly without hesitation, leaving Panamanian legend Braulio Baeza to partner the colt.

What followed on that hot 6 July afternoon in 1975 was unforgettable, but for all the wrong reasons. The public had been whipped into excitement, with the match race billed as the equal of both Man O' War vs. Sir Barton in 1920 and Seabiscuit vs. War Admiral 18 years later. 50,000 folk turned up in person, 20 million on TV, all armed with newspapers proclaiming the 'Battle of the Sexes' on their front pages.

Despite stumbling out of the inside gate and hitting her shoulder hard, Ruffian matched Foolish Pleasure for the first two furlongs, run at a ferocious 22.2 seconds. Then in the third furlong, she started to inch ahead ... which was when the audience heard a sickening crack. The sesamoid bones in Ruffian's right front leg had snapped. Yet the only thing that really beat Ruffian that day was Ruffian herself. Although in agony, and despite Vasquez's valiant efforts to pull her up, she refused to stop for what seemed an age, a fighter to the end who refused to yield.

When eventually she slowed enough for him to jump off and soothe her, as she circled him in confusion, her hoof was essentially hanging uselessly. All those watching were in horror, despite the vets arriving incredibly quickly to the scene, and loading her into a horse ambulance that went straight to the operating theatre to try to rescue her. One of those vets, Dr Manuel Gillman, had ironically only commented earlier that day after the compulsory inspection of the two horses that Ruffian was 'the finest anatomical specimen I've examined in 20 years as an NYRA vet'. Meanwhile, at the other end of the track, Foolish Pleasure came home on his own but, in an echo of Bernborough's last race, all eyes were elsewhere, the stunned silence of the crowd only punctuated by sobs.

Heartbreakingly, the news that followed the next day was even worse. After many hours of surgery, as the anaesthetic had worn off, and despite the efforts of the staff to calm her, a confused and terrified Ruffian had thrashed wildly on her side, spinning in circles, and smashing her plaster cast against her left elbow, leaving it like a piece of smashed ice. With her right foreleg also now rebroken in the commotion, the vets were left with no choice but to humanely euthanise her.

PUNCH A HOLE IN THE WIND

It was a brutal, sorrowful end to a life that had delivered so much, but promised to deliver even more. Ruffian was buried in the infield of Belmont Park with her head, poignantly, facing the finish line. Countless books were written about her, and later a movie, such was the impact that she had had on those who saw her. At the end of the century, *Sports Illustrated* compiled a list of the top 100 US female athletes of the century, and there sits Ruffian amongst the other legends, in splendid isolation as the only non-human.

Match races, mercifully, have become a thing of the past, spurred by the haunting vision of Ruffian's final few hours. I choose not to watch that race again. Instead, many of Ruffian's sensational victories are there to be admired online. Let those sublime moments, instead, be the true legacy of this scintillating filly.

Vasquez summed her up most poignantly: 'She was like Marilyn Monroe: there was everyone else. And then there was her.'

FACTFILE

Description: **Dark Bay Filly**
Size: **16.2 hands**
Dates: **1972-75**
Racing seasons: **1974-75**
Where were they trained?: **USA**
Trainer: **Frank Whiteley Jr**
Owner: **Stuart and Barbara Janney**
Jockey: **Jacinto Vasquez, Vince Bracciale**

Sire: **Reviewer**
Dam: **Shenanigans**
Damsire: **Native Dancer**
Record: **11: 10-0-0 (1 DNF)**
Most impressive victory: **Mother Goose Stakes 1975**
Nickname: **Queen of the Century, Black Terror, Sofie the Sofa**

SEATTLE SLEW

Seattle Slew – 'The People's Horse' – helps himself to a treat prior to winning the Kentucky Derby at Churchill Downs, May 1977.

Almost everyone – whether they choose to admit it, or whether it's simply a guilty pleasure – enjoys a good soap opera: the exaggerated emotions, the unlikely plot lines, the cliffhangers. The world of horseracing has had its fair share, but perhaps none as up and down as that revolving around Seattle Slew, who had a dollop of Cinderella thrown in for good measure. At one stage it almost felt like he was more of a commodity than a racehorse. But racehorse he certainly was, and in the golden years of 1970s US horseracing, he was unquestionably as good as any.

There were no aristocratic genes and millionaires in his story – at least, not at first. Two couples, Veterinarian Jim and Sally Hill from the swamps, or 'slews', of Florida, and Karen and Mickey Taylor from Seattle, found him at the Kentucky yearling sales – outsized, with a stumpy tail and a right forefoot that twisted outward from the knee down – yet Jim Hill on a whim pointed and said, 'Buy that one.' They fell in love with him and stretched their budget to $17,500 to secure him.

By Bold Reasoning out of My Charmer, he was sent to train with Billy Turner and quickly stood out – for good and bad reasons: ultra determined and quietly dominant, his messed up foot meant that he ran in a strange, gangly, splay-legged way, occasionally tripping over himself, earning himself the nickname Baby Huey after the duckling cartoon character. The latter displayed utter clumsiness, like Seattle Slew, but also unmistakeable idiocy too, which Slew in fairness did not.

PUNCH A HOLE IN THE WIND

Minor niggles initially kept him off the track while other two-year-olds made their name and won some big races. However, jockey Jean Cruguet, who would partner Slew through much of his career, was already telling fellow riders that there was a juvenile he had been riding out who would come out and blitz them all. They didn't pay much attention.

Yet when sent to the course three times as a two-year-old, he defied expectations, blitzing all-comers by increasing distances. His Grade 2 victory in the Champagne stakes by nearly ten lengths was the fastest mile ever run by a two-year-old in the US – a staggering 1min 34.4secs. The Hills and Taylors had accidentally found themselves a champion.

The brilliant form continued at three, where he had three warm-up races before trying for the Triple Crown. A rugged 16-hand colt, he took each as he pleased. Still clumsy looking when he ran, he had nevertheless filled out and had a progressively saggy back, not unlike Man O'War. It was now that Slewmania started in earnest, with the underdog colt in Everyman ownership paying lip service to the supposed sport of kings, and the public couldn't get enough. Even so, he sweated profusely before the Kentucky Derby, a situation not helped by fans seeking to pull hairs out of his tail as mementoes. Accompanied to the post as usual by the calming presence of a piebald stable pony called Steamboat, he still stumbled out of the gate, but regular Cruguet steered him skilfully and assertively through the field so that he led by the first turn and never looked back.

The Preakness at Pimlico proved easier, and he won in one of the fastest times ever for the race, and definitely the fastest opening mile in its history. That said, the owners – now known, together with Turner and Cruguet, as the 'Slew Crew' – were a little precious in keeping him away from the enthusiastic public at the course, a fact not lost by the more merciless members of the racing press who appeared, perhaps, jealous at the fortune of these 'amateur' owners. This escalated further by the time the Belmont Stakes arrived, with The Slew deliberately arriving 20 minutes late to the paddock, incurring a $200 fine, so minimising the chances of pre-race jitteriness. It worked, with a stunning four-length victory ensuring the Seattle Slew was the first horse ever to win the Triple Crown undefeated, as well as the first to have been sold at auction. The public couldn't get enough; the press instead chose, bizarrely, to round on jockey Cruguet even though he had never lost on the horse, and Turner was convinced that he was the perfect match for him.

But Slewmania now went into overdrive and it was here, at the horse's peak of greatness, that the soap opera took a new turn. With *Star Wars* proving that summer that merchandising could make a fortune when marketed right, The Slew Crew hired an advertising agency, made flak jackets, T-Shirts, and produced TV commercials for Xerox X-ray machines with their edgy colt, who needed to be tranquilised first. Despite his racecourse exertions and off-track schedule, a $300,000 purse for the Swaps Stakes lured the owners over to Hollywood Park, against Turner's wishes. Tranquilised again for the journey, the inevitable happened. A shattered and dopey Slew crawled home in fourth, 16 lengths behind J.O. Tobin. It was his only race out of the money.

With emotions sky-high, the owners needed a scapegoat, and rounded, of all people, on Turner, whose heavy drinking was well known. He was replaced later in the year by Doug Peterson, but now things took yet another turn as within weeks of Peterson taking charge the Slew was half-dead with colitis. He completely went off his food and would sweat uncontrollably for hours on end. He could barely stand, and often collapsed in his barn. Hill diagnosed a viral infection and feared Slew might die. It was touch-and-go, yet he pulled through, and an autumn 1978 campaign was planned. As he was recovering, the Taylors and Hills sold 50 per cent of their dream horse to a syndicate for $6 million.

The Slew – now sometimes referred to simply as 'The People's Horse' – returned successfully in a couple of low-key races before just being edged out by Dr Patches in the Paterson Handicap. Cruguet hinted strongly in post-race interviews that the Slew had been left a gallop or two short in training. Paterson took umbrage and sensationally sacked Cruguet, replacing him with Angel Cordero Jr. Another member of the Slew Crew was gone.

But the Slew wasn't done. He next took on Affirmed, that year's Triple Crown winner – the first time that two Triple Crown winners had ever met – in the Marlboro Cup over nine furlongs. The younger horse was the favourite, but The Slew unleashed his odd-looking stride in the home stretch in devastating style and won by over three lengths in near world-record time. After a follow-up win over Exceller in the Woodward Stakes, the Slew then ran possibly his greatest-ever race … in defeat. In the Jockey Club Gold Cup, both Affirmed and Exceller returned. But halfway through, as the two Triple Crown winners posted suicidal sections, Affirmed's saddle slipped and jockey Steve Cauthen could barely hang on. Bill Shoemaker on Exceller was 20 lengths adrift, but pacing much more steadily, and gradually ate into the Slew's lead until the home stretch where, despite his monstrous exertions early on, the Slew displayed astonishing courage and refused to yield. Exceller won it by a nose, but the Slew's sky-high reputation only grew.

PUNCH A HOLE IN THE WIND

One more commanding victory in the Stuyvesant Handicap and the great horse was retired, winning his third Horse of the Year award. And truly he was a star; the image of a horse that you can see on many licence plates in Kentucky is specifically that of The Slew.

He was expected to be a failure at stud, but again confounded the naysayers by becoming one of the US's most valuable and successful stallions. His dam, My Charmer, meanwhile, proved that Seattle Slew was no fluke and later produced Lomond, the English 2,000 Guineas winner, as well as Seattle Dancer, the most expensive yearling ever sold at public auction. That $17,500 initial outlay for The Slew really had been the steal of the decade. But as Taylor had once related, 'You don't go out and buy a horse like that. You don't go out and breed it. You just look up and there he is.' In a final, inevitable twist of the soap opera, in 1992 The Hills and Taylors had something of a falling out, with the latter buying out the former's remaining quarter share. There was never a dull moment with Seattle Slew.

Baby Huey never lost his idiosyncrasies: he was obsessed with grey mares, but was indifferent to bay and chestnut ones. He died on 7 May 2002, poignantly 25 years to the day after his Derby victory. But then The Slew always knew how to tell a good story.

FACTFILE

Description: Brown Colt
Size: 16.05 hands
Dates: 1974-2002
Racing seasons: 1976-78
Where were they trained?: USA
Trainer: Bill Turner, Doug Peterson
Owner: Karen and Mickey Taylor and Jim and Sally Hill

Jockey: Jean Cruguet, Angel Cordero Jr
Sire: Bold Reasoning
Dam: My Charmer
Damsire: Poker
Record: 17: 14-2-0
Most impressive victory: Marlboro Cup 1978
Nickname: The Slew, Baby Huey, The People's Horse

ALLEGED

Almost by accident, Alleged stole the limelight in the late 1970s, winning consecutive Prix de l'Arc de Triomphes in 1977 and 1978.

There must be something about dual Arc winners and jockey confidence. Just as Jacques Doyasbere never contemplated losing on Tantieme in the early '50s, so Lester Piggott displayed, during Alleged's fabulous career, all the behaviours that made him both utterly infuriating and an out-and-out genius. Still, it was just as well that Alleged was the kind of horse who would do exactly what you asked him to and would do it brilliantly. Almost by accident, he stole the limelight in the late '70s from other pretenders to the European throne.

Yet Europe was never his original target. Bred in the US as a son of Hoist the Flag and therefore great-grandson of Ribot, he was snapped up as a yearling for $34,000 in the Keeneland sales. Six months later he was sent back to the sales, where he was bought for $175,000 – a rather tidy profit – by representatives of English billionaire Robert Sangster, who was keen to run him in California. Soon, though, it became clear that the horse's knees and forelegs were rather suspect and racing in the usually firm California dirt was likely a recipe for disaster, and thus the two-year-old – now called Alleged, and part-owned by Robert Fluor – was sent to Ireland.

PUNCH A HOLE IN THE WIND

There he was trained by the indomitable Vincent O'Brien, who had already had a stream of champions come and go through his stable doors at Ballydoyle. It's fair to say that Alleged's start was underwhelming. One racing journalist recalled, 'No one took a great deal of notice. He was weak, backward, unfurnished and rather plain.' Further, there was an embarrassment of riches in the stable at Ballydoyle, so Alleged rather drifted into the background. But the team patiently plugged away at him, finally getting him ready for his first outing right at the end of his two-year-old season at a seven-furlong maiden at The Curragh. There was major surprise when, sporting Fluor's silks, he hacked up by eight lengths.

Yet as winter turned to spring, still he didn't thrill connections. Being seemingly slow to come to hand, he still won the Ballydoyle Stakes and then the Royal Whip Stakes over a mile and half. In the latter, so low were expectations that he started at 33-1, and had no trouble, with Paedar Matthews on board, in beating his stablemate and favourite Valinsky, the chosen ride of stable jockey Lester Piggott. The latter was not amused, although with his enigmatic face – once memorably described as resembling a well-kept grave – it was always hard to tell. They now realised that Alleged had plenty of ability, but the team had instead been priming another Sangster-owned stablemate, The Minstrel, to be their poster horse for the year. And the Minstrel didn't disappoint, taking in the Epsom Derby, The Irish Derby and the King George and Queen Elizabeth Stakes during the summer, won each time in close, very scrappy races.

Alleged then won the Gallinule Stakes, again showing that, for a colt who was supposedly 'backward', he was finding it enormously easy to win Group 2 races. By late summer, there was no pretence anymore, as Alleged took in the Great Voltigeur Stakes at York and cantered home seven lengths clear of Hot Grove, Classic Example and others – horses which The Minstrel had been all out to beat in his two Derbies. It was dawning on some folk that the best three-year-old running in Europe might not be The Minstrel after all. O'Brien therefore planned an autumn campaign for his fast-improving colt, culminating with a tilt at the Arc in October, but starting with the St Leger at Doncaster.

The St Leger proved not to be Piggott's finest hour. Up against him was the Queen's filly Dunfermline, who had won the Epsom Oaks to immense national joy during the Queen's Silver Jubilee year. Further, there were two pacemakers to keep the race honest. When they suddenly 'died' four furlongs out, Piggott was exposed at the front, a long way from home, and effectively acted as an easy target for Willie Carson on Dunfermline. The filly took her chance and crept past Alleged for a length-and-a-half victory. It was Alleged's first – and as it transpired, only – defeat.

ALLEGED

Sangster was livid, saying later, 'Lester was told to hold Alleged up, but he kicked on early in the home straight and acted like a pacemaker for Dunfermline. Vincent was so devastated he dropped his binoculars before the finish.' Yet it was well known that Piggott gave lip service when following instructions, once stating: 'A good jockey doesn't need orders and a bad jockey couldn't carry them out anyway, so it's best not to give them any.' Quite the team player was Piggott. Either way, a disheartened Fluor sold his share back, meaning that Alleged would now run exclusively in the Sangster colours.

In the build-up to the St Leger, Piggott had been asked if he thought he'd win, to which he nonchalantly replied, 'I don't know but I'll win the Prix de l'Arc de Triomphe.' Three weeks later, and the greater prize in Paris indeed beckoned. The huge, top-class field of 26 was a considerable mountain to climb for a horse that had hitherto – by accident rather than design – not won a Group 1, but O'Brien and Sangster were clear that this time Alleged should definitely be held up to play to his strengths. Piggott, never one to be kept awake late at night weighed down by the burden of self-doubt, did what he so often did and completely ignored them. When the field re-emerged on the back straight from behind the Petit Bois, there was Piggott's instantly recognisable backside perched on Alleged right at the front of the field, looking for all the world like a sitting duck. One assumes that this time O'Brien wasn't just dropping his binoculars but throwing them against the wall.

But 'The Long Fellow' knew what he was doing: keeping out of trouble, slowing things down, dictating the pace to stop it becoming muddled and saving his horse for a home straight sprint. And it all fell into place, with Alleged's crucial acceleration meaning none of the other quality horses got within two lengths of him, with Dunfermline a distant fourth. The jockey allowed himself a typically eldritch smile on returning to the enclosure. All was forgiven, and Alleged topped the inaugural international rankings, notably ahead of The Minstrel. Unlike his stablemate, he would be kept in training.

But 1978 proved to be immensely frustrating for him and his connections. It started promisingly enough, with Alleged ready to take in another Royal Whip Stakes at the Curragh in May. But the ground was rock solid and, although Alleged won easily, he had badly jarred those suspect knees of his; only his considerable class had seen him through. Just as he was recovering, disaster struck again, this time in the form of a virus that swept through O'Brien's yard, laying low pretty much his entire string, Alleged included. The summer was a complete write-off, and Alleged now faced a race against time to get him ready for a second tilt at the Arc.

PUNCH A HOLE IN THE WIND

O'Brien – the quintessential Irish horse whisperer – cannily handled his colt back to fitness as autumn approached, and knew that Alleged badly needed a warm-up race. They chose the ten-furlong Prix du Prince d'Orange at Longchamp, with relatively low expectations. Alleged – as he had throughout his career – proved everyone wrong again, storming home to win in course-record time, on ground that wasn't that firm. Come the second Arc, O'Brien and Sangster – huge figures in global racing and who, together with Coolmore Stud godfather John Magnier were known as 'The Brethren' – realised that it was now pointless to give Piggott riding instructions. True to form, and despite similar ground, field size and field quality, Piggott rode Alleged entirely differently to the year before, choosing instead to hang in behind the leaders and sprint past in the straight. Again – irritatingly – he was proved right, with Alleged an easy two-length victor over top mare Trillion, ridden by Bill Shoemaker. Alleged's season was another success, despite all that had been thrown at it. He finished the year even more highly rated in the rankings than the year before, and was syndicated to stud in Kentucky for a huge $13 million.

As a stallion, Alleged was a success, almost always imparting considerable stamina on his progeny – indeed, he was the grandsire of not one but two Aintree Grand National winners. Due to certain dominant genes, almost all his offspring were bay or brown, and never chestnut. But what most people remember from his stud days was how awful an individual he became. Just like his great-grandfather Ribot, he was obnoxious in the extreme: the words his handlers most commonly used to describe him were 'bad-tempered', 'dangerous' and 'savage' – and this from the people who liked him. He also grew to hate cold weather. But European visitors to Walmac International Stud forgave him, as they knew that winning one Arc was difficult enough, but winning two meant immortality.

FACTFILE

Description: Bay Colt
Size: 16.1 hands
Dates: 1974-2000
Racing seasons: 1977-78
Where were they trained?: Ireland
Trainer: Vincent O'Brien
Owner: Robert Sangster
Jockey: Lester Piggott, Paedar Matthews
Sire: Hoist The Flag
Dam: Princess Pout
Damsire: Prince John
Record: 10: 9-1-0
Most impressive victory: Prix de l'Arc de Triomphe 1978

AFFIRMED

Local boy Steve Cauthen drives Affirmed to victory in the Kentucky Derby, May 1978.

Salt and Pepper. Tom and Jerry. Gin and Tonic. Affirmed and Alydar. Some things must – simply *must* – be said as part of a pair. These two rivals lit up the US racing scene in the late '70s and, like it or not, you found yourself inexorably drawn into one camp or the other. Affirmed, though, proved on the racecourse that he was the better horse, even if it wasn't by much. More tellingly, he wasn't just talented but in possession of an indomitable will to win.

Affirmed was Florida-born, bred and owned by financier Louis Wolfson and his wife Patrice. Hugely wealthy, Wolfson had still had brushes with the law – including imprisonment, for securities violations, which were 'affirmed on appeal'. Canny to the last, he never confirmed, one way or the other, if this had provided the origin of his slightly undersized chestnut colt's name. It certainly had no connection to either his sire Exclusive Native or dam Won't Tell You, neither of whom could be called blue-blooded.

All connections agreed that Affirmed possessed not only an uncommon intelligence but an almost mystical ability to connect with humans. Patrice Wolfson recalled, '… there was something about his personality that was different. He'd work his way through the other foals to come up to me. And all through his racing career he loved to put his head in my arms when we'd come by his stall.' Even in his later years at stud, his handler recounted how '… he had a distinct and profound personality and was very understanding. He was like a friend in that you really felt like you could relate to him.'

PUNCH A HOLE IN THE WIND

He matured early too. A mix-up during some early training gallops saw him run a stiff training run against a multiple-winning older horse called Sparkling Native, and beating him. It was only after they realised that it was 'the baby' that they had been accidentally running that hearts fluttered a bit as to his potential, and Wolfson sent him to his retained trainer Laz Barrera in California. Soon enough, Affirmed won his first two-year-old race in May over five-and-a-half furlongs from pillar to post by nearly five lengths at Belmont. There was some excitement, but already the jungle drums had picked up that an as-yet unraced juvenile at Calumet Farm was burning up the gallops. His name was Alydar.

The following month, in the Youthful Stakes at the same track, they met for the first time – and most certainly not the last. This time Affirmed – ridden again by Angel Cordero Jr – came from behind, but the result was the same as his first race – an easy victory. Alydar, the 9-5 favourite, ran green and finished fifth. In July, however, he turned the tables in the Great American Stakes, again at Belmont. Barrera next sent his colt to California, where he crushed his opposition by seven lengths in the Hollywood Juvenile Championship. Back out East at Saratoga, Barrera chose a new jockey to partner his colt, an equally exciting 17-year-old sensation called Steve Cauthen, already known as the Kentucky Kid. It would be a partnership that clicked from the off, with the teenager as bowled over by the horse's human touch as others had been. 'My relationship with him was on his back and when I was up there, I knew he knew me,' Cauthen asserted later. 'He was a super intelligent horse, smart and willing.'

He trounced the field in Saratoga, returning there the following week to win the Grade 1 Hopeful Stakes, defeating Alydar by half a length. In the seven-furlong Futurity Stakes at Belmont a fortnight later, in an incredible duel, Alydar got to within a nose, with Affirmed's bottomless courage against the bigger colt just winning the day. It was a great spectacle, yet it wouldn't even be the best race that the two would have at Belmont. They exchanged one more victory each, again at top level, to finish their gruelling juvenile season with Affirmed 4-2 up, and claiming the two-year-old of the year as a consequence.

Yet that season ended up being no more than an amuse-bouche for what would happen during their Classic year. Wintering in California and growing a little, all Affirmed got in return was rain, which left him behind in gallops and races. Barrera eventually found a warm up before Affirmed took in the Santa Anita Derby and the Hollywood Derby, winning both easily, and by eight lengths at Santa Anita. The stage was set therefore for a Triple Crown like no other. At Churchill Downs, despite their head-to-head record, punters again sided with Alydar. Off a furious pace, Cauthen kept Affirmed handy, whilst Alydar was slow to start. With Affirmed two lengths clear throughout the home stretch, his rival came too late, and was still a length and half behind by the post.

Alydar got closer in the Preakness, but Affirmed dictated the pace from two furlongs in, helped by having Cauthen – one of the greatest-ever judges of pace – sitting on his back. Alydar was only a neck behind at the death after being closer to the pace. It was a fantastic race, yet paled when sat next to the Belmont. English trainer George Lambton once wrote that, 'About the best thing in racing is when two good horses single themselves out from the rest of the field and have a long drawn-out struggle'. Although this race happened 33 years after his death, no one could describe it better. It would be as memorable as Secretariat's five years earlier, but for vastly different reasons.

After a steady first half-mile, the two horses locked horns thereafter for a full mile, piling on the speed and with no other colt within neighing distance. The home stretch seemed to go on forever with, it seemed, each horse taking turns to literally inch ahead before the other, stung with pride, fought back. Despite being pinned hard against the rail, Affirmed it was who, with Cauthen urging him on his left side for the very first time, stuck no more than his nose in front when they flew past the post.

The familiar dichotomy of triumph for one and heartbreak for the other ensued. Cauthen of course was elated: 'I can't think of any moment that gave me any more thrill.' He also called it the 'Greatest Triple Crown race of all time', and no one could proffer an alternative. They met again – for a final time – in the Travers Stakes where Affirmed – with Laffit Pincay substituting for the injured Cauthen – cut up Alydar on the back stretch, meaning that, despite finishing first, he was disqualified, with Alydar earning something of a Pyrrhic victory. Final honours were therefore 7-3 in Affirmed's favour. Alydar was truly outstanding. Affirmed was just a bit better.

But Affirmed was far from finished. His next race, the Marlboro Cup, made history as two Triple Crown champions met for the first time. The great Settle Slew came out on top, although it was as much a race that Angel Cordero won as Affirmed lost. Riding the older horse, Cordero snuck three lengths at the start, and that was what separated them at the end. There was then frustration in the Jockey Club Gold Cup when the two champions met again, only for Affirmed's saddle to slip, with Cauthen working miracles simply not to fall. It was the only time he would finish out of the money. Despite the deflating finish to the year, he was a deserving winner of the Champion three-year-old honours.

It is arguable that Affirmed became an even better horse at four, although the start of the year was misleading. Coming placed in two Grade 2s at Santa Anita, Barrera blamed Cauthen's lack of confidence, and handed the ride to Laffit Pincay. Cauthen soon moved to England to become one of the stars of the 1980s, riding champion after champion, but was still adamant years later that Affirmed was his best-ever ride.

PUNCH A HOLE IN THE WIND

Affirmed, meanwhile, never lost again. Running almost exclusively in Grade 1s, he won the Charles H. Strub Stakes by ten lengths before returning for the Santa Anita Handicap and breaking the ten-furlong track record. He gave away lumps of weight in the Californian Stakes and Hollywood Gold Cup, but still found a way to win, running the latter in a blistering 1min 58.4secs. He finished in the Jockey Club Gold Cup, defeating his heir apparent Spectacular Bid in the process – the last time that champion would ever taste defeat. Affirmed had nothing else to prove and was syndicated to stud for a then record of $14.4 million, having become the first horse to win $2 million.

Alydar, in the minds of many, has the dubious distinction of possibly being the best horse in the modern era who could not be given that slippery, nebulous yet inspirational title of 'champion'. Perhaps only Reliance, fabulously unbeaten until conquered by Sea-Bird in that unforgettable 1965 Arc, can lay equal claim. 'A champion in any other year' is a descriptor that is as frustrating a complement as can be imagined; the only thing that had really defeated him was the bad timing of his birth.

His revenge – such as it was – lay in the breeding shed, where Alydar proved to be the more successful sire. Affirmed wasn't a failure; it was more that, like Sea-Bird, Secretariat and other magnificent racers before him, the unsaid expectation – desperation, almost – was always that he would sire one as superb as himself. He started as a stallion at Spendthrift Farms but was later transferred to Calumet Farm. There, in a neighbouring paddock, would stand an old foe. His name was Alydar, and one can only speculate as to how these two would have interacted into their old age over the paddock fence. Affirmed then saw out his years at nearby Jonabell Farm, being humanely put down aged 26 years when his laminitis became unbearable.

It is testament to the embarrassment of riches that was 1970s US racing that, even after winning the Triple Crown, Wolfson wouldn't be drawn into discussions of Affirmed's greatness. 'I want to see him run at four before I call him great overall.'

By the time he was retired in late 1979, no one needed any more convincing.

FACTFILE

Description: Chestnut Colt
Size: 16.1 hands
Dates: 1975-2001
Racing seasons: 1977-79
Where were they trained?: USA
Trainer: Lazaro Barrera
Owner: Harbor View Farm

Jockey: Steve Cauthen, Laffit Pincay Jr, Angel Cordero
Sire: Exclusive Native
Dam: Won't Tell You
Damsire: Crafty Admiral
Record: 29: 22-5-1
Most impressive victory: Jockey Club Gold Cup 1979

KINGSTON TOWN

Doting trainer Tom Smith relaxes with Kingston Town at Rosehill, September 1981.

'Kingston Town can't win.'

Any keen follower of Australian racing will be aware of this immortal line uttered in the heat of the moment by commentator Bill Collins – nicknamed 'The Accurate One' – during the 1982 Cox Plate. In the immediate short-term, it was a glorious gaffe, as Kingston Town, somehow, *did* win that race – and Collins's passionate call in the home straight more than made up for his earlier assertion. In the long-term, it is even more inaccurate: Kingston Town most certainly *could* win, with great frequency and awesome power. He was unquestionably one of the greatest Australian horses of the last half-century.

Yet as with so many heroes of the turf, his ability was not immediately apparent. Owned and bred by merchant banker David Hains, Kingston Town came into being because of Hains's experiment to match an Australian sire, most of whom were renowned for their speed, with a European mare, many of whom had a pedigree that screamed stamina. In this case, they were no ordinary mares, but ones brought over from the legendary Dormello Stud in Italy set up and run with such glory by the genius behind Ribot and Nearco, the late Federico Tesio. Thus the mare Ada Hunter, a granddaughter of Ribot, had a liaison with future Australian champion sire Bletchingly and 11 months later along came Kingston Town.

Initially, this nearly black yearling didn't do much to impress Hains visually, so he was sent to the sales in Flemington. Hains had a modest reserve price of AUS$8,000 on him, but everyone else thought as little of him as his breeder, and with no suitable bidders, he came home and Hains decided to keep him. As serendipity goes, it doesn't come much purer. Hains also knew where to put him in training: the stables of Tommy Smith, on the outskirts of Sydney. Smith, who had had the honour of training the great Tulloch 20 years before, and who had been leading trainer in Sydney *every single year* since 1953, was initially frustrated: 'When the youngster first came into the stable he was a holy terror. He would walk in his box and then try to climb up the wall, roaring all the time. He had speed but he just refused to go one yard.' Separately, one day, the young horse was being treated for a cut when he chose to bolt from his handler and ran straight into a wire fence, leaving him with a prominent and permanent scar on his face. He was quite the handful.

In March 1979 Smith finally tried out his two-year-old, in a low-key handicap at Sydney's Canterbury Park. Some legends are born straight away. Not in this case; Kingston Town was last out of the gate, last round the turn, and last at the finish post. His jockey that day was Mal Johnston, son of a truck driver, a recent champion apprentice, and a hit with the crowds, who had also done a short spell with Ian Balding in England. He was so small that he could only groom a horse by standing on a bucket. Johnston sensed – *knew* – that the horse was better than this, but coupled with his behaviours at home, Johnston and Smith convinced Hains that gelding the colt was the only option to improve him. Hains acceded, and the unkindest cut of all – as with Kelso – proved to be a most inspired one as well.

KINGSTON TOWN

Returning to the track three months later, focussed and stronger, Kingston Town ran his next races at distances between six and ten furlongs and proceeded to crush all his rivals, having developed – or perhaps finally choosing to reveal – an absolutely devastating turn of foot. This streak culminated in the Group 1 Spring Champion Stakes. It was abruptly halted, however, as soon as he went to Victoria for his next three races where, despite coming placed, it was clear to all what was happening: whilst the handsome black gelding loved turning right on the New South Wales (NSW) tracks, he was uncomfortable turning left on the Victoria tracks. Although imperious in Sydney, he wasn't down south, with race caller Collins describing his early performances in Victoria as though, '… he was lurching round Melbourne courses like a good-natured drunk'. Smith was happy to tell anyone who would listen that he was lengths better running one way than the other.

To prove his point, Smith next ran Kingston Town for 11 straight races only on the clockwise tracks of NSW and Queensland, and the powerful gelding won every single one. There was an eerie feeling of déjà-vu for anyone watching these. Johnston on Kingston Town would wait until the final bend every time before flicking his reins, whereby Kingston Town would take off with a sudden burst of speed, displaying an incredibly rapid stride cadence perhaps matched only later by Winx. Nor were these races all the same distance; to demonstrate his supreme versatility – and ultimately confirm the shrewdness of Hain's breeding logic – Kingston Town was winning over all distances between six and 16 furlongs, very often in Group 1 company, and including the AJC and Queensland Derbies. He was now known simply as The King, with Johnston reflecting simply, 'He is so relaxed. That is the secret of his greatness.' Smith, meanwhile, was beginning to talk about him in the same breath as Tulloch.

Yet with so many big weight-for-age races in Victoria, the urge to send him back there was overwhelming. Now aged four, Kingston Town therefore ran in the Caulfield Stakes and Caulfield Cup where again he ran well – coming second and third respectively – but clearly not to his best. Far from disheartened, Smith and Hains decided to give the big one – the Cox Plate at Moonee Valley – a go. This time, he absolutely trounced his rivals by five lengths, with connections believing not that it was going left-handed that was putting him off so much as specifically Caulfield racetrack that was spooking him. This blistering victory started another long winning streak of eight races over his four-year-old and five-year-old seasons, including the following year's Cox Plate. Smith throughout knew that his charge's front legs were more suspect than they seemed, so now only campaigned him in the late southern hemisphere winter and spring, allowing him a longer break between seasons.

Once again, it took a Victoria track to break the spell, namely Flemington for the Group 1 LKS Mackinnon Stakes, where Kingston Town still finished second. It was more of an experiment than anything that, a mere four days later, he turned out for the Melbourne Cup, having missed the previous year's due to sore legs. It was one race too many that season, with a visibly exhausted Kingston Town plodding around at the back of the field throughout.

Returning the following season as a six-year-old, Kingston Town started with what was now his traditional (third consecutive) Warwick Stakes victory. This marked a remarkable and unprecedented 21st consecutive victory on a Sydney track. That bubble then burst in the Chelmsford Stakes a fortnight later when Johnston, in what was not his finest hour, got boxed in on the rail for far too long, giving no time or space for Kingston Town to unleash his not-so-secret weapon. Further, Johnston collected a riding ban that day – his 26th in all – meaning Peter Cook would be in the seat for the Spring Festival races in Melbourne. But as one door closed, another door opened, with a final go at winning at Caulfield racetrack memorably succeeding with victory in the Caulfield Stakes.

A third trip to the Cox Plate ensued, but no horse had ever won it three times. Things weren't helped by Smith's instructions to Cook to keep the horse handy being completely compromised by Kingston Town taking an age to leave the stalls and get up to racing speed. Cook had to smack him a couple of times to give him even a half chance of keeping in touch with the other 13 horses. He kept changing his legs, and then got boxed in. It was as inauspicious a first three-quarters of a race as one could conceive. And yet …

Champions, more often than not, don't give up, even if commentators do. Collins emitted those immortal lines so confidently with barely two furlongs to go, which seemed to be the trigger for Kingston Town to do what he did best: unleash. First the camera zooms in to the two fighting out the finish, yet soon enough it pans out again, as Kingston Town, out of the clouds, storms wide to take his opponents out, ultimately taking an arguably cosy three-quarter length win. It was joyous, it was epic. It was horseracing. His record of three consecutive Cox Plates stood until the days of the mighty Winx.

Connections simply couldn't resist trying a final time for the Melbourne Cup, just one week later, and oh how close they came. With Johnston back in the saddle, and Kingston Town beautifully placed throughout, they went for glory, and were clear until the final ten yards when Gurner's Lane – a true two-mile stayer, carrying less weight – nicked him at the line. It was a glorious failure, not that this wonderful animal had anything left to prove. He finished off with a rare expedition out west to Perth and the Group 1 Western Mail Classic. He won well, and the race would soon be named after him. With his legs playing havoc again, happy retirement beckoned. Although not quite. First an attempt was made to send him to the US to see if the vets trying new techniques could rescue them from crumbling. Nine months of trying proved fruitless, and he was returned to finally see out his days in the paddock. He was only 15 when his playful antics with his paddock mate resulted in an injury that couldn't be fixed and he was put down.

Despite never running outside Australia, Kingston Town achieved ratings in the international system that put him at the pinnacle of racers from his country over the last few decades. And when you watch those electrifying bursts of speed that he displayed time and again to dispel his rivals with such disdain, it's really not hard to see why.

FACTFILE

Description: **Black Gelding**
Size: **16.1 hands**
Dates: **1976-91**
Racing seasons: **1979-82**
Where were they trained?: **Australia**
Trainer: **Tommy Smith**
Owner: **David Hains, G Monsborough**
Jockey: **Malcolm Johnston, Wayne Treloar, Roy Higgins, John Duggan, Ron Quinton, Peter Cook**
Sire: **Bletchingly**
Dam: **Ada Hunter**
Damsire: **Andrea Mantegna**
Record: **41: 30-5-2**
Most impressive victory: **Cox Plate 1980**
Nickname: **The King**

SPECTACULAR BID

Spectacular Bid (Willie Shoemaker) breaks another track record, this time at Delaware Park, August 1979.

Decades come and decades go, but with hindsight – rose-tinted or otherwise – we can be confident in saying that the 1970s truly were a golden age of US horseracing, with timeless champion after timeless champion gracing their numerous tracks, and displaying much evidence to suggest that the North American breeding programme and bloodlines had now overtaken the Europeans. Finishing off the decade in style was Spectacular Bid, an unassuming-looking colt who was anything but unassuming when he ran.

By the decent stakes winner Bold Bidder out of Spectacular, Spectacular Bid was bought as a yearling for $37,000 at the Keeneland sales by Harry Meyerhoff on behalf of his Hawksworth Farm in Maryland, and sent to the yard of the never-shy Grover 'Bud' Delp. Delp saw plenty of mileage in his charge and sent him out nine times as a two-year-old, usually ridden by teenager Ronnie Franklin. The highlight was winning the Laurel Futurity over eight and a half furlongs in a track record – very rare for an ever-maturing two-year-old. His fourth place in the Tyro Stakes at Monmouth Park in hideously sloppy conditions was the only time he ever finished out of the top three, and he was clear champion two-year-old.

Jockey Franklin, at only 4ft 7in, had predictably been picked on at school but had learned to toughen up, meaning he displayed disproportionate strength. Delp noticed this, encouraging the teenager to take up riding, and mentored

SPECTACULAR BID

him. Franklin only rode his first race early during Spectacular Bid's first season. He was green, but no one doubted his self-confidence or his work ethic, only his occasional bouts of anger.

The Bid – an unusual looking grey in that he looked silver if the sun caught his back but almost black when caked in sweat after a run – hit the ground running at three, with Delp amazingly squeezing in five races, three at Grade 1, before his Triple Crown bid, including the Florida Derby and Blue Grass. In the former he overcame all sorts of traffic problems which an angry Delp placed squarely at Franklin's feet, but he stuck by him nonetheless. The Bid passed each test with flying colours, with each race slightly longer than the last to prepare him for the ten furlongs of the Kentucky Derby. Delp, meanwhile, was not doing much to win the crowds over to his horse, boasting even at this stage that Spectacular Bid was the greatest horse ever to look through a bridle. For a racing public that had just seen three Triple Crown winners in six years, it didn't land well.

Even so, he started as 5-3 on favourite, with Delp – allergic, it seems, to humility – going to punters beforehand and shouting 'Go bet! Go bet!' Sure enough, The Bid confirmed his superiority over his rivals by despatching General Assembly by just shy of three lengths. Intriguingly, it would be the last time that the favourite would win the Run for the Roses in the 20th century.

Starting at a prohibitive 10-1 on, the Preakness proved even more decisive, where the easy-going colt's burst from the back saw him crush the opposition by five and a half lengths in one of the fastest times ever for the race, despite Franklin taking him incredibly wide for much of it – which he blamed on fellow jockey Angel Cordero Jr, with whom some bad blood was developing – and easing before the line. Regardless, the uber-talented horse was more than living up to his name. Franklin and Cordero meanwhile got into full-blown fisticuffs just two weeks later, when they were called in by the stewards to cool down, then left the room and did it all over again.

Just a year after Affirmed and two after Seattle Slew, the stage was all set for the Belmont Stakes and the coronation of the third successive Triple Crown winner. Even Franklin got in on the confident act, claiming that victory 'was a cinch'. Yet the records will show that he didn't win. Sweating and edgy before the off, but nevertheless leading from early on in Belmont's interminable back stretch, The Bid tired, was reeled in and cast aside by Coastal in the home stretch and then collared by Golden Act at the death. Both were horses that he regularly beat or would regularly beat, and the controversy still rages as to why and how he lost.

Three excuses did the rounds. Delp's was nothing less random than a safety pin which his champion had allegedly stepped on that morning – yet he had shown no sign of lameness in the run-up to the race, although he was sore the following day. There were suggestions too that he simply didn't stay 12 furlongs, and seeing as his only subsequent defeat would also be over that distance, it certainly had more merit.

But looking again at the race now, the most obvious reason is the one that all the racing analysts at the time instinctively believed: that Franklin – riding an utterly different race to the first two legs where he had dropped his mount well back – simply pushed Spectacular Bid too hard too soon, and unnecessarily so for a horse of unknown stamina, leaving the tank empty at the business end. There were strong suggestions that Delp had asked him to do so in order to 'do a Secretariat'. It was one of the great 'what might have beens' of US racing, and it ended poorly for Franklin, who both lost the ride and then, after a rapid descent into substance abuse, his jockey's licence.

The mount now went to US riding legend Bill Shoemaker, who rode him four more times that year, easily winning three – including a 17-length slaughter of his opponents in an allowance race at Delaware Park – and coming a fine second to Affirmed in the Jockey Club Gold Cup, showing again that he just didn't last home the mile and a half. He was never to lose again. Just as tellingly, in the Marlboro Cup back at Belmont, he trounced Coastal and Golden Act – the two horses who had beaten him in that final, infamous Triple Crown race.

But at four, as with so many racing legends, he found a way to get better still, cementing his place as an all-time great. He won every one of his nine races, sticking mainly to his unbeatable distance of nine or ten furlongs. Although he matched or beat the track record eight times in his career, it was in the Charles Strub Stakes at Santa Anita that he delivered his masterpiece. Off a blistering pace, he still found a way to accelerate and ran a mind-blowing 1min 57.8secs, a dirt world record that still stands to this day.

Crushing top-level victories continued around California and Arlington, often under top weight, and never getting anywhere near being beaten – as his regular starting price of 20-1 on would suggest. The final back-handed complement arrived for his swansong when literally not one horse was prepared to take him on in the Grade 1 Woodward Stakes. This hadn't happened for 32 years in a top-level race in the US, when Citation 'won' the Pimlico Special, and there has not been one since. That, as much as anything, summed up his stratospheric reputation. Shoemaker kidded that it was the race that he was most nervous of, as he would never hear the end of it if he fell off. More tellingly,

SPECTACULAR BID

for the jockey of such legends as Damascus, Swaps and Forego, Shoemaker was adamant that Spectacular Bid was the best he'd ever ridden. He was also the last US horse to be rated a champion at two, three and four.

A less-than-great career as a stallion ensued; he produced a good share of winners but expectations were sky-high, not least as he had been syndicated for a head-turning $22 million. Many of his progeny, for some reason, were very late maturers, which never helps in the impatient world of horseracing. He maintained a steady stream of visitors, though, and would always be willing to interact with them in exchange for his favourite food: a jelly doughnut.

When he finally passed away on 9 June 2003, he wouldn't have been aware that it was 24 years to the day since his infamous Belmont defeat. But he had proved his immense prowess so often since then that those excuses mattered less and less.

FACTFILE

Description: Grey Colt
Size: 16 hands
Dates: 1976–2003
Racing seasons: 1978–80
Where were they trained?: USA
Trainer: Grover 'Bud' Delp
Owner: Harry Meyerhoff/Hawksworth Farm
Jockey: Ron Franklin, Willie Shoemaker
Sire: Bold Bidder
Dam: Spectacular
Damsire: Promised Land
Record: 30: 26-2-1
Most impressive victory: Charles H Strub Stakes, 1980
Nickname: The Bid

SHERGAR

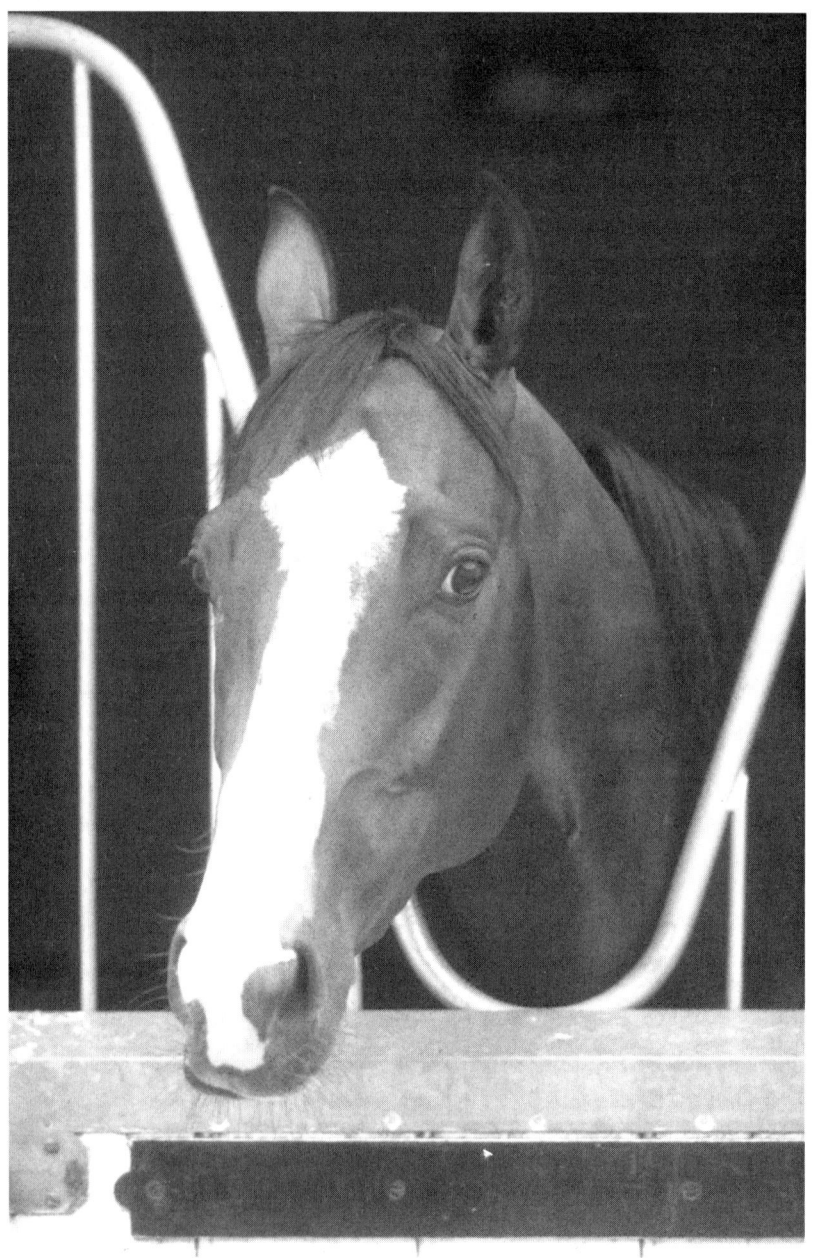

The ill-fated Shergar, seen here as a two-year-old at trainer Michael Stoute's stables in Newmarket, October 1980.

SHERGAR

The layperson will likely not know many of the names in this book, but depending on their age, you can be fairly sure that they will have heard of Shergar. It won't be for racing reasons, of course, but that shouldn't cloud the simple fact that, for the summer months of 1981, he showed that he was one of the most sublime racehorses to have ever graced the tracks of England.

Owned and bred by the Aga Khan, the son of Great Nephew was sent to Michael Stoute's impressive yard at Newmarket, soon becoming popular because of his fine temperament and instantly recognisable white blaze and matching four white socks. Ridden at two by Lester Piggott, he won his first race, the Kris Plate, at Newbury over a mile by two and a half lengths, displaying ample ability. Sent straight to Group 1 company thereafter, he was far from disgraced, coming second to Beldale Flutter in the Futurity Stakes at Doncaster, Piggott not having the smoothest of passages over the mile. But the colt clearly had bags of potential.

Shergar properly blossomed over the winter, packing on muscle, and displaying the clear stamp of a Derby horse. Two trials were chosen, and now with Stoute's new retained jockey on board, the 19-year-old Walter Swinburn. First, he headed to the Guardian Classic Trial over ten furlongs at Sandown, where he turned many heads in cruising to victory by ten lengths. Next, to try to practice for Epsom as much as possible, he was sent to Chester for the Chester Vase, over 12 furlongs of tight left-hand turns. It suited Shergar's instantly recognisable choppy stride well, and Swinburn let him loose, with victory this time by 12 lengths. He became a very hot Derby favourite.

At Epsom on 3 June, for once everything fell into place exactly as it was meant to. Rounding Tattenham Corner, four furlongs from the finish, Swinburn gave his mount a little rein, and he inexorably clipped his way further and further ahead, floating in the soft ground as others dragged. The distance over Glint of Gold at the line was ten lengths, which could easily have been 15 if Swinburn hadn't basically started pulling him up half a furlong from home, and remains to this day the greatest winning distance of this Epsom Classic. He had at one stage been so far apart that, after the event, Glint of Gold's jockey John Matthias stated, 'I told myself I had achieved my life's ambition. Only then did I discover there was another horse on the horizon.' England had a superhorse on its hands.

He was equally impressive later in the month in the Irish Derby, Piggott substituting for the suspended Swinburn. He sauntered to victory, with four lengths again a misleading guide to his colossal superiority over Cut Above.

PUNCH A HOLE IN THE WIND

Even commentator Peter O'Sullevan, never one to resort to cheap superlative or overstatement during his lengthy career, exclaimed dumbfounded: 'He's only in an exercise canter!' The US had taken notice too, with a group of American owners making a huge offer to the Aga Khan. He chose instead to split his champion into 40 shares, each worth a quarter of a million pounds, keeping six for himself.

It made no difference to Shergar, who next tried his luck against the older horses in the King George and Queen Elizabeth Diamond Stakes at Ascot in July, starting at 5-2 on. Despite finding himself boxed in on the rail for longer than he would have liked, Swinburn found a gap in the home straight and put the race to rest quickly, Shergar coasting home four lengths clear of Madame Gay. Stoute, a multiple British champion trainer, said simply, 'He's the best I've ever had,' something that he would repeat years later.

With the Arc as his predictable autumn target, there was surprise that the 14-furlong St Leger was chosen as his 'prep race'. Rumours also swirled in the lead up – swiftly denied – that he had become a bit rascally in training. In the event, Shergar did something for the one and only time: he ran an ordinary race. He simply couldn't accelerate in the soft ground, finishing fourth behind Cut Above and nine lengths behind Glint of Gold, each of whom he had destroyed in the two Derbies. Once again, lessons about the growing risks of using the St Leger as a trial for the Arc had not been heeded.

No one could find anything wrong with him other than tiredness, with the Aga Khan rapidly deciding that he had nothing left to prove, thus retiring him to stud at the Ballymany Stud in County Kildare in his birthplace of Ireland, a recognised middle-distance champion who annihilated worthy opposition in those first five races. And there the story should conclude with his success, or otherwise, as a sire.

But of course, tragically, it doesn't.

On the night of 8 February 1983, just 18 months after his last race, three masked gunmen, very likely IRA criminals needing to raise funds to buy arms, raided the stud, holding the head groom at gunpoint as he loaded one of the most famous stallions in the world into a horsebox. What happened over the next few days has been captured in immense detail by many articles and documentaries, but two things always shine through: the gunmen knew absolutely nothing either about how racehorse syndication worked – they thought the Aga Khan was still the single owner, when in fact there were now 40 – nor about how to look after a half-ton stallion. It was also staggering to some that stud farms like this, holding multimillion-dollar thoroughbreds, should have no meaningful security. But then again, nothing as brazen or thoughtless as this had ever been attempted before.

The entire process was front-page news for days in the global press. Comparisons with the celebrated disappearance of British socialite Lord Lucan in the 1970s were spuriously made – a rather lazy analogy when one considers that Shergar wasn't in charge of his own destiny and was accused of nothing other than being immensely valuable ($10 million in 1981 money). Indeed, it was his incredible success and the manner of doing so that had first made him headline news around the world as a racehorse, and in turn most likely lured the kidnapper – amongst a host of valuable stallions – to zoom in specifically on him.

Negotiations soon went dead, and it became apparent within days that their ignorant demands simply couldn't be met. No one was keen to pay a ransom and therefore set a potentially lucrative criminal precedent, but the logistics of doing so were essentially impossible anyway. Although hard to prove with conflicting IRA reports since emerging, a detailed *Sunday Telegraph* investigation 27 years after the event spelled out what they believed had transpired. It was a truly stomach-churning turn of events. Senior IRA leaders – likely unsighted on the 'plan' – initially wanted the poor horse released, but soon realised that with a huge search underway and the media all over the issue, the kidnappers – and possibly others – would soon be compromised.

By this stage, it is probable that a distressed and manhandled Shergar had in any case injured himself, likely a broken leg. One secret source claimed, 'Shergar was machine gunned to death. There was blood everywhere and the horse even slipped on his own blood. There was lots of cussin' and swearin' because the horse wouldn't die. It was a very bloody death.' What was left of Shergar was then allegedly buried in a bog in county Leitrim. We may never know exactly when or where the shameful deed happened, or indeed whether this absurd and horrific plot ever resulted in internal retribution within closed IRA circles, as certainly no one was ever brought to justice in the courts.

Shergar had only covered 44 mares before his disappearance. In a horrible irony, the first of his 42 offspring was born the very week that the stallion was taken. Needless to say, their pedigree coupled with their rarity made all of his offspring treasured more than most foals.

But this dreadful episode should simply not be the final word on this magnificent thoroughbred. He brought a rare talent to a glorious summer,

PUNCH A HOLE IN THE WIND

during which he would likely have beaten any horse in the world. He set records that look like they won't be beaten anytime soon. He inspired non-racegoers to start visiting the racetracks, hoping that they would see 'the next Shergar'. As one journalist put it, his '... series of spread-eagling victories ... seemed to define supreme excellence in the middle-distance thoroughbred.' He was indeed truly special.

And those are the memories, above all others, that we should cling to.

FACTFILE

Description: Bay Colt
Size: 16 hands
Dates: 1978-83
Racing seasons: 1980-81
Where were they trained?: UK
Trainer: Michael Stoute
Owner: HH Aga Khan IV
Jockey: Walter Swinburn, Lester Piggott

Sire: Great Nephew
Dam: Sharmeen
Damsire: Val De Loir
Record: 8: 6-1-0
Most impressive victory: Epsom Derby 1981
Nickname: The Wonder Horse

DANCING BRAVE

Dancing Brave – his parrot mouth clearly visible – in training for the Epsom Derby, May 1986.

When we watch a horse race, we are ultimately seeing who can run the distance in the shortest – and therefore quickest – time possible. But when we analyse it closer, what really gets most people excited is watching a horse *accelerate and overtake* faster than the other competitors. It can send shivers down the spine when timed well. And more often than not, that was the effect that Dancing Brave had on the racecourse. He had a gear that others simply couldn't find, and it was electrifying. Yet, ironically, he will be remembered just as much for a race he didn't win as for the ones he did.

It is fair to say that Dancing Brave would never win the gold medal for beauty. He was an ordinary size, had a plain head, was famously parrot-mouthed and had rather imperfect forelegs. Bought by Prince Khaled Abdullah for $200,000, his principal trainer Jeremy Tree was given first dibs over all of Prince Khaled's new crop of yearlings. It was perhaps no surprise, therefore, that the underwhelming son of Lyphard was passed over in favour of others, and went into training instead at the yard of Guy Harwood at Pulborough, near England's south coast.

Quite soon Harwood realised that Jeremy Tree had made a rare mistake, and the horse – now called Dancing Brave – began setting the gallops alight. Even so, Harwood didn't rush. He had an unwritten rule that a two-year-old horse shouldn't run until he or she was actually two years and three months old, and Dancing Brave had been a very late foal (11 May). When he did appear, in the eight-furlong Dorking Stakes at Sandown, it was telling that he started odds-on against three opponents – others had clearly seen his performances on the gallops. He duly obliged in easy fashion by three lengths, and backed this up with a victory by a similar distance in the Soham House Stakes at Newmarket. His jockey, veteran Greville Starkey, instantly recognised the class oozing underneath him, dismounting from his first race and announcing to his trainer: 'I've found my Derby ride!'

On both occasions, albeit against slightly inferior colts, he demonstrated at eye-catching acceleration towards the end. Having never run a Group race, it was impossible to class him at – or even near – the top of the end-of-season ratings, but the public weren't fooled and made him winter favourite for the next year's 2,000 Guineas. At his reappearance at three, he took in a comfortable warm-up, albeit in unpleasant soft ground, at the traditional Guineas trial at Newmarket's Craven Stakes, making him a warmer favourite still. And on the day itself, he didn't disappoint. Despite still technically not having reached his actual third birthday, he burst clear with a glorious turn of foot to beat a class field decisively by three lengths. Second-place Green Desert franked the form during the season, winning two of England's top sprints – the July Cup and the Haydock Sprint Cup – that summer.

Inevitably, talk thereafter could only be of the Epsom Derby. The Brave's pedigree was ambiguous regarding stamina. Harwood was circumspect, having seen the incredible speed which his charge had shown. Conversely, the increasingly confident Starkey had no doubts. In the run-up to the race he even stated that The Brave was 'bomb-proof'. They were words that he would soon bitterly regret. On the day itself, all knew that to protect Dancing Brave's unknown stamina, Starkey would play the waiting game. What no one foresaw was how much he would overdo it. Perhaps over-imbued with confidence, the colt was being held right back when clearly being keen to move on. He also didn't seem to take the idiosyncratic Tattenham Hill and Epsom's other unique contours with much relish.

From a truly impossible position at the back of the field with just two furlongs left to run, Starkey finally decided to press go. The reaction was astonishing. Dancing Brave stormed past almost all the field with a sustained burst, covering the penultimate furlong in an inconceivable 10.3 seconds – thought to be the fastest single furlong ever covered in the Derby. Yet it wasn't enough. Walter Swinburn had already set sail on the Aga Khan's handsome colt Shahrastani, and despite The Brave eating prodigiously into his lead, the post came two strides too soon.

Dancing Brave had tasted unthinkable defeat, and the journalists' pens scorched the papers thereafter with one accusation after another aimed at Starkey's perceived arrogance. The *Daily Telegraph* was lenient on him, claiming that '… Starkey lived through the original jockey's nightmare,' putting most of the blame on the horse's lack of balance. Others were less forgiving, accusing Starkey of a 'fatal misjudgement'. Looking at it again, it remains very hard to be certain one way or the other – except that it is screamingly clear that the best horse didn't win. When the dust had settled, Dancing Brave was sent to test himself over ten furlongs against his elders in the Eclipse Stakes. Starkey made amends, with Dancing Brave annihilating top French filly Triptych and a high-class field by four lengths.

The next obvious step to reset the colt's journey to immortality was at the King George And Queen Elizabeth Stakes, back over 12 furlongs. It is only with the perennial benefit of hindsight that we are surprised that this colossus of the '80s didn't start favourite. With the jury still out in some corners over whether he truly stayed 12 furlongs, and Shahrastani having in the interim cruised to an eight-length success in the Irish Derby, it was the latter who was thought most likely to win. Dancing Brave also had a new jockey, multiple UK champion Pat Eddery, as Starkey was injured. The Brave beat Shadari and another top field comfortably, if not sensationally, with his Epsom conqueror running a sub-par race.

A short August break followed before Dancing Brave was brought back in the low-key September Stakes at Goodwood, nothing more than a facile ten-length win around Goodwood racecourse to tune him up for his true Autumn target, the Prix de l'Arc de Triomphe. The only thing to note at Goodwood was that Eddery was once again in the saddle, even though Starkey was now fit. It would stay that way for the rest of the colt's career. Quietly, it seemed as though connections were still blaming Starkey for the Epsom failure, although none would say as much.

Come early October in the Paris sunshine, the lucky crowd was able to witness something truly special. The line-up for any Arc is usually of the highest order, but few could remember the race dripping with such a profusion of talent as the 1986 iteration; only Sea-Bird's 1965 Arc was mentioned in the same breath regarding strength in depth. France's main hope was Bering, a grandson of the 1965 Arc hero. Unbeaten, with a course record Prix du Jockey Club

(French Derby) under his belt, he posed a huge threat. The amazing and durable filly Triptych was there, as were the Prix Vermeille winner Darara, the German champion Acatenango, as well as Shahrastani, Shadari and many more. Run at breakneck speed, the huge field swung around the final bend of Longchamp with one of the aforementioned after the other each taking a turn to briefly lead. For a moment, Bering looked to have it sewn up, but like a falcon swooping from the cliffs, Dancing Brave – the ugly duckling who ran with the imperiousness of a swan – overtook the entire field in another electric burst of speed, this time with no one beyond him at the finishing post. He was going away by nearly two lengths at the end, and broke the course record in the process.

It had been a magnificent display against a raft of outstanding thoroughbreds running true to form, and earned him the highest international rating since the European classification system had been introduced in 1977. But this was 1986, and with the recently established Breeders' Cup capturing the imagination of global racing as the *de facto* World championships, it was felt that he needed to prove himself there too.

As it transpired, it was a race too far, and The Brave ran the only lacklustre race of his illustrious career, coming a never-threatening fourth behind excellent US colt Manila, whom he nevertheless really should have beaten. Three decent reasons were given. First, he had been on the go since April, and it was November. Very few horses could maintain form for even most of that period, and he was likely over the top. Second, he had lost considerable weight on the journey over and didn't look his best. More prosaically, he came back with an eye injury, with Eddery confirming what the cameras had picked up, that a clod of earth had struck the horse's eye hard during the race, meaning that he had run in considerable pain and with hazy vision.

Gracefully retired to stud, Dancing Brave's life as a sire was complex. He initially seemed to have fertility problems, although this may have been from his contracting the rare Marie's Disease. The Japanese made Dalham Hall Stud an offer they couldn't refuse, but only then did The Brave start producing top-class winners, including Epsom Derby winner Commander in Chief and Italian Derby winner White Muzzle. But his racing legacy was secure, and perhaps most succinctly summed up in *Racehorses of 1986*: 'He possessed an extraordinary range for a top horse, combining outstanding qualities of speed and endurance. Had he been campaigned in the major summer and autumn events at a mile or a mile and a quarter he'd almost certainly have dominated his generation as peerlessly as he did at a mile and a half. There are precious few champions about whom that can be said.'

DANCING BRAVE

FACTFILE

Description: Bay Colt
Size: 16.05 hands
Dates: 1983-99
Racing seasons: 1985-86
Where were they trained?: UK
Trainer: Guy Harwood
Owner: Prince Khalid Abdullah
Jockey: Pat Eddery, Greville Starkey
Sire: Lyphard

Dam: Navajo Princess
Damsire: Drone
Record: 10: 8-1-0
Most impressive victory: Prix de l'Arc de Triomphe 1986
Nickname: The Brave

MIESQUE

Freddie Head, in the 'Ride of the Year', celebrates as Miesque storms to a blisteringly fast victory in the Breeders' Cup Mile at Hollywood Park, November 1987.

When the Breeders' Cup series was inaugurated in the 1980s as the unofficial end-of-season global world championships, it was always going to favour North American horses, whether due to the running surface, track conditions, track configurations or the travelling involved. It therefore may have been something of a surprise to the locals that the first-ever winner of back-to-back Breeders' Cup races should have hailed from France. But in fact it wasn't unexpected to anyone who followed European racing, because Miesque had been sensational since she had first stepped on a track.

Bred in Kentucky by shipping magnate and long-term racing enthusiast Stavros Niarchos, she was moved to France to be trained by the legendary Francois Boutin, who had also conditioned her sire Nureyev. Like that other great French filly Allez France, you'd be hard pushed to call Miesque 'pretty' in the conventional sense. Whilst no horror, her head was quite plain, her build rather masculine, and she had a distinctly fractious temperament.

It was to her eternal luck therefore that she had Boutin, a man who had always commanded immense respect, as a trainer, and would be ridden throughout her career by multiple French champion Freddy Head, who possessed a knack for calming skittish fillies. They say that the way to a man's heart is through his stomach, but Boutin realised that it would be the path to Miesque's too. Noting that she had a very sweet tooth, he indulged her both with sugar cubes as well as her all-time favourite, honey, which she loved having slathered all over her oats. Fiercely intelligent, she was also an eternal nosy parker at home, constantly peering round the corner of her barn to see who was getting up to what, earning herself the nickname 'La Concierge'.

She was ready for her first race in August of her two-year-old campaign and readily took the Prix de Lisieux at Deauville. Sensing something special, Boutin threw her straight into the deep end next in the Group 1 Prix Morny where, despite running green and getting slightly boxed, she still finished third, just a length behind Sakura Reiko. It was to prove her worst-ever finish. At Longchamp, at the seven-furlong Group 1 Prix de la Salamandre, she bounced back, and now that she had a clear run she easily reversed the form with her Deauville conqueror, displaying an eye-catching turn of foot. Finishing the season impressively with another top-level victory at the Prix Marcel Boussac on Arc Day, she was an obvious recipient to be France's Champion juvenile filly. Boutin and Head already anticipated greater things.

Returning in Spring, she breezed through her warm-up in the Prix Imprudence at Maisons-Lafitte before Boutin sent her over to England to take on their best in the 1,000 Guineas at Newmarket. Niarchos and Boutin undoubtedly had unfinished business there. Miesque's sire Nureyev had been first past the post in the 1980 2,000 Guineas, but was controversially relegated to last for a rather trivial infringement, causing a minor diplomatic incident. This was to be his daughter's revenge. With just a furlong to go, however, Miesque found herself boxed in and going nowhere. Her situation looked hopeless, until Head thrust her out left, whereby she unleashed breath-taking acceleration to charge past the other top fillies and win going away, leaving dropped jaws everywhere.

She repeated the trick in the French equivalent at Longchamp later in the month, winning even more comfortably despite coming from last to first. Boutin knew he had a potential great on his hands, but wanted to see if she could stretch out further. In the Prix de Diane (French Oaks) at Chantilly over ten and a half furlongs, he experimented, but Miesque clearly didn't have the stamina to last out, and it was only her class that saw her still take second place behind Henry Cecil's excellent Indian Skimmer. Sticking to a mile therefore, it was time to take on the colts in France's two top summer mile races, the Prix Jacques Le Marois at Deauville and the Prix du Moulin at Longchamp. It was a golden age of European milers, but she walloped them all, displaying in Deauville in particular a turn of foot which left every journalist the next day using the same word: devastating.

PUNCH A HOLE IN THE WIND

Returning to the UK, Miesque endured a rare reversal in the Queen Elizabeth II Stakes at Ascot. Having easily beaten the British filly Milligram on numerous occasions, on this day, for some reason, she could not. Some blamed stand-in jockey Steve Cauthen, deputising for the injured Head, but there seemed no obvious reason why. He was in the right place at the right time but Miesque's usually dependable acceleration never came. 'The sensation of the year,' wrote one breathless journalist with more than a hint of hyperbole, but it reflected the fact that she had by now garnered a lot of fans and a huge sense of expectation.

Far from crestfallen, connections decided to try their luck in the Breeders' Cup Mile, held that year at Hollywood Park, and unquestionably the highest-quality international mile race of 1987. Head, in what most agreed was the ride of the year, kept Miesque in fourth throughout, hugging the rail obsessively despite the track's very sharp turns, and waiting for the gap to appear as they entered the home stretch. Sure enough, when it did, he asked his filly to quicken, and she proceeded to obliterate them, storming home in isolation in the sensational course record time of 1min 32.8secs. Now a global conqueror, Miesque was crowned champion turf horse in the US, champion three-year-old filly in England and France, and champion miler in England and France. Better still, Niarchos agreed to keep her in training for another year.

She started her next campaign in the Prix d'Ispahan, over nine furlongs instead of her preferred eight, but, although rusty, she snuck home cosily enough. Returning in the summer a red-hot Prix Jacques Le Marois in Deauville, she was joined by top milers Soviet Song and Warning. She beat both of them fair and square, with Warning franking the form a few weeks later by blitzing the field in the Queen Elizabeth II Stakes at Ascot. She then had a blip when defending her crown in the Prix Du Moulin, with Head finding himself boxed in and Soviet Song managing to get first run on her, just beating her by a rapidly diminishing head – a surprise, as she had taken his scalp more than once in the past.

Boutin didn't rush Miesque out again to make amends, however. Instead, history beckoned with an attempt to become the first horse to win a Breeders' Cup race twice. As with other championship races like the Arc or the King George, to win two means having an awful lot of stars aligning, and all presupposing outrageous talent in the first instance. The 1988 iteration was to be held at Churchill Downs with arguably even tighter corners than Hollywood Park. To that end, Head chose to ride her differently, keeping her wider, further back but timing his move to perfection. Despite the sloppy turf, she still found her turbo in the home stretch and it was all over in a matter of strides, and she won by almost four lengths, as she had 12 months previously.

MIESQUE

History had been made, and the US fans were as effusive as their European counterparts. Here was a true – and truly consistent – world champion. Laffit Pincay Jr., on board runner-up Steinlen, admiringly spoke for many afterwards: 'I saw her move, but nobody could do anything to stop her.' 'Twas ever thus with Miesque. This time Niarchos decided that it was best to retire her whilst still on top. The end-of-year awards could go nowhere else but her, and alongside that came comments like those of revered US handicapper Steve Davidowitz, to whom cheap superlative was usually anathema: 'Frankly, I doubt there was a better turf miler, male or female, since grass racing began in this country.'

So often, great fillies flatter to deceive once they become broodmares, yet now and again they almost match their on-track abilities. Miesque showed that she was still a champion in a different way by, incredibly, producing two Classic winners from her first two offspring (Kingmambo winning the French 2,000 Guineas, East of the Moon the French 1,000 Guineas the following year). Living to the admirable age of 27, even at stud 'La Concierge' apparently maintained her endless curiosity. But she had more than earned her right to be a busybody.

FACTFILE

Description: **Bay Filly**
Size: **16 Hands**
Dates: **1984-2011**
Racing seasons: **1986-88**
Where were they trained?: **France**
Trainer: **Francois Boutin**
Owner: **Stavros Niarchos**
Jockey: **Freddy Head, Steve Cauthen**

Sire: **Nureyev**
Dam: **Pasadoble**
Damsire: **Prove Out**
Record: **16: 12-3-1**
Most impressive victory: **Breeders' Cup Mile 1988**
Nickname: **La Concierge**

DAYJUR

'He left you feeling that a thoroughbred simply couldn't go any faster.' The quintessential sprinter Dayjur and Wille Carson, June 1990.

Speed. All good horses need to show it, of course, even the stayers. But actual out-and-out *raw* speed? That is the preserve of the sprinters. It seems a straightforward challenge: exit the stalls, and go flat out over five or six furlongs. Easier said than done. But Dayjur's lasting impression on those who saw him was unanimous: he left you feeling that a thoroughbred, physically and mechanically, simply couldn't go any faster.

A beautiful, dark brown, small yet muscular colt, Dayjur (Arabic for 'Darkness') was by Danzig, yet another son of omnipresent super-sire Northern Dancer, and came with a hefty $1.65 million price tag. But his true speed came from his dam, American champion sprinter Gold Beauty. Owned by Hamdan al-Maktoum, trained by veteran Dick Hern from his base in Berkshire in the UK, and ridden throughout his career by multiple UK champion jockey Willie Carson, Dayjur proved that even experts can get it badly wrong.

Tested at six and seven furlongs throughout his two-year-old and early three-year-old races, and attempting to come from behind in each, he was good without being spectacular. He won minor races at Newbury and Nottingham, but equally was beaten in lesser company too. The cultural obsession with preparing a horse of such a rich pedigree uniquely for the Classics was blinding connections from the evidence in front of them.

With hindsight, it seems obvious. As Hern's then assistant – and later a successful trainer in his own right – Marcus Tregoning would later recount, Dayjur ' … didn't care for trotting. It was always a bit hair-raising and he was quite tricky. He always came out jumping and kicking every morning – it was just a nightmare getting him down to the ride. He'd bounce all the way.' There was always something of the coiled spring about him.

He nearly didn't have a three-year-old season at all, however. Over that winter, whilst attempting to get the horse to trot and keep him active, his leg caught a piece of metal that had fallen off a nearby tractor. A deep and nasty cut to the tendon in his hind leg had connections worry that he wouldn't be able to run again, but it ended up healing fine.

Back on the racecourse, the horse clearly had pace but his seventh place in the seven-furlong Free Handicap at Newmarket, his prep race for the 1990 2,000 Guineas over a mile, still had connections scratching their heads. Carson remarked how quickly Dayjur could break from the gates. Only then did the no-nonsense, wheelchair-bound Hern suggest, 'Why don't you just let him go?'

And so they did. In May Dayjur was next tested in Group company for the first time, in the Temple Stakes at Sandown, his first foray at the minimum trip of five furlongs. He bolted from the stalls and nothing got within two lengths of him throughout. From there, the King Stand Stakes at Royal Ascot beckoned. The dead ground meant that Hern was in two minds about running. Sheikh Hamdan had no reservations though, and insisted. And the owner is always right.

Outstanding French sprinter Ron's Victory, who would go on to win the Diadem Stakes by ten lengths, only got to within two and half lengths; the rest were a further six lengths behind *him*. You would be hard pushed to see a five-furlong race anywhere finish with a field as spread-eagled as this. Already Dayjur was being touted as the fastest in the world, but for once the words were not premature.

Next up was the Nunthorpe Stakes in August, the sprinting centrepiece of York's Ebor meeting. This time it was one of the US's top sprinters, Mr Nickerson, who decided to take the challenge. It was in vain. Dayjur's acceleration from the stalls was electric, and he poured it on, furlong by rapid furlong. His margin of victory over Statoblest was four lengths, and his time of 56.16 seconds beat the course record by over a second, and would stand until 2019. Amongst a summer of glorious performances, it was perhaps his finest.

PUNCH A HOLE IN THE WIND

Haydock's Ladbroke Sprint Cup followed, this time back up to six furlongs. More top sprinters were thrown his way – Royal Academy, the July Cup winner who would go on to win the Breeders' Cup Mile, and Dead Certain, the Prix Maurice de Gheest winner. It made no difference to the result. Despite very heavy going, which concerned connections as it was the only thing likely to blunt his speed, Dayjur and Carson repeated their usual catch-me-if-you-can tactics; and they couldn't, with only Royal Academy getting to within a length-and-a-half as Dayjur was eased well before the line. It could have been five lengths – again, unheard of victory distances for a sprint race, and Carson confirmed afterwards that he was 'taking it easy'.

With nothing left to prove in the UK, Dayjur next went on Arc weekend to Longchamp for France's top sprint, the Prix de l'Abbaye. It was notable for two reasons. First, it was clear that he was now scaring away the European competition, with only five turning out to oppose him. He won as he pleased by two lengths, at the prohibitive odds of 10-1 on. But the significance of the second thing of note would only become apparent a month later. As Dayjur crossed the line, few noticed that he appeared to jump a shadow running across the track, slowing him down, although his victory was already well sewn up by then.

There could only be one race for Dayjur to finish his season, and indeed his career, namely the six-furlong Breeders' Cup Sprint, held that year at Belmont Park. The Americans had, as usual, a fine deck of sprinters, notably Eclipse award winner and champion US four-year-old sprinter Safely Kept, who would win 24 of 31 races in her illustrious career. But Dayjur faced other challenges: He was completely new to running on dirt, and he was drawn on the extreme outside of a sharp turning track. As it happened, these didn't matter as, despite an uncharacteristically lethargic break from the gates, he used his immense speed to catch Safely Kept, within a furlong. And for the final four furlongs it was a pure match race, with each on level terms, and both pulverising the opposition.

In the final furlong, Dayjur started to inch ahead, first a head, then a neck, as Safely Kept started to tire slightly. There were just 50 yards to go … which was when Dayjur saw the dark shadow of the grandstand across the track and once again chose to jump it. His momentum was briefly checked as he landed, but it was enough to hand victory at the death to Safely Kept.

Even the partisan US crowd couldn't help but feel that Dayjur had been desperately unlucky and deserved to win. It was heartbreak for all his supporters, and a deeply frustrated Carson was unrepentant in his post-race interview: 'We

DAYJUR

don't get the money but we got the best horse.' Few argued. It had a profound impact on the jockey, as he was still reflecting on their bad luck many years later: 'Half an hour before or half an hour after, that wouldn't have happened. The sun wouldn't have been hitting those turrets at Belmont. What do you say?' What indeed.

Hern, meanwhile, unnecessarily blamed himself for knowing that the great horse had done the same at Longchamp, but did not address it. Only Sheikh Hamdan was positive and philosophical about it after, safe in the knowledge that Dayjur had done more than enough to prove himself a highly desirable sire. Whilst it had been an extraordinary end to an electrifying year, the memories of Dayjur's incredible pace, even many years later, are still etched into the minds of those who were fortunate enough to witness it.

Dayjur duly went to his owner's Shadwell stud in 1991, doing his business for 19 years before earning his pension. Although never a champion sire, there were several group winners dotted in amongst his offspring, and even a Brazilian champion, Eyjur.

The most amusing of all though was a horse from Dayjur's very first crop, who was given the name 'Jump the Shadow'.

Who says that there's no humour left in horseracing?

FACTFILE

Description: Brown Colt
Size: 15.3 hands
Dates: 1987-2013
Racing seasons: 1989-90
Where were they trained?: UK
Trainer: Major Dick Hern
Owner: Sheikh Hamdan Al-Maktoum

Jockey: Willie Carson
Sire: Danzig
Dam: Gold Beauty
Damsire: Mr Prospector
Record: 11: 7-3-0
Most impressive victory: Nunthorpe Stakes 1990
Nickname: The Darkness

CIGAR

Cigar and Jerry Bailey's long winning streak continues in the Massachusetts Handicap at Suffolk Downs, June 1995.

Some human joggers prefer to run on the concrete of a road; others like a little more tenderness underfoot and run on grass. Horses are no different in that regard. Where they do differ, though, is the potentially huge difference in how fast they can run on each in comparison to their rivals. Cigar was a fairly ordinary horse on turf; on dirt, he was a world-beating legend.

It wasn't the only transformation he underwent. As a foal at Country Life Farm in Maryland, he was a feisty little one, kicking out at anyone who came too close, and earning himself the nickname 'The Hammer'. It also provided him with a scar on his chest when he came off second best with a fence. But he eventually calmed down. Being by Palace Music, a Grade 1 winner on the turf in both Europe and the US, no one early on considered running him on anything else. His name had nothing to do with tobacco but everything to do with navigational checkpoints for airplanes – unsurprising as his owner Allen Paulson had owned Gulfstream Aerospace, which made private jets. Technically, he had been owned by Paulson's wife Madeleine, who, in a game of swapsies that only the fabulously wealthy could even conceive let alone indulge in, exchanged him with her husband for top filly Eliza.

Sent into training with Alex Hassinger in California, Cigar didn't run at two. At three, although he won two minor races, Cigar was not setting the racing world on fire, and finished out of the money on several of his nine starts, with various jockeys trying out on him. Connections sensed that he was better than he was letting on, with Paulson deciding to send him to be trained instead by Bill Mott on the east coast. Mott eventually tried him in a couple of conditions races where he came third. His jockey that day, Julie Krone, suggested to Mott that the colt's next race should be on dirt instead. And that was the day that everything changed.

With Mike Smith on board next, Cigar trounced his rivals by eight lengths in a one-mile allowance race on Aqueduct's dirt. Mott then plunged Cigar straight into the Grade 1 NYRA Mile, with Jerry Bailey now his rider. Cigar mopped it up by seven lengths, and Bailey had no intention of letting the ride ever go elsewhere. Suddenly it was plain as day what the horse had been trying to tell them: 'Grass no, dirt yes.' It being already the end of his four-year-old campaign, everyone was impatient to see what he could do aged five. And they were right to be excited.

Always running between his favoured distances of a mile and ten furlongs, Cigar kicked off with an allowance race warm up before taking on the previous season's champion Holy Bull in the Donn Handicap. The latter sadly broke down in the backstretch, making Cigar's impressive victory slightly hollow as few were paying attention to him. Remaining in Florida, he again crushed his rivals by over seven lengths in the Gulfstream Park Handicap, before beating reigning Breeders' Cup Classic champion Concern at Oaklawn Park in a quick time. Six straight victories; many other top horses defeated with ease. Mott carried on sending his wonderful colt to all four corners of the country to share the joy, always accompanied by white stable pony Snowball to keep him relaxed. Pimlico was next, then Suffolk Downs in Massachusetts, with Cigar storming to victory and building up a nationwide momentum of fans who began to realise that something historic was happening.

Poignantly, he returned to his original stomping ground of California for the Hollywood Gold Cup, but this time on the dirt – albeit the notoriously quick dirt of the west coast tracks that not all east coasters adapt to. The challenge was considerable, with winners of many of the big stakes and handicap races of the year set to take him on and Cigar lumbered with top weight. Bailey didn't panic, kept his mount wide and stormed home by nearly four lengths in a blisteringly fast time.

Indeed, Cigar was more than another top racehorse for Bailey; the colt offered his jockey a cathartic experience of what it was really like to connect with a horse in a way that this vastly experienced jockey had not previously experienced. 'It was his personality – he was just so cool,' recalled Bailey later. 'I wanted to spend as much time with him as I could. I would go back to the barn just to be around him and just to watch him graze.' With his growing fan club loving experiencing this rare colt's new lease of life as a dirt runner, they were also aware that, with each victory, he was creeping closer towards Citation's US record of 16 consecutive race wins, once thought to be essentially untouchable.

There was an obvious and ultimate target of his end-of-season: The Breeders' Cup Classic, that year run at Belmont Park. He warmed up in the Woodward Stakes over nine furlongs and the Jockey Club Gold Cup over a furlong further, taking both as he pleased, and was the warmest of favourites for the big one. But it was a very tall order. Being drawn on the outside, and with the heavens opening beforehand to make the track muddy, it was going to test all the skill and talent of a great horse who was at heart a miler, but had a canny trainer who could draw him out to ten furlongs – on a dry track, at least. It being the Classic, the quality of the competition was watertight too.

Cigar was in the zone that day. He so clearly wanted to unleash, and it took all of Bailey's considerable strength to rein in his mighty mount's enthusiasm. As they entered the final turn, Bailey couldn't hold him anymore – 'The feeling was going out of my fingers, they were completely numb. He was pulling that hard' – so he let Cigar have his head and hoped that he would have enough in the tank. He certainly did. His low, skimming action gripped into the mud and Cigar wasn't for catching. As he scorched past the post, in an incredible sub-two-minute time bearing in mind the ground, another moment of instinctive commentator history was made, as race caller Tom Durkin belted out that he was 'the unconquerable, invincible, unbeatable Cigar'. And at that moment in time, it was both a nod to the bombastic, and yet profoundly true.

Cigar had won all ten of his races that year, eight at Grade 1, naturally winning Horse of the Year and was on an unbeaten streak of 12. He started his six-year-old season as he had left off, gaining another win in the Donn Handicap, but the lure of more global fame – not to mention vast pots of cash – beckoned on the other side of the world with the inaugural running of the Dubai World Cup, now the world's richest race. Over ten furlongs in the dirt, it was a race whose credentials fitted Cigar like a glove, and to his connections' credit they didn't shirk the challenge. Cigar, as ever, duly delivered against an international cast list, showing all his usual ability and enthusiasm. He returned to the Massachusetts Handicap at Suffolk Downs in front of the biggest audience the track had ever seen, and kept them happy with another easy victory, despite carrying top weight.

How and where would the mighty Cigar aim to match that incredible winning streak? Such was the profile of Cigar's every race by now that Arlington Park cleverly put on a specially conceived race, the nine-furlong Arlington Citation Challenge, where again he would have to take on top horses Unbridled

CIGAR

Song and Dramatic Gold as well as the burden of top weight. Bailey, as ever, kept Cigar out of trouble on the outside, and in the home stretch he met his date with destiny with ease, and had incredibly won his 16th race in a row.

Cigar, meet Citation. Citation, meet Cigar.

As though this mythical number doubled up as a glass ceiling, the enormity of Cigar's achievement seemed to get to him. As he went next to Del Mar for the Pacific Challenge Stakes in front of a record crowd, Bailey kept the same tactics. But for once he couldn't keep Cigar's enthusiasm in check, as the great colt got sucked into a speed duel, again with Dramatic Gold, but outsider Dare and Go was able to come from behind under a steadier pace and streak to victory. The bubble had finally burst, and the intelligent Cigar knew it: Bailey would offer Cigar his favourite treat, a peppermint, after every race. This time, the colt rejected it in disgust. Horses can show pride too, and Cigar that day believed he didn't deserve it.

More victories and a couple more defeats followed before Cigar was gracefully retired at the end of the year, winning champion older horse honours and falling agonisingly short of $10 million career winnings by a mere $185. He was surely the American horse of the '90s. Paulson sold 75 per cent of his great horse to the Coolmore set-up for Cigar's breeding career. It was just as well that they took out insurance: Cigar was utterly sterile, and couldn't get a single mare pregnant the entire season. He was therefore sent to Kentucky Horse Park where visitors could enjoy seeing him during his long, leisurely retirement, before he passed away aged 24 of osteoarthritis in the neck.

Bailey summed up his favourite horse pithily: 'He had great speed, acceleration, and there wasn't a situation in a race that he couldn't get you out of ... Good horses can win over broken glass and he didn't care ... There really was no one else like him.'

FACTFILE

Description: Dark Bay Colt
Size: 16.1 Hands
Dates: 1990-2014
Racing seasons: 1993-96
Where were they trained?: USA
Trainer: Alex Hassinger, Bill Mott
Owner: Madeleine and Allen Paulson
Jockey: Jerry Bailey, Pat Valenzuela, Chris McCarron, Mike Smith, Julie Krone

Sire: Palace Music
Dam: Solar Slew
Damsire: Seattle Slew
Record: 33: 19-4-5
Most impressive victory: Hollywood Gold Cup 1995
Nickname: The Hammer

DUBAI MILLENNIUM

Frankie Dettori and Dubai Millennium storm to victory in the Dubai World Cup, March 2000.

Names matter. Just consider the serendipity of naming a champion French filly Allez France, or of the Japanese horse making the biggest impression on his adoring public being called Deep Impact. The world's biggest racehorse owner and ruler of Dubai, Sheikh Mohammed Bin Rashid Al-Maktoum, was only too aware of this, and so he did something that only seldom happens: he renamed a racehorse. As it turned out, it was an utterly inspired decision, because Dubai Millennium represented his owner's ubiquitous colours in a way that none of his regally bred thoroughbreds, before or since, has been able to match.

It started prosaically enough. The son of Seeking the Gold was sent into training as a two-year-old at David Loder's Newmarket stables, and was assigned the name Yaazer (Arabic for 'White Gazelle' – ironic, as the bay colt didn't have a single splash of white on him). But with an eye to showcasing the transformation of his home city state into a global training and racing hub, Sheikh Mohammed was scanning his entire two-year-old string for a horse to be its flagbearer, and Yaazer appeared to be the best prospect, hence in 1998 he was renamed Dubai Millennium. His sole two-year-old outing that October, over a mile at the English seaside course at Yarmouth, left an impression on many, winning by five lengths pulling up under Frankie Dettori.

DUBAI MILLENNIUM

The decision was therefore taken to base him henceforth in Dubai, under the supervision of Saeed Bin Suroor. He thrived, growing into a hefty animal over the winter, and when he reappeared at Doncaster in the Sponsorship Club Stakes, he walloped the opposition by nine lengths. The Epsom Derby loomed, so the recognised trial of the ten-furlong Predominate Stakes at Goodwood later that month beckoned. Looking stunning in his coat, he breezed past the entire field, going away by three-and-a-half lengths at the post.

But the Epsom Derby was not to be. As his pedigree might have suggested, he patently didn't stay the 12 furlongs and pulled hard throughout, trailing in ninth behind Oath. It was clear too that his beefy build was never going to be suited to Epsom's idiosyncratic undulations. It was to be his only defeat. To rebuild his confidence, he was next sent to Maisons-Laffitte, on the banks of the River Seine, and the ten-furlong Prix Eugene Adam, where he powered home once more. Staying in France, he was then brought back to the mile, this time for Deauville's summer showpiece the Prix Jacques Le Marois where, despite quagmire ground blunting his natural speed, he ploughed through from the front to win easily by nearly three lengths from a small but strong field.

A final outing in the UK was planned at the Queen Elizabeth II Stakes at Ascot, again at a mile, where Dettori punched Dubai Millennium clear in the final quarter-mile, crushing the opposition by six lengths. Godolphin was convinced: this was the classiest horse they had yet produced in their behemoth breeding programme. Yet incredibly, the best was yet to come.

Returning to winter in the Emirati warmth, Sheikh Mohammed mollycoddled the apple of his eye so that, after a bloodless warm-up victory to get used to the local dirt at Nad-Al-Sheeba, he would be tip-top for the richest race in the world at the time, the ten-furlong Dubai World Cup – the Sheikh's brainchild to bring Dubai racing properly into the global fold. But by the same token it was somewhat more. As one British daily paper slyly remarked: 'The Dubai World Cup is not a race meeting at all but a pageant of power, an expensively staged piece of one-upmanship.' But everyone was having too much fun to really care.

It was a race two years in the planning, and the fairy tale came true spectacularly. Taking the lead after just a furlong, the chunky bay piled on the pressure throughout against a properly international field, thundering clear by six lengths from US invitee Behrens in a lightning 1min 59.5secs. If the Sheikh had written the script, it couldn't have been more word-perfect. Dettori – by now, like Madonna or Beyonce, universally recognised by the single name Frankie – was beyond effusive: 'I could afford to have a look round but I nearly broke my neck because I couldn't see anybody. I almost had tears of disbelief in my eyes.' A palpable feeling of controlled destiny imbued the course that evening, and the colt's official rating was now stratospheric.

Three months later in June, he jetted back to Royal Ascot for the Prince of Wales Stakes where he took on hitherto unbeaten French champion miler Sendawar. This time it was Jerry Bailey who was flown over from the US to sit on top, as Dettori had suffered nasty injuries from a horrific light aircraft crash that had claimed the life of the pilot. Nevertheless, the exuberant Anglo-Italian was cheering from the stands, plaster cast and all.

Whether Sendawar – an exception miler by any standards – ran his true race was unclear, finishing a tame fourth. But even at his best he wouldn't have held a candle to Dubai Millennium, who skipped effortlessly to an eight-length victory. Noticeable then, as it had been at Nad-Al-Sheeba, was the incredibly high cruising speed that Dubai Millennium had. To the others it felt like they were being led out by a pacemaker who was a sprinter. The difference here was that this pacemaker simply didn't relent. Bailey afterwards rated him the equal of Cigar.

It is not traditionally all that common for many US racing fans and reporters to stretch their interest beyond their borders; after all, they have their own embarrassment of riches to keep them sated. But Dubai Millennium beeped on the radar of many. Consider this from an ESPN reporter: 'Is he the new Secretariat? My fervent hope is that Dubai Millennium stays healthy, because it will give racing fans in the United States a chance to see one of the best horses ever. Yes, *ever*.' Further, with his monstrous performances on both turf and dirt – and only a few truly master both – there was no end of championship races across the Atlantic for him to choose from.

First though, Sheikh Mohammed wanted to settle something closer to home. He was now convinced that he had the best horse in the world and was gagging to take on Montjeu, the previous year's Arc winner who that summer also claimed a jaw-droppingly impressive victory in the King George VI and Queen Elizabeth Stakes (see next chapter). Although almost extinct as a concept in the UK, on 4 August the Sheikh suggested a match race to Montjeu's owners: it would be over ten furlongs – the upper limit for Dubai Millennium, the lower limit for Montjeu – to be held at York, Newmarket or Ascot before the end of September, with an eye-watering winner takes all purse of $6 million.

Before anything was finalised – indeed, just as it was being made public – the fates intervened. On 5 August – just 24 hours later – Dubai Millennium shattered his leg on the gallops. His career was over, and thus the race to salivate over would never happen, but most importantly outstanding veterinary intervention saved his life. It provided an eerie echo of the Mill Reef/Brigadier Gerard saga 28 years previously. In retrospect, though, one wonders if, a quarter of a century after the Ruffian horror-show, it was actually a good thing to be spared another artificial race where anything could happen – good or bad. He was sent to Dalham Hall Stud, but after covering less than a full book of mares, tragedy struck in April 2001. Dubai Millennium got grass sickness and was operated upon. Initially there was a sense that all was not lost, with a press statement saying, 'While the stallion continues to remain in intensive care in Newmarket his condition is diagnosed as critical but stable … we can offer a feeling of cautious optimism.' But sadly his condition worsened and two further emergency operations were not enough to save him.

A distraught Sheikh Mohammed made it his mission to buy up every offspring of his favourite son, including future Group 1 winner and star sire Dubawi. And when we watch again those colossal victories by this superhorse, who could blame him?

FACTFILE

Description: Bay Colt
Size: 16.1 hands
Dates: 1996-2001
Racing seasons: 1998-2000
Where were they trained?: United Arab Emirates and UK
Trainer: Saeed Bin Suroor and David Loder
Owner: Godolphin/Sheikh Mohammed bin Rashid Al-Maktoum

Jockey: Frankie Dettori and Jerry Bailey
Sire: Seeking the Gold
Dam: Colorado Dancer
Damsire: Shareef Dancer
Record: 10: 9-0-0
Most impressive victory: Dubai World Cup 2000

MONTJEU

Cash Asmussen steers the unpredictable Montjeu to an easy victory in the Prix du Jockey Club, June 1999.

In researching this book, it has been striking to me how many of the great horses were actually slightly mad. Be it the hyperactivity of Count Fleet, the pig-headedness of Sun Chariot or the sheer cussedness of Native Dancer, it shows that you don't have to be level-headed to be a champion – indeed, perhaps many excelled *because* of their odd behaviours. Montjeu was another who had to do things his way – and *only* his way – before he deigned to deliver. But deliver he did, usually in truly sumptuous style.

By the end of his career, everyone wanted to claim Montjeu as one of their own. Born in Ireland, bred by a Franco-Brit, but trained in France by another Englishman, he was a proper European. As a son of all-conquering sire Sadlers Wells, he was always going to be the apple of someone's eye, and initially it was that of Sir James Goldsmith, tycoon, financier and occasional politician, who bred the horse and named him after his stunning chateau in the Burgundy region of France. Yet after his death when Montjeu was a yearling, the colt was passed to Goldsmith's ex-partner Laure Boulay de la Meurthe, who decided to keep the horse trained in France by ex-pat Englishman John Hammond. The latter knew what it took to train a champion, having conditioned Suave Dancer to Arc glory in 1991, and he soon saw something equally impressive in his new charge. He also saw a streak of bizarre, diva-like behaviour in the colt which would need every ounce of the trainer's gentle handling to contain.

Montjeu's two races as a juvenile were seemingly low-key, albeit impressive. An easy debut victory over a mile at Chantilly in the Prix de la Maniguette was soon followed by a cosy victory in the Prix Isonomy at Deauville, but it was only after the horse he conquered there, Spadoun, mopped up the Group 1 Criterium de Saint Cloud a fortnight later, that people started paying more attention to Montjeu. Amongst them was the hugely powerful Coolmore outfit from Ireland led by John Magnier, who made an offer that Mme Boulay de la Meurthe couldn't refuse, and thereafter the colt would run in the colours of business partner Michael Tabor.

There were thus very high hopes for Montjeu's three-year-old campaign and he ultimately, somehow, exceeded them. Ridden initially by American veteran Cash Asmussen, he started in the ten-and-a-half furlong Prix Greffulhe. Asmussen rode him in his favourite 'catbird' seat, blasting past the Aga Khan's highly rated Sendawar in the last 100m. Although it was further than Sendawar's ideal, the fact that he then proceeded to mop up most of Europe's top mile races that year, yet was clearly second-best here, showed that Montjeu was indeed a class act. The Prix Lupin, his main prep race for the French Derby, was, however, something of a farce. They crawled through the early stages, before Montjeu started twisting his head stubbornly to the side and hanging badly, failing to catch up in time with leader Gracioso.

Punters who had made him 10-1 on were bemused, but hoped for better in the Prix du Jockey Club itself. They weren't disappointed. Settled in the rear, Montjeu unleashed a pulverising turn of foot in the straight to take the Classic by four lengths without being tested by the other top-drawer colts. The Irish owners then decided to bring him over later in the month for their home equivalent. Despite another class field, it was clear that Asmussen was just itching to unleash his colt for several furlongs. When he finally pressed the button, the response was electric, and Montjeu was suddenly five lengths up, head turned this time to the crowd on the left, as though seeking their approval. The following day's *Irish Times* summed it up best: 'Only good horses win Classics but yesterday's Budweiser Irish Derby had a feeling of coronation about it as Montjeu completed the French and Irish Derby double with an overpowering display of dominance. And the clear impression that will reverberate around Europe is that he can only get better.' Asmussen was adamant afterwards that the mighty colt had five kilos in hand, and there were only nods from witnesses. Hammond called the performance 'frightening', and confirmed that the Arc was the autumn target.

PUNCH A HOLE IN THE WIND

For the rest of his career, Montjeu would be ridden by Irish great Michael Kinane, who was essentially Coolmore's retained rider. His first ride almost went against the script in the traditional Arc warm up for three-year-old colts, the Prix Niel. Montjeu was having one of his naughty days and not responding to urges. When he finally decided to, he snuck up and won by a head. No one was too put out, but more discouraging was the ground for the Arc itself. Little short of a quagmire after days of rain, it was disastrous for Hammond's colt, whose unparalleled turn of foot was infinitely more effective on good or firm ground than in the mud. In a race featuring top horses from France, England, Ireland, Japan and even Norway, Kinane would have to keep him handier than usual.

In fact, the rider of the day wasn't European, but Masayoshi Ebina from Japan. Partnering El Condor Pasa, the highest internationally rated Japanese runner ever to that point, he took the lead early and deceptively moved gradually clear round the long final turn, his colt floating on the heavy ground. By the home straight the Condor seemed to have flown; no one got near him … except for Montjeu. Kinane asked his mount to unleash everything he had in the last two furlongs, and remorselessly, despite the appalling conditions, he ground down the five lengths to his Japanese opponent, passing the finishing post half a length in front. The rest were nowhere. It had been an outstanding effort, and broke Japanese hearts.

Fortunately, though, Montjeu was to stay in training as a four-year-old, with a second Arc his long-term target. Returning to Ireland to kick off his season, he cruised to victory in the ten-furlong Tattersalls Gold Cup in what looked like little more than an exercise canter, again a proper Group 1 field. Back in France, he took in the Grand Prix de Saint-Cloud, outclassing his rivals by five lengths. It seemed as though the two biggest fears for connections – would he be as good, and would he learn to behave – were allayed. In fact, they were only half right.

Montjeu next made his only trip to the UK, where the midsummer centrepiece of the King George VI and Queen Elizabeth Stakes at Ascot would be his target. It was now that he decided to play the pig-headed diva. As the other horses walked calmly into the paddock beforehand, there was one horse missing – the big favourite. Hammond, who was convinced that Montjeu had never been in better form, later reminisced, 'It was soon obvious that Montjeu had decided, as had become his inclination, that he had no intention of going in to the paddock itself. No amount of pushing, pulling or being offered a 'lead' by another horse was working.'

MONTJEU

Montjeu wasn't getting fractious, far from it. He was playing games, and just wanted a particular thing to happen, and it was up to his charges to work out what that was. Just as Hammond was about to lose his own mind, it clicked: Montjeu wanted Hammond's Head Lad, Didier Foloppe – and *only* Didier Foloppe – to ride him into the parade ring. Left with no other option, Hammond hoisted on Foloppe – suit, tie, brogues and all – onto Montjeu's back, and suddenly the colt acquiesced and walked happily into the parade ring as though it was the most normal thing in the world.

To his credit, Montjeu paid back his handlers a few minutes later with one of the most sumptuous displays of class ever witnessed on a British track. Against another field oozing with quality, Kinane didn't have to move a muscle as Montjeu strode past the others with almost contemptuous ease. Only Nijinsky's 1970 performance was even remotely comparable in the history of this championship race. His behaviour that day summed up Hammond's nickname for him – 'the Eccentric Genius' – perfectly.

Yet Montjeu was never quite the same animal again. He won his Arc warm up the Prix Foy easily enough, but in his last three performances – the Arc, the Champion Stakes and the Breeders' Cup Turf – it was clear that his heart wasn't really in it, finishing fourth, second and seventh to horses whom he would likely have beaten well in the past. His oddness was beginning to get the better of him, and it was time for stud. There, Montjeu was every bit as much a stunning success as on the course, siring champions around the globe, including no less than four Epsom Derby winners before his premature death at the age of 16 from sepsis.

'He had a few issues,' Kinane once said euphemistically – by which he actually meant that Montjeu was as mad as a box of frogs. Indeed. And he was also a wonderful champion who helped us see in the millennium with a rare talent.

FACTFILE

Description: Bay Colt
Size: 16.1 hands
Dates: 1996-2012
Racing seasons: 1998-2000
Where were they trained?: France
Trainer: John Hammond
Owner: Michael Tabor, John Magnier, Laure Boulay de la Meurthe
Jockey: Cash Asmussen, Michael Kinane
Sire: Sadlers Wells
Dam: Floripides
Damsire: Top Ville
Record: 16:11-2-0
Most impressive victory: King George and Queen Elizabeth Stakes, 2000
Nickname: The Eccentric Genius

SILENT WITNESS

Silent Witness and Felix Coetzee are all business in training at Sha Tin, February 2006.

SILENT WITNESS

A passionate and knowledgeable audience, a tremendous atmosphere, fantastic facilities … all that was missing from Hong Kong were world-class horses who could look any other thoroughbred in the eye over their distance and soundly beat them. But the blossoming in the East happened pretty much simultaneously. At around the time that Deep Impact was shaking up the world order from Japan (see next chapter), Hong Kong discovered that it, too, had a world-beater on its hands; Asia was no longer the poor horseracing cousin. For the first time in history, the international ratings were agreed that the fastest sprinter on earth for three years running was plying his trade at Sha Tin racecourse. And his name was Silent Witness.

Silent Witness's stellar performances could not have come at a better time for the Hong Kongers. Whilst nearly two decades later the world would fall into the clutches of a pernicious pandemic, those in Hong Kong had seen it all before, as in the early years of the century the territory was gripped by the SARS epidemic, meaning masks, social distancing, economic downturn and lockdowns were already well known to them. There was a yearning for a hero, of any description, and he filled that hole magnificently.

So many of the best racing stories display humble origins, and Silent Witness was no different. Foaled in Australia, his sire El Moxie had never hitherto set the world alight either on the course in the US or in the breeding shed, and had been, in the words of one unforgiving hack, 'relegated to the Tasmanian bush'. His dam, Jade Tiara, matched that level or ordinariness, so expectations were hardly elevated. He was bought by a shipping magnate from Macau called Arthur Antonio Da Silva – Archie to his friends – and brought over to run in Hong Kong, almost exclusively at the oasis of green within a concrete quagmire that is Sha Tin racecourse. He was placed into training by Tony Cruz, a familiar figure to European racegoers in the '80s when, as a jockey, he had partnered the fantastic mare Triptych on several of her top-level victories. Silent Witness would be partnered throughout his 29 races by top South African jockey Felix Coetzee.

Maturing slowly, but gradually turning into a handsome, chunky gelding, Cruz saw plenty of speed in him so tried him over five furlongs for his first race in December 2002, which the three-year-old polished off four lengths clear of the field. The following month he had a go over a furlong further, and he found that just as easy. Back at five furlongs for his third outing, and he blitzed it in a mouth-watering 55.50 seconds. Those two sprint distances would be his bread and butter for the next three seasons.

What Silent Witness achieved in those years was something that the race-mad public of Hong Kong, and the racing world beyond, would never forget. Seldom had anyone – from any country – seen such a sense of inevitability pervade the usually risky mix of thoroughbreds running together around a tight circle at over 40 miles an hour. Whether he started slowly or, more often, with an electric burst from the starting gates ('He has the reflexes of a springbok,' Coetzee would reflect), the only two things that were certain were that night would follow day, and that Silent Witness would win his races. Many were Group 1s, and some were against fields attracting top international sprinters, enticed by Hong Kong's generous prize money. But all were swatted away with contemptuous ease.

Quickly a proper fan club grew, and the word phenomenon was seldom more apt. Many would watch his races wearing colours to match their hero's black and green silks, and he was the first horse in Hong Kong to have his own website. By the end of his second season, Silent Witness had won his first 11 races, thus beating the long-standing Hong Kong record of Co-Tack – ridden, ironically, by Cruz. Race commentator David Raphael's elated outburst as he crossed the line to break the record – 'Think of the best; he's better!' – soon entered local racing lore. International judges were unequivocal too, and named him world champion sprinter for each of his first three seasons – a novelty for a horse trained in Hong Kong, but questioned by absolutely no one. His ability to quicken towards the end of races which were designed to be run flat out from the start was mesmerising. In some of the victories, Coetzee didn't move on him. You sometimes see this in middle distance races, very occasionally in top-drawer ones, but pretty much never in Group 1 sprints.

By now he had taken all the top sprint prizes in Hong Kong: the Bauhinia Sprint Trophy, the Centenary Sprint Cup, the Chairman's Sprint Prize, the International Sprint Trial, and the Hong Kong Sprint. In the latter race, he raced against several top European sprinters, all of whom were gasping by half way before he pulled further away. Loving every moment of it was owner Da Silva, thunderously popular, extrovert, and a man who never believed in washing his mouth out with soap and water. 'We fucking shat on them!' he exclaimed in the aftermath, and he wasn't wrong.

The next target was to break the number of consecutive victories by horses in the post-war era, with the magic number 16 held by three legendary champions: Cigar, Citation and Ribot. With crowds 50 per cent bigger than usual – as they always were when he ran – he won the six-furlong Chairman's Sprint Prize for the second time to equal the record and then, three weeks later, running over seven furlongs for the first time in the

SILENT WITNESS

Queen's Silver Jubilee Cup, he led from pillar to post to win 17 out of 17. To say that the locals were excited would be underplaying it. During the day, the Hong Kong Jockey Club (HKJC) had let in free anyone wearing official Silent Witness T-Shirts or even displaying the latest merchandising gimmick: a Silent Witness credit card. They had also run a competition with Silent Witness baseball caps as prizes. But every single one of the 60,000-strong crowd wanted one as a souvenir of the day, and the ensuing mini-stampede put 26 people in hospital.

This would prove to be the zenith of this incredible gelding's career. Never ones to shirk from a challenge, and with absolutely nothing to prove, connections wanted to see if there was any chance that he could last out a full mile. The HK$8 million Champions Mile was chosen, where he would come against star miler – and stablemate – Bullish Luck. Despite the unknowns, the crowd still made Silent Witness the odds-on favourite, most with no intention of cashing their tickets in, but rather to be part of more history.

In rain-softened ground, Coetzee sprang his charge straight to the front so that he could control the pace and preserve his horse's stamina. In the home straight he pulled away, and déjà vu nearly kicked in. But in the final furlong the question was answered, and there was nothing left in the sprinter's tank. Meanwhile, Bullish Luck, under a canny rail-hugging ride from globetrotting French jockey Gerald Mosse, crept up in the last 80 yards, and pipped the hitherto unbeaten gelding by the shortest of heads.

Sha Tin was in shock. As Coetzee later reminisced, 'That day it was very loud, all the way down the straight, but in the final strides something very strange happened ... All of a sudden, it was like somebody switched off the volume. I was just so disappointed for not only Silent Witness, after all the hype, but for the people. I had to come back and it was as if I didn't just have to face the crowd, but all of Hong Kong.' The journalists didn't need asking twice to switch on the hyperbole. One even wrote: 'The painted ones in the stand looked bereaved, silent witnesses to the death of their dream.'

Connections, for some reason, were desperate to show that he could indeed last out the mile, and therefore sent him a month later on his first foray abroad, to the Yasuda Kinen in Tokyo. The same thing happened, this time with their charge coming a close third. Finished for the season, he nevertheless started the next back in Japan, this time over his preferred six furlongs at the Sprinter's Stakes in Nakayama. It was both a stunning victory in an incredibly quick 1min 7.3secs, and was also his last. He was beginning to show less enthusiasm and his weight – always considerable – had begun to steadily go up before each subsequent race.

The glory days were over, and his legs were getting old, but the public still adored him, and not just in Hong Kong. Americans saw a clear parallel between him and Seabiscuit, their underdog hero of the 1930s Depression era. *Time* magazine thought nothing of including him in their list of '24 people *[sic]* who mattered most in 2004'. The HKJC didn't hesitate to put his statue at Sha Tin, in glorious full gallop with a celebrating Coetzee on top.

As Da Silva would reflect, 'Sporting heroes mean a lot in hard times. You would turn around and see the crowds cheering, stomping their feet for him and you suddenly realised this horse was making people happy just when they needed it.

'He touched people with the spirit of Hong Kong.'

FACTFILE

Description: Bay Gelding
Size: 16.1 hands
Dates: 1999–
Racing seasons: 2002–07
Where were they trained?: Hong Kong
Trainer: Tony Cruz
Owner: Arthur Antonio and Betty Da Silva
Jockey: Felix Coetzee

Sire: El Moxie
Dam: Jade Tiara
Damsire: Bureaucracy
Record: 29: 18-3-2
Most impressive victory: Cathay Pacific Hong Kong Sprint 2004
Nickname: Master of the Elite, Spirit of Hong Kong

DEEP IMPACT

Yutaka Take cannot hide his delight as Japanese legend Deep Impact wins the Japan Cup in his final racecourse appearance, November 2006.

PUNCH A HOLE IN THE WIND

Japan adores its horseracing but, like Hong Kong, it is undoubtedly playing catch-up: Only with the trillions of yen poured into bloodstock since the 1980s have top-class stallions started plying their trade there in numbers, to produce the next generation of local and potentially international stars. Which is all to say that one doesn't need to go that far back to find the truly great Japanese horses that could have gone hoof-to-hoof with the best anywhere. Deep Impact – a 2002 son of late 80s US Champion Sunday Silence – was unquestionably the horse that Japanese racing had been waiting for.

He was out of Wind in Her Hair, a granddaughter to Queen Elizabeth's dual Classic winner Highclere, and a great-grand-daughter of Northern Dancer on her other side. With Sunday Silence the champion sire in Japan 12 times, Deep Impact certainly had a regal head-start with his breeding. An impressive dark bay colt with a hint of a white star on his forehead, he was consequently purchased for 70 million yen ($750,000 at the time) by businessman Makoto Kaneko and sent into training with Yasuo Ikee.

At aged two, he made his debut at Hanshin racecourse on the outskirts of Osaka a winning one, showing little sign of greenness. But it was all prep for his tilt at the Classics the following year. Ikee already had his eyes on the Japanese Triple Crown, only won five times previously. It started with the ten-furlong Satsuki Sho at Nakayama. With Japanese legend Yutaka Take on board, as he would be throughout Deep Impact's career. He won in a blistering 1min 59.2secs, displaying what would become his trademark of being dropped in near last, coming wide around the home bend and then quickening effortlessly.

What may have helped with his speed was that there wasn't a great deal of him in the first place. When racing he never weighed more than 452kg, distinctly on the slight side, and well over 100kg less than bulky mares like Black Caviar or Zenyatta. He didn't shirk from his feed either, with handlers calling him 'surprisingly gluttonous'. He just seemed to possess a magic metabolism. Ikee's farrier also pointed out that, perhaps because of his light frame, he wore out his horseshoes much slower than other stablemates.

The Tokyo Yushun (Japanese Derby) came next, and the same pattern was followed, this time with Deep Impact having to run eight horses wide on the bend, before thundering down the centre of the wide track in splendid isolation, winning by four lengths being eased down, yet still posting a remarkable 2min 23.3secs. A love affair between horse and public had properly begun. To complete the Triple Crown, he then needed to tap

DEEP IMPACT

into unknown stamina reserves for the Kikuka Sho (St Leger) at Kyoto. It unfurled in identikit fashion, with a devastating burst in the home straight from far back to win going away by two lengths over Admire Japan. He had conquered.

Yet at the height of his powers, he tripped up at his next outing, for the only time in his domestic career. Needing to prove himself against the older horses, in December he went to Nakayama to contest the Arima Kinen, one of Japan's premier all-aged races, over an extended 12 furlongs. Take adopted his usual fall-back tactics, but the pace wasn't strong, and he was simply outfoxed by Christophe Lemaire on the very decent Heart's Cry, who ran much closer to the pace. By getting first run for his sprint in the straight, Lemaire gained enough distance that even Deep Impact couldn't make it up, going down by half a length.

Disheartened but not crestfallen, connections plotted ambitiously for his four-year-old campaign. After an easy warm up in the Grade 2 Hanshin Daishōten, he was prepared for another marathon, this time the Spring edition of the Tenno Sho, the 'Emperor's Prize' over a full two miles (16 furlongs) at Kyoto. He showed he still had it in him by sailing away and setting a staggering new world record of 3min 13.4secs, and the public couldn't get enough of him. To display his versatility, he then dropped right back to 11 furlongs to take in the other top aged race in Japan, the Takarazuka Kinen, run that year at Kyoto. He won in a canter, with Take describing being on board him more like flying than riding. But the true prize lay abroad …

Japan's love affair with the Prix de l'Arc de Triomphe borders on obsession. Europe's premier middle distance race, always run on the first Sunday in October at Longchamp, it is the prize that the Japanese crave to win more than any other as it will symbolize their unequivocal arrival on the international racing scene. In 1999 they came agonisingly close when only the mighty Montjeu prevented El Condor Pasa from creating history. But this time they felt it was their turn.

Arc fever gripped the nation. Something approaching 9,000 Japanese racing fans – nicknamed the 'idolatrous thousands' and many of them teenagers who had saved for the trip, rather than dip into the bank of mum and dad – cheerfully descended onto Paris. Meanwhile, 21.6 million Japanese – fully 16 per cent of the population – was to watch it live on TV.

The fans put not just their hearts but their pockets into Deep Impact, ploughing over 1.5 million Euros into the Pari-Mutuel on the big day, meaning Deep Impact would go off one of the shortest priced favourites in the history of the race. Indeed, at one stage in the run-up he had been as ludicrously short as 10-1 on, with the second favourite at 23-1. What made it all the more bizarre was that most of the Japanese punters freely admitted that they had no intention to cash in their winnings if their wonder horse won; they just wanted a memento of their trip.

It was a muddling pace throughout, but it looked halfway down the straight that Deep Impact, run more handily than usual, would make it. However, within the last furlong, he was passed by both Rail Link and Pride, coming a close third.

But drama followed a fortnight later. Deep Impact had had a respiratory illness, which may have affected his performance at Longchamp, and had been administered Ipratropium via an inhaler. Misunderstandings about how long it would remain in his bloodstream meant it was still there when he ran. Although legal in Japan, it contravened French rules, and so he was sensationally disqualified. Frustrated but with something to prove, Ikee sent the horse back to Japan where he first won the Arima Kinen at the second time of asking, before rounding off his career in style against all-comers at the Japan Cup. He was still mighty.

Retiring to Shadai Stud Station in Hokkaido under a whopping $43 million syndication didn't mean that Deep Impact's superstar status ended. Far from it: he had his own uniformed security guard and each summer up to 400 adoring fans would visit him daily. It didn't seem to have put him off his day job though. Although quite small framed, his handlers were always impressed at how he was super relaxed when walking into the breeding shed and then could turn on the goods in the blink of an eye. Indeed, often they were only too happy to offer intimate detail of his technique, hip flexibility and durability.

By any calculation, Deep Impact was hugely successful, becoming champion sire seven years in a row from 2012 and siring 45 Group 1 winners, including two-time Japan Cup winner Gentildonna and A Shin Hikari. But also, crucially, he sired Classic winners abroad, including Study of Man (Prix du Jockey Club), Snowfall (Epsom Oaks) and Saxon Warrior (English 2,000 Guineas).

But Japan woke up to tragic news on 30 July 2019. Having initially undergone successful neck surgery, the following morning Deep Impact couldn't stand, and x-rays revealed a cervical fracture that stood no chance of healing. The nation's equine hero had been euthanised aged 17. The Japanese Racing Authority immediately dubbed two upcoming meetings as 'Deep

DEEP IMPACT

Impact Memorial days', and condolence books and flower stands were set up spontaneously at racecourses and even racing museums. It is hard to think of an equine hero in the west ever transcending their sport so much as to be this level of a social phenomenon.

But watching his races again, it somehow becomes less surprising. He was that good, and the public were only too happy to display the true depth of their love and respect for their world-class hero, who did more than any horse in cementing Japan's place at the international flat racing top table.

FACTFILE

Description: Dark Bay Colt
Size: 16.1 hands
Dates: 2002-19
Racing seasons: 2004-06
Where were they trained?: Japan
Trainer: Yasuo Ikee
Owner: Kaneko Makoto
Jockey: Yutaka Take
Sire: Sunday Silence
Dam: Wind In Her Hair
Damsire: Alzao
Record: 14: 12-1-0 (1 DSQ)
Most impressive victory: Tokyo Yushun 2005
Nickname: Wing To Fly

ZENYATTA

The huge – and hugely talented – Zenyatta (Mike Smith up) becomes the first mare to win the Breeders' Cup Classic, Santa Anita, November 2009.

'Popular' doesn't always equate to 'great'. Many of our heroes from bygone eras would best be categorised as plucky losers, or perennial try-hards who entertain us year after year. But occasionally there is crossover, where immense ability, limitless courage and a huge fan club meet. And at the hub of that Venn diagram you would find Zenyatta.

Zenyatta's career was a compendium of superlatives and firsts, yet she never really seemed destined to socialise in such stratospheric circles. A daughter of Dubai World Cup winner Street Cry out of Kris S mare Vertigineux, when she went to the Keeneland yearling sales in 2005 she brought with her a rather unappealing (but thankfully temporary) skin condition that made her almost-black coat look underwhelming and blotchy. Many prospective buyers were put off, but not Jerry and Ann Moss, who paid $60,000 for her. It was to be a sensational investment.

She was given her name due to the 1980 album *Zenyatta Mondatta* by UK band The Police, who were signed by Jerry Moss to A&M Records and whose singer/bass player Sting was a close friend. And as The Police had grown gradually in stature, so did Zenyatta, who eventually filled a huge 17.1-hand frame – some swore it was even more – and tipped the scales at nearly 560kg at her racing peak. Her massive shoulders were a sight to behold, augmented by freakishly high withers (not unlike Man O' War's) which could only be accommodated by a custom-made saddle. To round it off, she had an invisible on/off switch, meaning that she was a delightful patient, kindly filly at home but turned into a fierce, no-nonsense professional once on the track.

Trained in California by John Shirreffs, he was canny enough to know that this outsized filly would take considerable time to mature and reach her peak. It was therefore not until late November of her three-year-old season – when certain horses are already being retired – that the big filly made her racecourse debut over six-and-a-half furlongs in a Maiden at Hollywood Park. She soon took to her task and stretched away to win by three lengths under David Flores. Three weeks later at the same venue she was tested over eight and a half furlongs in an allowance race, winning easily by the same distance.

Even at this early stage in her career, three very telling facets of her racing were already in clear evidence. First was her instinct to turn her switch 'on', and become mentally prepared to race. She did this by demonstrating a unique action in the parade ring that her burgeoning band of followers soon called the 'Zenyatta dance'. Clearly filling with adrenaline in anticipation of the rigours ahead, she would thrust out her front legs alternatively, almost goose-stepping her away around the ring, expelling excess energy. It was as though a highly strung dressage horse was on display. That, plus her jockey thereafter, simply letting her survey the crowd and her rivals whilst motionless, was all she needed to warm up.

Second was her perennial battle with her arch-nemesis: the starting stalls. Her huge bulk clearly felt constrained by them, and no amount of patient training over the years could make her either accept them or, ironically, leave them fast enough. She therefore started all her races immensely slowly, losing lengths to rivals before properly starting. And third was her stretch run. Many horses display a stunning turn of foot, but few would do it with the metronomic regularly of Zenyatta, each time from seemingly hopeless positions, using her 26ft stride to maximum effect.

No time was wasted for her four-year-old season, and she was upped in January to the Grade 2 El Encino Stakes at Santa Anita, and won in identikit fashion, this time against Grade 1 winners, and displaying her Count Fleet-style tendency of running very wide around the bends. Now only being ridden by Mike Smith, she was sent on what would be a rare foray for her out of California, for the Grade 1 Apple Blossom Handicap at Oaklawn Park in Arkansas, where she dispatched Breeders' Cup Ladies Classic winner and strong favourite Ginger Punch. She returned to Hollywood Park in May for the Milady Handicap where, despite the crawling early pace, she still stormed past the others in the stretch to win easily. A besotted Ann Moss commented, 'She always makes everyone look like they stopped.'

PUNCH A HOLE IN THE WIND

And so it continued throughout the season, demolishing all-comers in the same inexorable way, taking in a track record at Del Mar for eight-and-a-half furlongs in the process. Her year culminated in the Breeders' Cup Ladies Classic, run in her home state that year, and now starting as at odds-on, she gave the high-class field another drubbing in the second-fastest running of the race since its inauguration, her seventh victory of the year confirming her inevitable Eclipse award for Champion Older Female Horse. She celebrated – in her typically different way – by guzzling a fair amount of her favourite drink: Guinness Stout. She loved the stuff, whether neat or drenching her oats. They tried other beers with her, but she would only ever touch that brand, and even then it had to be ice cold. Her fan club was now an adoring one, nicknaming their new hero Queen Z.

Despite being given a lengthy winter break thereafter, only returning in May, Zenyatta carried on regardless on her return in the Milady Handicap, giving weight and a comfortable beating to her Grade 1 winning stablemate Life is Sweet. Three more Grade 1 victories followed with deja-vu growing. All the races were in California, and she didn't change her running style once, despite Smith's occasional urgings. On more than one occasion she was timed at having hit 40 miles an hour in the final quarter-mile – a speed usually reserved for the early stages of a race.

Despite such apparent untouchability, there were still sneers from certain quarters. She usually only ran against other mares (albeit very good ones) rather than colts, and had barely raced outside California, usually on synthetic tracks which her doubters claimed exaggerated her apparent supremacy over opponents. Her connections calmly countered this, Shirreffs pointing out that she disliked the synthetic track too and had to be trained on dirt track at Hollywood Park. As if to prove a point, she was entered for the Breeders' Cup Classic, which happened to be run in Santa Anita anyway that year, leaving Life is Sweet to take the Ladies Classic as she pleased, thus already countering her naysayers.

In the Classic itself against the best colts that the US and Europe had to offer, she started even slower than usual, and was still seven lengths back in ninth with two furlongs to go. Yet still she found a way, reeling them in one by one and winning by a length from Gio Ponti, notching up win number 14 from 14 starts and thus becoming the first mare to win the Classic, and the first horse to win two different Breeders' Cup races. Only Serena Williams beat her to US female Athlete of the Year for 2009, such was her popularity outside traditional racing circles.

Initially the Mosses planned to retire their champion but then decided to give her one more year. She went back for another bite at the Apple Blossom, where her intended main rival Rachel Alexandra didn't turn up, giving her a

ZENYATTA

bloodless victory. She returned to California for four more Grade 1 victories, including the Lady's Secret Stakes and the Clement L. Hirsch Stakes, giving her an unparalleled 19 out of 19. Her last hurrah would be an attempt to repeat her victory in the Breeders' Cup Classic in what would be only her third outing outside California, this time at Churchill Downs. No champion horse had ever retired undefeated in the US, and the international competition was exceptionally deep. Even by her standards, she dawdled from the stalls, and had fully 15 lengths to make up after only four furlongs. Top colt Blame had got the run on her and started his run much earlier. The mare, blocked by a wall of slowing horses, went wide and unleashed her breathtaking turn of foot, crushing all before her ... except Blame. At the post, he was a rapidly diminishing neck in front – a position reversed just half a second after the finish line.

With such impossible distances to make up, she had lost nothing in defeat, Smith even (wrongly) blaming himself. Shirreffs casually said, 'You run that race nine more times, she probably wins all nine of them,' and even Blame's connections weren't arguing. As a consolation, by coming second she was still able to claim the title of highest-earning horse in US history (at the time).

The breeding shed at last beckoned. Nevertheless, authorities saw to it that Zenyatta's electrifying performances would not be quickly forgotten. The Group 1 Lady's Secret Stakes was inevitably retitled the Zenyatta Stakes, with Santa Anita also erecting her statue just 18 months after her final race. Oprah Winfrey even named her in the 'O Power List' for 2010. She continues to have a slew of visitors to this day, far more than any other broodmare, and happily eats every carrot, peppermint, banana and pint of Guinness offered to her. They make Queen Z happy, just as she in turn made her fans delirious during her sensational career.

FACTFILE

Description: Brown Filly/Mare
Size: 17.1 hands
Dates: 2004-
Racing seasons: 2007-10
Where were they trained?: USA
Trainer: John Shirreffs
Owner: Jerry & Ann Moss

Jockey: Mike Smith, David Flores
Sire: Street Cry
Dam: Vertigineux
Damsire: Kris S
Record: 20: 19-1-0
Most impressive victory: Breeders' Cup Classic 2009
Nickname: Queen Z

SEA THE STARS

'He is the point to which thoroughbred breeding, after 300 years, has arrived': Sea the Stars (Mick Kinane) breaks the track record in winning the Juddmont International at York, August 2009.

July 2008, The Curragh, outside Dublin. An ordinary day. The Djebel Ali Stables Maiden Stakes at the Curragh, over seven furlongs. Lots of two-year-olds getting blooded on the racecourse in a run-of-the-mill maiden. Driving Snow, a future Grade 1 winner in the US, wins. In fourth, running very green and having been trapped on the rails, but just a length behind at the finish, is a colt called Sea The Stars. It was impossible to guess on that day what the next 18 months would have in store: that Sea The Stars would never be beaten again, would become undisputed European champion, and would be Ireland's horse of a generation.

As with so many other champions here, he had the advantage of fabulous genetics: by top miler Cape Cross, out of Arc heroine Urban Sea, he was half-brother to the 21st-century's top stallion Galileo. Owned by Hong Kong businessman Christopher Tsui and trained by the understated but gifted John Oxx, he went on from his debut to score impressively in Leopardstown before Oxx thought him capable of winning a Group 2, the Beresford Stakes, which he again took readily if unspectacularly, beating a slew of future big winners in the process. It was clear that he had bags of ability but his chilled demeanour meant that he was never going to win by a street. His jockey Mick Kinane, one of the world's leading big-race riders for two decades and in his final season, sensed that there was something special in the bay colt's engine.

Therefore ambitions were high for his three-year-old campaign, but they almost derailed at the start as he caught a virus in March, making it touch-and-go as to whether he would reach the 2,000 Guineas at Newmarket. He just made it but bookmakers were aware of his disrupted training, letting him go off at 8-1 – a remarkably large price with the gift of hindsight. Having blossomed into a beautiful, strong animal over the winter, and with his preferred good ground underfoot, he quickened readily to win by a length from Gan Amhras. Kinane, who had ridden so many top horses in his long career, was purring afterwards, and thought that, unlike his sire, he would get better over middle distances.

The Epsom Derby was consequently a no-brainer, but still he had his doubters, and favouritism eventually went to Fame and Glory, winner of the top Derby trial the Dante Stakes at York. It was the last time that Sea the Stars would start odds-against. Once again, in remorseless style, he overcame the competition easily, running within himself and still nearly two lengths clear at the finish. In Epsom's small, intense winners' enclosure, amongst the usual hubbub, the inscrutable Kinane jumped off, went to his trainer's ear, and whispered, 'This is one of the greats. He's the best I've ever ridden.' He would later tell journalists that he was going so easily that it felt as though the other horses had been racing in slow motion.

His next intended target, the Irish Derby, had to be missed as the ground at the Curragh was bottomless, which Sea The Stars hated, so he was instead pointed at the ten-furlong Eclipse Stakes, the first big race in the UK calendar where the Classic generation meet their elders. Despite finding himself in front too early with two furlongs still to go, none of his rivals could find a way past him, and again the winning distance of one-and-a-half lengths from Rip Van Winkle did not do justice to his evident superiority.

In each race the behemoth of Ballydoyle, Ireland's all-conquering stable run by Aidan O'Brien, threw a different battalion of their colts to try to find flaws in Oxx's champion. They always failed. In the Juddmonte International at York over an extended ten furlongs, it was the turn of Mastercraftsman, who had won several Group 1s since defeat in the Guineas. But it was a repeat of the Eclipse: a thunderous pace set by the pacemakers, who then tired early leaving Sea The Stars in front too soon, and yet still he galloped on, with no one getting within striking distance. The one-length victory this time was supplemented with a huge new course record.

Oxx was acutely aware that the Irish public was by now desperate to see their hero run on home soil, and the Irish Champion Stakes at Leopardstown fitted the bill perfectly. But again the ground was soft as the day approached.

The cunning staff at the course put on a charm offensive and even moved the rails of the course to use slightly better ground and Oxx decided to take a chance. Ballydoyle threw Mastercraftsman and runaway Irish Derby winner Fame and Glory at him to probe the seemingly exposed champion. It was a fruitless endeavour. He powered away from both in front of a mesmerised crowd, earning a huge *Timeform* rating in the process. Oxx reflected: 'He's one of those landmark horses that come along every 25 to 30 years and people will always remember him.'

Of note here is that nowhere along the line did connections even contemplate running in the St Leger where, had he won, he would have been the first UK Triple Crown winner in 39 years. Venerable and historic this old Classic may be, but time and again it has proven a step too far to take it in as well as any other major race that autumn.

Indeed, the inevitable finale – as with all European middle-distance contenders – was the Arc in early October at Longchamp. But Sea The Stars had been on the go since April, with no mid-season break. He was surely being asked the impossible, in a very high-class field of 19. He sweated beforehand, and didn't look like the peach he had earlier in the season. Seasoned experts asserted that he was probably over the top and would go the way of so many champions-elect of the past, finding this challenge one step too many. Sea the Stars indeed pulled hard in the early stages, and the magic hands of Kinane let him drop back and find his rhythm. Entering the straight, he was boxed in and seemed to be without options. And then Kinane spotted a gap in the rail and didn't need asking twice. The mighty colt found his turn of foot once more and powered through the field, at once stage three lengths clear before being eased at the line. In a strong year, he had become the first – and still only – horse to win the arduous, season-long Guineas/Derby/Arc treble.

His luscious pedigree meant that the lure of the breeding shed was preferred to a four-year-old campaign. By the 21st century, the old days of covering 40 mares a year had been steamrollered by some fertile types to take in up to 100 mares in the northern Hemisphere, and then the same again in the Southern. Money definitely spoke, but no one really begrudged his retirement. As Sea The Stars took every award going at the end-of-season awards, the verbal battles started about how good he was.

In the blue corner, superlatives were thrown around with reckless abandon. Both Ian Balding and Pat Eddery, forever associated with other greats Mill Reef and Dancing Brave respectively, echoed each other's words in calling him 'right up there with the best'. The different ratings organisations were notably

SEA THE STARS

equivocal, with his figures and accompanying commentary varying considerably. Part of this was because it was hard to gauge the quality of his opponents and part was because he never did more than he had to: crushing his opposition by ten lengths was not for him.

In the red corner, Brigadier Gerard's former jockey Joe Mercer was less enthused by the apparent hype: 'You can't have a best horse you've ever seen every other year ... Half the people who are saying he's the best they've ever seen aren't old enough to have seen the best horses. I'm going back to the 1950s with Ribot.' Sea The Stars' own jockey, Mick Kinane, begged to differ, and when posed the hypothetical question a few years later about whether he thought his mount or the mighty Frankel was better, he didn't hesitate: 'Sea the Stars. There was never a horse that could drag him to his limit. Sea The Stars was never tested'. As stated repeatedly in these pages, it is essentially an unwinnable debate, fuelled more by emotion that cold hard logic.

Regardless, all agreed that this colt was special. Oxx spoke for many: 'He's perfect, the perfect racing machine. He is the point to which thoroughbred breeding, after 300 years, has arrived.' And for once, the hyperbole felt justified.

FACTFILE

Description: Bay Colt
Size: 16.2 hands
Dates: 2006–
Racing seasons: 2008–09
Where were they trained?: Ireland
Trainer: John Oxx
Owner: Christopher Tsui
Jockey: Michael Kinane
Sire: Cape Cross
Dam: Urban Sea
Damsire: Miswaki
Record: 9: 8-0-0
Most impressive victory: Prix de l'Arc de Triomphe 2009
Nickname: The Star

BLACK CAVIAR

Black Caviar and Luke Nolen complete the mare's 25th and final race with another flawless performance in the TJ Smith Stakes at Randwick, April 2013.

Some great horses have statues in their honour. Others have movies made about them. But how many can boast being on the front cover of one of the world's most iconic fashion magazines? Black Caviar for one. And it wasn't just because she was gorgeous that she was a poster girl for *Vogue*; it was because she was unbeatably brilliant.

Her start in life wasn't so auspicious, as 'issues' with her dam Helsinge meant that she had to be bottle fed at her farm in Victoria. It seemed to have a positive effect on her, though, as she would grow to 16.2 hands and weighed in at her peak at a huge 575kg – heavier than some sizeable steeplechasers. Having been picked out of the yearling sales by trainer Peter Moody, she was bought by a consortium of friends – the Maddens, the Wilkies and Neil Werrett – who had known each other since primary school and had always wanted to buy a horse together. Serendipity played its part as Werrett knew Moody, who showed them the big, near-black filly and they took the plunge, buying her for AUS$210,000, with friends Pam Hawkes and David Taylor joining in – in Taylor's case behind his wife's back as he knew she wouldn't approve. As first purchases go, only Seattle Slew's was comparable in terms of sheer, outrageous luck.

The group called her Black Caviar, partly to reflect her colour and partly because the filly's grand dam was called Scandinavia, home to the exotic fish egg dish. In turn, choosing her colours as salmon pink with black dots to reflect the caviar felt instinctive. She ran just twice as a two-year-old, both times bolting up without showing any sign of greenness, the second by six lengths in the Blue Sapphire Stakes, but that was barely the hors d'ouevre. She continued to improve at three and, now ridden almost exclusively by Luke Nolen, she started specialising at six furlongs, taking in a listed race and then two Group 2s, despite stumbling at the start of the latter. A ligament injury meant that she had to be put away for the rest of the season, but owners and trainer sensed that the best was yet to come.

Taking in two more Group 2s with facile ease at the start of her four-year-old campaign, connections decided to take the plunge in Group 1 company, at the Patinack Farm Classic in Flemington, with a high-calibre field assembled. She utterly destroyed them by four lengths, Nolen motionless, and now the star could properly be said to have been born. She followed this up quickly with easy victories in more Group 1s, the Lightning Stakes and the Newmarket Handicap, making a mockery of her top weight and breaking the Flemington five-furlong course record in the process, giving her a rating which made her the top-rated horse in the world. But she was just warming up.

Caviar-mania was beginning to grip Australia and after another easy Group 1 she made her first visit to New South Wales, for the TJ Smith Stakes. The usual crowd of 3,000 was now ten times bigger, and her new army of fans were not disappointed as she crushed the field of almost exclusively Group 1 winners. Venturing further north to Doomben near Brisbane for the BTC Cup, the situation was repeated: huge crowds, spread-eagling victory, adoration.

Unbeaten over three seasons and with the owners loving every minute, it could be argued that she was even better the following season. She polished off Group 1s and Group 2s as though they were exercise canters, usually winning by no less than three lengths and often with Nolen merely a passenger. This included a repeat of her victory in the Lightning Stakes where, true to the race's name, she ran the middle furlong of five in an unbelievable 9.98 seconds – no one could recall another thoroughbred in Australia recording a furlong in under ten seconds. Yet for her it seemed easy, as her monstrous 27ft stride meant that she took 24 strides to cover a furlong, compared to the average for a thoroughbred of 30. The win took her to 19 straight victories out of 19, beating the Australian records set the previous century by legends Phar Lap and Bernborough. She then went to Morphetville in South Australia to spread the love there, annexing the Robert Sangster Stakes by four-and-a-half lengths.

But it wasn't just all of Australia who wanted a piece of her. On the other side of the world, the authorities at Ascot were desperate to do anything to bring her over to the Royal Meeting – specifically the Diamond Jubilee Stakes – and pitch her against Europe's best. The charm offensive worked and her incredibly sporting owners put her unbeaten record and her international reputation on the line. It wasn't the cheapest option either, with the 30-hour flight in a specially designed compression suit costing them £100,000 ($150,000) just to get her there. The weather was typically June-like for England, i.e. wet, which shouldn't have put her off as her favourite activity was a trip to the seaside for a swim.

Black Caviar, despite her epic journey, prevailed, but only just. Palpably better than her opposition, she sustained a muscle tear in her shoulder halfway through the race, but still pulled away. Then Nolen, in a moment of madness, dropped his hands far too early, perhaps misjudging the finish line. French challenger Moonlight Cloud got to within a head of her by the finish line, with Nolen profusely apologetic in the aftermath, calling his action 'brain failure' as Queen Elizabeth II admired the Wonder from Down Under in the flesh in the winner's enclosure. Tight it may have been, but her supremacy had been clear to all and she was named later in the year as European champion sprinter – the first time the award had gone to a horse not trained on the continent.

Given time to recover from her injury, it was during her recuperation that she did her cover shoot for Vogue, maintaining her incredibly calm demeanour throughout like a true professional. She only reappeared eight months after her previous race, as a six-year-old, but carried on regardless, taking her third Lightning Stakes and breaking the Flemington course record in the process, covering the five furlongs in a blistering 55.42 seconds. Just five days later, the Australian racing authorities broke with tradition and inducted her into their Hall of Fame. Only Sunline had previously joined this exalted circle whilst still actively racing. But Nelly – as her owners affectionately called her – wasn't done yet. The following month she pulverised the field in the William Reid Stakes at Moonee Valley before sauntering clear to take a second TJ Smith Stakes at Randwick, after which she was once again placed at the head of the international rankings. Starting at odds-on for the 24th consecutive time, she had now won 25 races, 15 at Group 1. What else did she have to prove?

Nothing, as it transpired. Later that month, journalists were called to a hastily organised press conference at Moody's stable, where the emotional trainer, on behalf of the owners, announced his superstar's retirement. 'At the end of the day we believe she's done everything we've asked her to do and she could possibly have done no more,' he said. 'We thought, "what else can we achieve?" The connections of the horse and I decided 25 was a great number.

BLACK CAVIAR

She's been a great shining light for racing.' Indeed she was, as her name trended on social media worldwide in minutes in a way that few of her species had. She was a truly global phenomenon who genuinely transcended her sport. Indeed, earlier in her career, Australian Rules Football star Dale Thomas had a bet with owner David Taylor that Black Caviar couldn't win 20 consecutive races. To his credit, after the inevitable happened, Thomas fulfilled his end of the bet and had Black Caviar tattooed on his posterior.

A career in the breeding shed beckoned, although sadly not with her legendary peer Frankel; rumours of a dream coupling had been circulating for years. As one Australian wag reminisced, 'Built like a bulldozer, performed like a ballerina.' Massive she may have been, but there was seldom a horse that captured the public's hearts as she had.

FACTFILE

Description: Brown Filly/Mare
Size: 16.2 hands
Dates: 2006–
Racing seasons: 2008–13
Where were they trained?: Australia
Trainer: Peter Moody
Owner: Werrett Bloodstock Pty Ltd, G.J. & K.J. Wilkie C.H. & J. Madden, P.A. Hawkes, D.M. & J. Taylor
Jockey: Luke Nolen, Jarrad Noske, Ben Melham
Sire: Bel Esprit
Dam: Helsinge
Damsire: Desert Sun
Record: 25: 25-0-0
Most impressive victory: Patinack Farm Classic 2010
Nickname: Nelly, The Wonder from Down Under

FRANKEL

Jockey Tom Queally kisses Frankel after his unbeaten mount's 14th and final victory at the Champion Stakes at Ascot, October 2012.

When, in 2013, The World Thoroughbred Rankings Supervisory Committee undertook a rather drastic retrofitting of some of their figures on horses of times gone by, there were mixed feelings. On the one hand, some horses from their earlier days had clearly been over-indulged and were cut down to size, even if some seemingly arbitrary downgradings from more recent heroes felt quite disrespectful. On the other hand, there was a seemingly good reason: recalibration was needed because this venerable organisation believed that they had just witnessed the greatest horse in their history.

Frankel, named after owner Khalid Abdullah's recently deceased US trainer Bobby Frankel, had supersire Galileo as a father and Danehill mare Kind as a mother, so there were expectations. His career became intertwined with that of his trainer, ten-times British Champion trainer Henry Cecil, who suffered punishingly from stomach cancer throughout the time he was in charge of this special colt. Even at two, Frankel's nickname at the stable was Pegasus; they knew they had something mythical on their hands. As Cecil's widow Jane recalled later: 'Shortly before his first race he galloped with a highly rated three-year-old and left him for dead. He drew clear by 20 lengths. Everyone who saw it could hardly believe their eyes.'

One of his traits, however – which many humans can relate to – was that Frankel didn't like change. Racehorses often change barn as they grow, and Frankel was put in the yearlings' barn when he arrived at Warren Place. At two, when all the juveniles were moved to their new, larger and fancier rooms, the others were fine. But not Frankel. He was clearly unsettled, so they moved him back to his smaller shed where he was immediately placated. It may have been because he wanted to be near his best friend, Bullet Train, a horse who would often act as Frankel's pacemaker and who, Frankel may have sensed, was his three-quarter brother.

Ridden by Tom Queally throughout his 14-race career, Frankel first won a maiden readily at Newmarket from future King George winner Nathaniel, before trouncing a small field by 12 lengths at a conditions race at Doncaster. Stepping up in class, at the Royal Lodge Stakes over a mile in September, he bounded past a decent field to win as he pleased by 11 lengths from future Irish Derby winner Treasure Beach, before comfortably beating a field of future Group 1 winners in the Dewhurst stakes back at Newmarket. He became a predictably hot favourite for the following Spring's 2,000 Guineas. At three, stable staff once again attempted to move him to a new part of the stable where he would be more comfortable. Again, he made it clear that he was unhappy, so they took him back. They didn't bother trying again.

Preceded by an easy prep race in the Greenham Stakes at Newbury to fine-tune him, Frankel's 2,000 Guineas was something to behold. Only Tudor Minstrel's iteration of this race was as mesmerising, and never was Frankel's ground-devouring stride more evident than on that day. Utterly spread-eagling the field, with Dubawi Gold a remote second, everyone was left in stupendous shock, with Ian Bartlett's commentary having shades of Chic Anderson's timeless call at Secretariat's Belmont Stakes: during one of the great Classics, each is gradually overcome with disbelief, yet makes sure that we are focussed on the uniqueness of what we are witnessing.

Displaying so much speed meant connections were unsure if he would stay the 12 furlongs of the Epsom Derby, so he went to Royal Ascot instead and won the St James Palace Stakes in what was his least impressive display, Queally taking him into the lead too early where he idled and then scrambled home by just under a length from Zoffany.

Older horses beckoned, first champion older miler Canford Cliffs in the Sussex Stakes at Goodwood, who was despatched easily by four lengths. The normally reserved Cecil finally started being more assertive: 'I know it's a facetious thing to say, but I think he's the best I've ever seen.' Fewer and fewer were arguing. He was only seen once more as a three-year-old, back at Ascot at the Queen Elizabeth II Stakes, where he won easily by four lengths from a field with numerous Group 1 runners including Prix Du Moulin winner Excelebration, whom he was beating for the third time that year.

It was to Prince Khalid's sporting credit that Frankel was enjoyed by the racing public for another year despite the lure of the lucrative breeding shed. Reappearing in the Lockinge Stakes at Newbury, he won smoothly by five lengths from Excelebration again, Cecil claiming that he still wasn't fully fit. As it transpired, he was right.

Royal Ascot beckoned once more, this time in the opening race of the Queen Anne Stakes. Starting at 10-1 on, it was in this race that Frankel produced what remains the highest-ranking single performance by a racehorse – if those international ranking calculations are your barometer. Either way, the 11-length demolition of (who else?) Excelebration was breathtaking, the latter going on to show that he had improved too, winning two of Europe's other top-mile races, the Prix Jacques Le Marois and that year's Queen Elizabeth II Stakes. Frankel covered the third-last furlong in 10.58 sec. That was faster than any of the top sprinters could achieve in the Group 1, five-furlong King's Stand Stakes later that day.

What made him so frighteningly good? Perhaps it was his calorie intake. Chomping through an impressive 23 pounds of Canadian oats each day, as well as plenty of English hay – he apparently found US hay too rich – it was conspicuously more than his fellow colts and fillies at Cecil's yard. Maybe it was his disproportionately large hooves (and in parallel, we might find out one day that – like Secretariat and Phar Lap – he had a huge heart too). Revered racing and breeding correspondent Tony Morris believed it to be more straightforward:

FRANKEL

'I've never known another horse with such a high cruising speed and the capacity to sustain maximum velocity for so long.'

After a routine follow-up for a second Sussex Stakes, at the unthinkable odds of 20-1 on, a clearly ailing Cecil finally gave Frankel his chance over a longer distance, at York's ten-Furlong Juddmonte International Stakes, sponsored by Abdullah's breeding interests. Relaxing well, Frankel surged clear to win by seven lengths, without breaking sweat, from Group 1 winners Farhh and St Nicholas Abbey. There were rumours that he would go for his final race at the Prix de l'Arc de Triomphe over 12 furlongs. But instead, connections kept him for the ten-furlong Champion Stakes at Ascot. Despite bottomless ground, and missing the break, Frankel pulled through, for once being tested, winning by just shy of two lengths from top French middle-distance gelding Cirrus Des Aigles.

With his great horse now being retired, Cecil went a step further: '... the best I've ever had, the best I've ever seen; I can't believe that in the history of racing there has ever been better.' His patient handling of his crowning glory now complete, the master trainer had nothing left to prove, and quietly succumbed the following June to his debilitating disease, and much heartache in the racing community. Frankel, meanwhile, went to Banstead Manor Stud, producing a hefty number of increasingly important winners each year, as he tries to unwittingly outdo his sadly deceased champion sire.

In amongst the avalanche of ensuing hagiographies, let us offer some temperance here and try to play Devil's Advocate. Frankel was utterly spectacular, but there was a feeling with some that he only beat (the admittedly very good) Excelebration again and again. He also stuck relentlessly to a mile throughout his career until his last two victories of ten furlongs, so was never given the opportunity to display the same versatility as others in this book – and as such a classy son of Galileo, surely 12 furlongs would have been within his reach. And thirdly, at a time when flat racing has become so instinctively global, many thought it a shame that Frankel never ventured beyond his home shores to prove his superiority against the best that France, the US or even Australia had to offer; in the twilight of his great career, Cecil increasingly shied away from sending *any* of his horses abroad.

But this is being picky. The memories of his outrageous displays remain seared in our minds. Frankel was – and likely always will be – one of the all-time greats, and for that we are eternally thankful. As Queally reflected after Frankel's demolition job at York: 'I could stand here all day and go about trying to describe him, but words *don't* describe him.'

PUNCH A HOLE IN THE WIND

FACTFILE

Description: Bay Colt
Size: 16.1 hands
Dates: 2008-
Racing seasons: 2010-12
Where were they trained?: UK
Trainer: Henry Cecil
Owner: Prince Khalid Abdullah

Jockey: Tom Queally
Sire: Galileo
Dam: Kind
Damsire: Danehill
Record: 14: 14-0-0
Most impressive victory: Queen Anne Stakes 2012
Nickname: Pegasus

WINX

Hugh Bowman celebrates on the inimitable Winx after winning the George Rider Stakes at Rosehill Gardens, March 2017.

Some horses get a high official rating based on just one brilliant – but rather anomalous – performance. There are plenty of examples. We shouldn't automatically be suspicious of these assessments, but by the same token there is little doubt that, overall, most of us are impressed far more by the horses that manage to find a way to win again and again, no matter what competition is thrown their way, no matter what the going underfoot. And in the modern era, no colt or mare has managed that more regularly and more gloriously than Australian legend Winx.

Foaled at the Coolmore stud in the beautiful wine region of the Hunter Valley, she had, in Street Cry, the same sire as US supermare Zenyatta. It was Winx's dam, Vegas Showgirl, who shaped her name, as it was tradition during Las Vegas burlesque shows of the 1970s and 1980s for men in the front row to wink at the dancers. She was bought in the yearling sales by Magic Bloodstock Racing, an enterprise set up by a trio of friends – Peter Tighe, Debra Kepitis and Richard Treweeke – who had long supported racing but had hitherto never had a Group 1 winner. Winx soon make a mockery of that.

Choosing her for no other reason than she fell within their budget, the filly had an 'average' look to her – not huge and imposing like Phar Lap, not all bulging muscle like Black Caviar, but in the goldilocks zone of 'just right'. She was placed into training at New Zealand-born Chris Waller's stables in Rosehill,

Sydney. Not overly exerted as a two-year-old, she still readily won both her races, at local tracks under Jason Collett, and in eye-catching times bearing in mind the conditions. Returning as a three-year-old in September, she was upped straight away to Group 2 company, and ran away with the six-furlong Furious Stakes at Randwick. Connections started to dream, although that was slightly tempered during a successful, but not perfect, campaign where Winx, still coming into herself, notched up some promising second places in Group 1 company, as well as a couple more lacklustre efforts. Noticeable to all, though, was her incredible versatility, as she was holding her own in six-furlong spring races, yet still coming second over 12 furlongs in the Australian Oaks.

She finally broke her Group 1 duck in her final race of the season, the 11-furlong Queensland Oaks at Doomben. The race was notable for two reasons. First, it was the first time that she would be partnered by Hugh Bowman, who would also sit on her back in all but one of her 32 subsequent races. Second, it started an astonishing streak that was unprecedented in modern thoroughbred racing, as she would win every single one of them.

The numbers associated with Winx's career thereafter beggar belief and almost threaten to undermine the sheer enormity of her achievements. It is worth highlighting a few. As a four-year-old, in the Group 1 Epsom Handicap at Randwick over a mile, she was baulked rounding the turn, enough to crush the chances of normal horses. Yet she gathered herself to pass the field and win, carrying 57kg – a record for a mare in the race. Next she went to Moonee Valley to contest Australia's top weight-for-age race, the Cox Plate over an extended ten furlongs. Top English, French and Irish raiders tried to lower her, but she sprinted clear to win by five effortless lengths, in course record time. By the end of the season, Bowman was unsurprisingly calling her 'the best I have had anything to do with'. She finished the season tied as the world's highest-rated racehorse.

Coming back aged five, Winx was even better. Taking in eight races, all bar one at Group 1 level, she flitted between seven furlongs and ten, and was barely stretched. In her second Cox Plate, against another field of fellow Group 1 winners, she drew gasps as she flew eight lengths clear, making her 13th consecutive victory once again look so easy. Her rating now matched Black Caviar and she was undisputed turf world champion.

Bowman and Waller, who knew her best, were keen to point out that she had an indomitable will to win, almost as though she took huge affront to being beaten. Whilst undoubtedly true, there were two other factors that equine specialists pointed to. The first was her balance. Most animals, including humans, aren't as symmetrical as they at first seem, and horses can consequently display an imbalance that is exaggerated when running at speed around turns. Not so Winx. She was almost perfectly symmetrical, meaning that it didn't matter whether she ran on the clockwise tracks of New South Wales and Queensland or the anticlockwise tracks of Victoria; she was equally smooth and balanced on either.

Second was her stride. It wasn't big – far smaller than Black Caviar's, for example – but what it lacked in size it more than made up for in cadence. In a mile race, the average horse will take 140 strides per minute. Winx, however, was clocking in, incredibly, at 170, an almost unheard of rate that she could somehow maintain throughout the race, when her competitors would be slowing. It proved to be her magic-bullet time and again, as more often that not she would come from behind, accelerating past her hapless opponents.

And she kept winning. Her sporting owners were enjoying every moment, as was Winx, so they kept her in training. The distances varied, the ground could be firm or heavy, but Winx always found a way. Her six-year-old season followed a similar pattern of eight races, largely Group 1s, and with a strategic break in the middle over the Christmas period to preserve her. Her closest shave that year was in her first race, the Warwick Stakes, where she completely missed the break, starting many lengths down in a seven-furlong race. A patient ride by Bowman saw him finally unleash her in the home straight where, despite looking for all the world that she would get beaten, she won by a neck from stablemate Foxplay.

She later took in a third Cox Plate, a feat only ever achieved by Kingston Town, and making her Australian racing's highest-ever earner. She then put in a race record time of 1min 33.65secs in the George Main Stakes at Randwick. Two of her races saw her coast clear by seven lengths, performances that would normally cause stampedes in a Group 1, yet with Winx it had become an expectation. She finished the season once more at the head of the international rankings. In winning the George Ryder Stakes at Rosehill, she broke the world record for most Group 1 victories – a hugely impressive 17. She was then inducted into the Australian Racing Hall of Fame – an exceptional rarity for a still-active horse. But she wasn't done yet.

As had happened with Black Caviar the previous decade, authorities at Royal Ascot turned on the charm offensive to lure the superstar to that prestigious meeting on the far side of the globe – and with her versatility she could have the pick of the races. Winx's connections thought long and hard but eventually turned it down, saying, 'The Royal Ascot carnival is one of the greatest in the world and would provide Winx the opportunity to be showcased on a global stage. It has been our dream to have a horse race in front of Her Majesty the Queen at Royal Ascot. However, this decision is not about us and must be based on the best interests of Winx.' It was completely understandable, and horse welfare was necessarily paramount, but it did rob the wider racing world of being able to see the wondermare from Down Under for themselves.

Instead, it was agreed that Winx would have one more season, running at home. Eight again felt like the right number of races, seven at the top level. Aged seven she may have been, but this incredible mare showed no sign of diminishing talent, and taking in a couple more race records in the process. In the ten-furlong Turnbull Stakes at Flemington, she completed the last four furlongs in under 44 seconds. She then did something unthinkable by winning a fourth consecutive Cox Plate, a truly outstanding achievement. Her usual mid-season break was followed by four more races, three at Group 1, culminating at Randwick in the Queen Elizabeth Stakes where the huge crowd, knowing it to be her last-ever race, roared her on to a victory that was never in doubt. Bowman didn't want to leave the scene as the adulation poured in. He bent forward to give her a kiss on the neck, at which the cheeky mare made it clear who was boss and headbutted him, giving him a juicy split lip. The crowd loved it. Bowman was too emotional to care.

Winx then retired, having won her last 33 races, 25 of which were at Group 1 level. A three-time world's top-rated horse, she had developed a fan club that stretched well beyond her Antipodean homeland. Records may be there to be broken, but one senses that it will be a long time before any horse approaches, let alone beats these figures, or even approaches the cult-like status that Winx achieved in the process. As one admiring commentator pointed out, 'It's a story that goes beyond sport, embraced by young and old alike; one that will be told for generations to come.'

FACTFILE

Description: Bay Mare
Size: 16.1 hands
Dates: 2011-
Racing seasons: 2014-19
Where were they trained?: Australia
Trainer: Chris Waller
Owner: Magic Bloodstock Racing
Jockey: Hugh Bowman, Jason Collet, Tommy Berry, James McDonald, Larry Cassidy, Joao Moreira
Sire: Street Cry
Dam: Vegas Showgirl
Damsire: Winkie
Record: 43:37-3-0
Most impressive victory: Cox Plate 2016
Nickname: The Wondermare

AMERICAN PHAROAH

Victor Espinoza is overjoyed to win the Kentucky Derby at Churchill Downs on the mighty American Pharoah, May 2015.

After Seattle Slew and Affirmed won back-to-back Triple Crowns in the late 1970s, with the afterglow of Secretariat still visible, some observers understandably became complacent; it seemed like the US Triple Crown was becoming commonplace – easy, almost. With the advantage of history we can now say with certainty that it was anything but, and the US had just been spoiled with an abundance of riches in that decade. The wait for the next would be fully 37 years. Yet a horse shouldn't just be included here because they win a Triple Crown; many on both sides of the Atlantic haven't made that cut. But American Pharoah does make it, not just because of what he did but how he did it.

The gentle bay colt's name was both appropriate and frustrating. Appropriate, because as a son of Pioneer of the Nile, grandson of Yankee Gentleman, and being owned and bred by flamboyant Egyptian-American businessman Ahmed Zayat, it all made sense. All, that is, except for the infuriating misspelling of 'Pharoah'. The story goes that Zayat's son Justin ran a naming competition for the horse, and copied and pasted the winning suggestion before sending it on to the Jockey Club. Before anyone spotted the mistake it was in the system and too late.

It wasn't just his name that was 'wrong'. His tail was far shorter than average, although he hadn't been born that way. Some later detective work concluded that his paddock companion as a yearling at the breeding farm in Florida, a certain Mr Z, chewed it off, possibly out of hunger or perhaps – sensing later greatness – out of jealousy. Not reaching his reserve price at the yearling sales, likely because of a slight swelling on his leg, Zayat kept him and put him into training with Bob Baffert. It didn't take long for the experts to spot that there was something different about the colt's movement. His smooth stride and athletic movement drew one observer to compare him to basketball legend Michael Jordan: 'When he would go up in the air with his stride, he seemed to stay up in the air longer and cover more ground than other horses.'

Yet he disappointed on his first track run, a six-and-a-half maiden at Del Mar, coming only in fifth, and displaying uncharacteristic jitters before and after. Baffert worked out that American Pharoah was acutely sensitive to the shouting of the crowd and would run him thereafter with noise-drowning ear buds. Undeterred, and now with Victor Espinoza in the saddle, Baffert sent him to the Grade 1 Del Mar Futurity, where his calmer juvenile displayed what they knew he was capable of and bolted up by just shy of five lengths. He backed this up three weeks later in the Grade 1 FrontRunner Stakes where, in a neat case of nominative determinism, he led the entire way to easily dispatch his rivals by three-and-a-half lengths. The race would later be named after him. Despite being pulled out of the Breeders' Cup juvenile with a bruised foot, officials had seen enough to give him end-of-year top juvenile honours.

For his sensational Classic season, Baffert chose a low-key start, preferring to warm his colt up at Oaklawn, Arkansas, first in the Rebel Stakes and then the Arkansas Derby. In those he confirmed his versatility. He won the former from the front in wet conditions (with a loose shoe), the latter from behind on drier ground. And in both he finished many lengths clear of the opposition. He was an obvious favourite for the Kentucky Derby at Churchill Downs, which as usual attracted a line-up that included many proven Grade 1 performers. There were concerns before the off, as a skittish America Pharoah was unhappy, needing four grooms to calm him. It seemed that even the ear-buds were not keeping out the volume of the epic 170,000-strong crowd.

Once the race was underway though, and despite having used up too much energy with those pre-race nerves, Espinoza felt in control, although he had to fight to his one-length victory over Firing Line. Even so, Espinoza was criticised for hitting his horse too often during the race, although closer scrutiny suggests that as often as not he was simply waving his whip or hitting the saddle cloth.

As if to make a point, Espinoza didn't hit American Pharoah once during the Preakness Stakes a fortnight later, as it was clear he didn't need to. Despite exiting from an unfavourable inside stall, he had the advantage of having proven himself before in similar muddy conditions. Mr Z also raced, this time showing no interest in his friend's tail, probably because he couldn't get near it. American Pharoah romped clear in the stretch to a seven-length victory. By this stage, Zayat's handsome, kindly colt was gaining a proper fan club ('Pharoah's Phans') who would dress in ancient Egyptian-style clothing in the yellow and blue colours of their hero. For once the spillover from his victories was seeping into wider US sporting consciousness in a way that few horses manage.

Since Affirmed 37 years previously, nine horses had won the first two legs of the Triple Crown only to be thwarted by 'The Test of the Champion', The Belmont Stakes. It has never been easy. There was something in the air, though, as this time felt decidedly different. It was not hope in the air, but a sense of fate and expectation, matched by the disproportionately large audience of 22 million watching it live on TV. The Pharoah knew his lines, and owned the track that day as he had done so often previously. Pushed to the front straightaway by Espinoza, he bossed them from the off, gradually increasing the tempo, and storming clear for a five-and-a-half length victory, as commentator Larry Collmus screeched, 'American Pharoah is finally The One!' on the tannoy. And that he was – the stars had finally once again aligned. In an echo of Secretariat's Belmont, very few of the $2 winning tickets bought on-course were cashed in. They were now souvenirs of history being made.

After a short break, the Pharoah was next out at the nine furlong Haskell Invitational at Monmouth, for no other reason than Zayat wanting him to run on a Sunday in New Jersey in front of a big crowd. It was little more than a stroll in the park for the colt, with Espinoza motionless and pulling him up for the whole final furlong. Second that day was Keen Ice, and it was that very horse who caused a sensation when they met again at Saratoga for the Travers Stakes. The course once again lived up to its 'Graveyard of Champions' moniker, with American Pharoah, harassed and unsettled throughout by Frosted, unable to respond to the from-behind finish of Keen Ice, going down by three-quarters of a length. It appeared that the repeated travelling across the country was taking its toll.

But the Pharoah wasn't finished. He had another date with destiny to fulfil. When last the Triple Crown was won, the Breeders' Cup had only been an idea on paper. The addition of the Classic to the three venerable races was together seen as an unofficial – and season-long – 'Grand Slam'. Held that year in Keeneland, the Classic was so steeped in quality that few could remember anything comparable; six of his seven rivals were Grade/Group 1 winners. With crowds 20-deep, and ear buds firmly in place, the favourite was there to prove that the Travers had been a blip, rather than the start of a decline. In control throughout, he thundered down the stretch with his light, bouncy stride to destroy all-comers by six-and-a-half lengths in course-record time. The Slam was his, and it will only be another true great that wins another. As Baffert pointed out after when comparing to other top horses: 'They have a small window of greatness where Pharoah, he had a window all year long.'

It had long been known that Zayat had sold breeding rights for his hero for the following season, meaning that he was retired to Ashford Stud farm in Kentucky with a distinctly European-looking record of a mere 11 races, making him the most lightly raced Triple Crown winner – a record which would only stand for three years until Justify came along. *Sports Illustrated's* readers easily voted him their 'Sportsperson of the Year' – a vote that the editors promptly ignored, opting for Serena Williams instead.

But American Pharoah had by then easily proven that, even in the 21st century with such immense competition from wealthy sports that are marketed to the hilt to an entranced American public, a great horse can still burst through into wider US consciousness. Horses like him don't come around often. That was why, after he retired, the US Jockey Club took the precaution of registering the correct spelling of his name as well. He was unique and they wanted to keep it that way.

FACTFILE

Description: Bay Colt
Size: 16.2 hands
Dates: 2012-
Racing seasons: 2014-15
Where were they trained?: USA
Trainer: Bob Baffert
Owner: Ahmed Zayat
Jockey: Victor Espinoza, Martin Garcia

Sire: Pioneerof The Nile
Dam: Littleprincessemma
Damsire: Yankee Gentleman
Record: 11: 9-1-0
Most impressive victory: Breeders' Cup Classic 2015
Nickname: The Pharoah

EPILOGUE

This book captures the lives of 50 horses who were born over a period of almost exactly a hundred years. It doesn't neatly fit across an actual century, but it does encapsulate many of the greats during the first hundred years of horseracing being captured on film for posterity. These horses were chosen for the extraordinary abilities that they displayed; we are simply fortunate that a lot of them had fascinating tales to tell. There are no patterns, as such, that make themselves evident here – other than their unequivocal brilliance – but a few themes really came to the fore as I delved deeper into these stories.

The first is not an original conclusion, but this book further cements it: the balance of thoroughbred breeding – and in turn the balance of racing power – has shifted both east and west from its European origins. With the exception of the currently mighty Coolmore empire, dominant breeding lines are now mainly found in the US, but with ever-increasing quality bloodstock being exported to both Japan and Australia. Anyone who writes the next version of this book in a quarter of a century is likely to have a greater proportion of new horses from these continents than from Europe. A controversial assertion, perhaps, but you can only tell me that I was wrong in 25 years' time.

The second conclusion is a play on the first. As horseracing becomes more and more mobile, and even more instinctively global, the flags that I have arbitrarily assigned the horses here – based purely on where they were trained – will become more and more meaningless. Already, we have plenty of examples of horses being bred in the US, owned by an Irishman, trained in the UK, running in France and Australia and ridden by an Italian. What can be gained by saying the horse was 'from' country X or 'represented' country Y? I, for one, hope that this becomes an irrelevance so that the thoroughbred, above all, is the hero, not the flag.

Which, in turn, makes me want to highlight a third point. We know that, sadly, every living creature has to pass away. What struck me during the research of this book was how many of these heroes had endings that were simply not fitting for the champions that they once were. Some, like Ruffian, had their demise brought about by the track itself. With Shergar, it was criminals, and for Epinard, it was the horrors of war. Meanwhile, in Ribot's case, it could well have been undiagnosed illness. Whether we like it or not, death for any of us is seldom dignified, but whilst I hope that we never forget these legends, likewise I hope that there will be more and more stories of our future heroes passing away quietly due to the infirmities of old age after a long and happy retirement. If we don't regard the horse's welfare as absolutely paramount, then we surely have no right to pass judgement on their abilities on the racetrack.

Finally, and to stress for a final time, this book is not an attempt to rank thoroughbreds, or to open up a can of worms about who should and shouldn't be included here. Any feedback that starts, 'But what about X? Why isn't he in here?' is rather missing the point. I could (almost) have produced an equally valid group of 50 completely different horses without sacrificing credibility – indeed, maybe I shall one day. The point here is to revel in and marvel at the rare abilities, quirky behaviours and poignant stories that these 50 horses have given us. And, in turn, if you own a thoroughbred horse, or a share in one, and wherever that horse may run, you may well have entered this game thinking that maybe – just maybe – your colt or filly will one day rank amongst these immortals.

Indulge that dream. It's what makes it all worthwhile.